DUQUESNE STUDIES

Philosophical Series

22

PHENOMENOLOGY OF NATURAL LAW

DUQUESNE STUDIES

Philosophical Series

22

PHENOMENOLOGY OF NATURAL LAW

by
William A. Luijpen, Ph.D.

Duquesne University Press, Pittsburgh, Pa.
Editions E. Nauwelaerts, Louvain

DUQUESNE STUDIES

Philosophical Series

Andrew G. van Melsen, D.Sc., D.Ed., and Henry J. Koren, C.S. Sp. S.T.D., editors.

Volume One—*Andrew G. van Melsen,* From Atomos to Atom. Pp. XII and 240. Published also in Dutch, German, Spanish and Italian editions. Available only in Torchbook paper-back edition.

Volume Two—*Andrew G. van Melsen,* The Philosophy of Nature. Pp. XII and 265. Third edition, fifth impression. Price: cloth $4.50. Published also in Italian, Dutch and Polish editions.

Volume Three—*P. Henry van Laer,* Philosophico-Scientific Problems. Out of print.

Volume Four—*Cajetan's* The Analogy of Names and The Concept of Being. Pp. X and 93. Second edition. Price: $2.25, cloth.

Volume Five—*Louis de Raeymaeker and others,* Truth and Freedom. Pp. VII and 132. Second impression. Price: $3.00 cloth. Published also in French and Catalan.

Volume Six—*P. Henry van Laer,* The Philosophy of Science. Part One: Science in General. Pp. XVII and 164. Second edition. Price: cloth $3.75.

Volume Seven—*Stephen Strasser,* The Soul, in Metaphysical and Empirical Psychology. Pp. X and 275. Third impression. Price: cloth $6.00. Published also in German, Dutch and French.

Volume Eight—*Albert Dondeyne,* Contemporary European Thought and Christian Faith. Pp. XI and 211. Third impression. Price: cloth $5.75. Published also in French.

Library of Congress Catalog Card Number: 67–17123

Volume Nine—*Maxwell J. Charlesworth*, PHILOSOPHY AND LINGUISTIC ANALYSIS. Pp. XIII and 234. Second impression. Price: paper $4.75, cloth $5.50.

Volume Ten—*Remy C. Kwant*, PHILOSOPHY OF LABOR. Pp. XI and 163. Price: paper $4.50, cloth $5.25. Italian and Spanish editions in preparation.

Volume Eleven—*Remy C. Kwant*, ENCOUNTER. Pp. VIII and 85. Second impression. Price: cloth $3.25. Published also in Dutch.

Volume Twelve—*William A. Luijpen*, EXISTENTIAL PHENOMENOLOGY. Pp. XIII and 355. Fifth impression. Price: cloth $6.25. Published also in Dutch. German and Spanish edition in preparation.

Volume Thirteen—*Andrew G. van Melsen*, SCIENCE AND TECHNOLOGY. Pp. X and 373. Price: paper $6.20, cloth $6.95. Published also in Dutch and German.

Volume Fourteen—*P. Henry van Laer*, PHILOSOPHY OF SCIENCE. PART TWO: A STUDY OF THE DIVISION AND NATURE OF VARIOUS GROUPS OF SCIENCES. Pp. XIII and 342. Price: paper $5.75, cloth, $6.50.

Volume Fifteen—*Remy C. Kwant*, THE PHENOMENOLOGICAL PHILOSOPHY OF MERLEAU-PONTY. Pp. IX and 257. Price: paper $4.50, cloth $5.25.

Volume Sixteen—*John A. Peters*, METAPHYSICS: A SYSTEMATIC SURVEY. Pp. XVIII and 529. Price: paper $9.00, cloth $9.75.

Volume Seventeen—*William A. Liujpen*, PHENOMENOLOGY AND ATHEISM. Pp. XIV and 342. Price: paper $5.75, cloth $6.50.

Volume Eighteen—*Martin G. Plattel*, SOCIAL PHILOSOPHY. Pp. XI and 346. Price: paper $7.20, cloth $7.95. Published also in Dutch and German.

Volume Nineteen—*Andrew G. van Melsen*, EVOLUTION AND PHILOSOPHY. Pp. 208. Price: paper $4.75, cloth $5.50. Published also in Dutch.

Volume Twenty—*Remy C. Kwant*, FROM PHENOMENOLOGY TO METAPHYSICS. Pp. 247. Price: paper $7.20, cloth $7.95.

Volume Twenty-One—*Joseph J. Kockelmans*, PHENOMENOLOGY AND PHYSICAL SCIENCE. Pp. 208. Price: paper $6.20; cloth $6.95.

Volume Twenty-Two—*William A. Luijpen*, PHENOMENOLOGY OF NATURAL LAW. Pp. 249. Price: paper $6.20; cloth $6.95.

"The natural law is dead;
long live the natural law."
Erich Fechner

PREFACE

The American edition of this work has been translated directly from the author's original Dutch manuscript by the undersigned. The Latin, French and German footnotes have also been translated for the convenience of the reader.

The ambiguity of the Dutch and German term *"Recht"* and the French *"Droit,"* which have no corresponding English equivalent, was solved by selecting "law," "justice," "right," "legal order" or combinations of these words as required by the context.

Henry J. Koren, C.S.Sp.

TABLE OF CONTENTS

INTRODUCTION

The value of a society is not commensurate with the principles embodied in its constitution. From the inscriptions on its monuments and the slogans of its orators no one can determine how far a society has advanced on the difficult road toward a community worthy of man. The value of a society depends on the importance it attaches to the relationships of man to his fellow-men in its community.[1]

It often happens that the value of the actually existing relationships is camouflaged by references to principles and concealed under mystifications. The principles are often called "sacred" and of "everlasting" validity; they are frequently justified by an appeal to divine guarantees.

Meanwhile, however, it is and remains an indisputable fact that such an appeal to a "sacred," "everlasting" principle endowed with a "divine guarantee" cannot make the actually existing relationships between men human. These relationships are human only when they embody and give concrete form to the recognition of man by his fellow-men.

The conviction expressed in these two paragraphs underlies the content of this work. We shall try to justify this conviction in the course of this book, but it seemed useful to explicitly state this leading idea at the very beginning of our study.

Despite the fact that many abhor even the very term "natural law," we have not hesitated to use it. The existence of such an aversion should not surprise anyone. The mere mention of the term more or less spontaneously brings to the mind certain historical views of the natural law, and it is possible that someone may feel compelled to reject *all* the views that have been presented in the course of history. In such a case one can hardly be surprised to hear that he objects even to the use of the term "natural law."

Our use of the term is not based on the suspicion that those people have overlooked one view of the natural law. If we want to maintain the expression "the natural law," the reason is that for the past twenty-

---

[1] Maurice Merleau-Ponty, *Humanisme et Terreur,* Paris, 1947, p. X.

11

five centuries there has existed a *tradition* of thinking in terms of natural law. Abstracting for the present from the value of this thinking, it seems to us that the very existence of such a long tradition implies at least that thinking mankind has "seen" something here which continues to draw attention in spite of everything. For this reason we are justified in retaining this term.

There is a second reason, however, for retaining the term "natural law." Contemporary philosophers often object against the use of certain terms, even if they know that those who use them do not attach to them an interpretation that is no longer tenable. They simply want to force everybody to give up using the offending term; they simply fix the meaning of the term in an unacceptable interpretation and look upon any use of this term as implying *per se* this untenable interpretation.

Such a procedure causes great confusion. To limit ourselves to the term "natural law," one who *unqualifiedly* rejects this term can expect that he will be accused of legal positivism. If, however, he is not an adherent of legal positivism, he will try to justify his position by showing that he does not absolutize the value of the legal order, but accepts that this order is based upon a justifying ground and subject to a critical norm. The position assumed by Hans Welzel is particularly illustrating in this matter. This author rejects natural law;[2] at the same time, he does not want to join "ordinary" positivists, for he accepts a principle that can deprive any positive law of its obligatory character though not of its coercive power.[3] In other words, according to Welzel, the legal order has a justifying basis and is subject to a critical norm. Now, if precisely this point is the fundamental inspiration of traditional thinking in terms of natural law, only confusion can result from the unqualified rejection of the term "natural law."

The second term occurring in the title of this book is "phenomenology." This word should not be taken to mean only that we employ a certain "method," at least not if by "method" one means a complex of technical aids in the search of truth. Like existential thought, from which today it can no longer be distinguished, phenomenological thought

---

[2] Hans Welzel, "Naturrecht und Rechtspositivismus," *Festschrift für Hans Niedermeyer,* Göttingen, 1953, pp. 279-289.

[3] "Where, then, a government order degrades the person to a mere thing . . . , this order can perhaps still force him insofar as the government's power is strong enough and the evil inflicted in the case of refusal to obey is sufficiently grave, but the order can no longer oblige him." Welzel, *art. cit.,* pp. 293-294.

can be called a "method" only if this term is taken to refer to the internal life of a philosophy as determined by its "primitive fact," its central reference point or fundamental inspiration. For us, phenomenology simply means philosophy, albeit a particular type of philosophy.

In spite of the fact that hitherto relatively little reflection has been devoted to law from an existential and phenomenological standpoint the opinion has already been voiced that this philosophical approach will not make any contributions to the philosophy of law, and it is even said that nothing must be expected from it precisely because of the way of thinking adopted by existentialism and phenomenology. Thijssen argues in this way with respect to the philosophy of Karl Jaspers,[4] and Welzel[5] and Hommes[6] make a like negative judgment in reference to all existential and phenomenological thought. Erich Fechner[7] and Werner Maihofer,[8] however, object to this motion of no confidence.

As the title of this book shows, in the author's opinion a phenomenology of the natural law is possible. It is up to the reader to judge to what extent we have managed to do justice to both phenomenology and the natural law. At present we merely want to indicate briefly on what grounds certain thinkers consider the junction of the two terms "phenomenology" and "natural law" impossible.

Insofar as the term "law" is taken to refer to positive law, the opponents of the phenomenology of the natural law point out that positive law presents itself as a regulating, schematizing and generalizing reality. It produces interconnection, security, safety and predictability among men. It is *par excellence* a social reality which safeguards the individuals' security. It imposes itself in a compelling way, so that even those of ill-will find it difficult to escape from its grasp. Positive law brings uniformity to human behavior.

These descriptive qualifications would seem to indicate that the legal order belongs to the realm of the impersonal "they" (*das Man*). But,

---

[4] Johannes Thijssen, "Staat und Recht in der Existenzphilosophie," *Archiv für Rechts- und Sozialphilosophie,* vol. XLI (1954-55), pp. 1-18.

[5] Welzel, *Naturrecht und materiale Gerechtigkeit,* Göttingen, 1951, pp. 187-198.

[6] H. J. Hommes, *Een nieuwe herleving van het natuurrecht,* Zwolle, 1961, pp. 135-142.

[7] Erich Fechner, "Naturrecht und Existenzphilosophie," *Archiv für Rechts- und Sozialphilosophie,* vol. XLI (1954-55), pp. 305-325.

[8] Werner Maihofer, *Recht und Sein. Prolegomena zu einer Rechtsontologie,* Frankfurt a.M., 1954.

so they add, this is precisely what phenomenologists and philosophers of existence consider to be the realm of inauthenticity, of inauthentic being-man.   The impersonal "they" is the negation of what is meant by "existence."   The fact that man "exists" means that man is an irreducible, wholly unique and radically original self; by giving way to regulative and generalizing schemata, he attains safety and security but perishes as a self.   Authentic existence implies a victory over the uniformity, safety, security and predictability of the impersonal "they."   He who realizes his existence in accordance with the norms of established juridical rules loses the authenticity of his selfhood.   Therefore, phenomenological or existential thought contradicts itself when it thinks that a value can be assigned to positive law.[9]

Insofar as the term "law" is taken to refer to the natural law, certain thinkers claim that this sense is utterly foreign to phenomenology or philosophy of existence.   The reason is that the emphasis placed on subjectivity as *selfhood* by phenomenology and philosophy of existence is so strong that both in theory and in practice there is no room for "pre-given norms."[10]   Hence all existing norms must be reduced to the subject's decision.   On the other hand, traditional thinking in terms of natural law precisely affirms this natural law as the justifying ground and the critical norm of positive law.   Thus it follows that such a natural law must be meaningless for a philosophy which does not recognize any "pre-given norms" and makes all existing norms depend on decisions of the subject.

This is the reason why Thijssen rejects phenomenological and existential thinking about the natural law.   He illustrates the meaning of his rejection with a clear example.   When Luther, he says, at the Diet of Worms declared: "Here I stand; I cannot do otherwise; may God help me," he made a decision in the full sense of the term.   In his decision, however, he was governed to the best of his knowledge and conscience by the New Testament, which for him functioned as a "pre-given norm." Such a dependence on a norm, Thijssen argues, cannot be recognized by the phenomenologists and the philosophers of existence, because of the emphasis they place on the subject's selfhood and his decisions.   Those

---

[9] Fechner, *art. cit.,* pp. 307-311.

[10] "The philosophy of existence denies that norms are pre-given. It assigns the original decision wholly to man's freedom. Man's *Dasein* as a 'thrown project' ultimately must be shaped from within man himself because there are no pre-given norms." Fechner, *art. cit.,* p. 320.

philosophers, Thijssen continues, would say that the norm of the New Testament received its binding value from Luther's own conscientious decision.[11] But if this principle is applied to the natural law, how can one continue to call the natural law the justifying basis and critical norm of positive law? In other words, are we not forced to conclude that phenomenological and existential thinking must of necessity lead to positivism of law?[12]

The questions raised by these objections will not be evaded in this study. On the other hand, they will not constitute the sole topic of this book, for we want to write a philosophy of law. All the traditional topics of the philosophy of law will be discussed here, in addition to those raised by existential phenomenology. We hope that the debate about the natural law, as well as that about phenomenology, may contribute to bring greater clarity to both.

---

[11] Thijssen, *art. cit.,* p. 10.

[12] "Existentialistic philosophy of law seems of necessity to terminate in legal positivism." Fechner, *art. cit.,* p. 315.

CHAPTER ONE

THE EVER-RECURRING DILEMMA

A global survey of the history of philosophy soon demonstrates that the questions raised by living philosophy are somehow always the same. They are the eternal questions of mankind. This constant recurrence of the same questions occurs also in the philosophy of law. One does not need a profound knowledge of the philosophy of law to realize that there exists very little unanimity in the fundamental issues raised in the philosophy of law. This situation often results in the discussions of the philosophers of law being listened to with a kind of benevolent boredom and pious scepticism. One who surveys the history of this branch of philosophy easily gets the impression that every conceivable solution of the problem of law, right and justice has already been proposed and rejected.[1]

In spite of the many answers, however, it remains indisputably true that the *questions* remain perennially the same. Is this fact of any importance? Has it any significance? It is unthinkable that mankind, from the moment it reached the level of authenticity till the present, would have occupied itself with questions devoid of importance. Questions pertaining to the philosophy of law unmistakably impose themselves as soon as man becomes authentically man.[2] The reason is not far to seek. As soon as man manages to reach the level of authentic existence, it becomes obvious to him that even the most elementary level of authenticity is impossible unless existence is co-existence. To be man is

---

[1] A. Struicken, *Recht en gezag,* Gouda, 1916, p. 7.

[2] We have in mind here one of the fundamental insights of phenomenology, which says that man is not man just as a rain storm is wet or a table square. Phenomenology's distinction between inauthentic and authentic existence makes it possible to add relief to the difference between primitive man and the cultural man of the twentieth century.

to be a fellow-man. But even the most simple and most elementary level of co-existence calls for rules and regulations to make this co-existence possible and to preserve it when it has been achieved.[3] This means, therefore, that there is positive law wherever there is co-existence and that there is authority wherever there is positive law. It stands to reason, of course, that at first this law and authority will be of a very rudimentary and primitive type. Nevertheless, as soon as man begins to reflect in a critical fashion, he is bound to raise questions about the foundations of positive law and authority due to their far-reaching influence on his life.

All this is not merely a theoretical necessity; as a matter of fact man has asked these questions. The history of the philosophy of law manifests a striking unity and coherence, derived from the task given to man, viz., to establish order in human society. Beyond any possible doubt, this ordering of society is a work of man. Thus it is impossible to avoid the question of whether or not this work can be left to man's arbitrariness. Are there norms regulating the order to be established in society? Does every regulation of this order satisfy what man has in mind when he sets about regulating society? What exactly does man have in mind? And is that which he has in mind *per se* what he ought to have in mind? What does it mean "to have something in mind"? The history of the philosophy of law is the history of the answers given to these questions.[4] Man's questioning in this matter is endless because every answer that imposes itself has a future; it evokes a more profound and "better" question. And every "better" question demands a "better" answer.

1. Legal Positivism

We do not want, however, to raise questions here concerning the historical origin of the philosophy of law, for what interests us especially are the fundamental questions of this philosophy itself. Strange as it

---

[3] "The vital importance of law for society cannot be denied. There is no way human beings can live together without a legal order." Fechner, *Rechtsphilosophie, Soziologie und Metaphysik des Rechts*, Tübingen, 1956, p. 265.

[4] "Precisely the history of the natural law offers a striking example, illustrating the unity of the 'historical' mind in its orientation to an objective (*sachlichen*) problem. This history constitutes . . . an internally connected train of thought, in which each succeeding generation takes over and continues the state of the question attained by the preceding generation as an objective problem." Welzel, *op. cit.*, p. 8.

may seem, today it is precisely the jurists, the students of the positive sciences of law, who openly profess the necessity of reflecting philosophically upon the law. This fact is all the more striking because not so very long ago it was generally admitted that nothing more could be said about law and right after the specialists in the various positive sciences of law had said everything they could say *as jurists*. In the nineteenth century jurists were generally convinced that right and positive law were identical; hence we may call that century the era of legal positivism.[5]

A positivistic view of right and law obviously leaves no room for a philosophy of law. For, no matter how one wants to define the philosophy of law, it always intends to say something about right, justice or injustice. But if just or unjust are identical with what is permitted or forbidden by positive law, there remains no room for a philosophy of law to say anything which has not yet been said by the positive sciences of law.

The Occasion for Asking Philosophical Questions About Law. As a matter of fact, the positive sciences of law themselves occasioned the asking of a number of questions which could not at all be conceived as questions of positive law. As early as 1920 Kranenburg[6] enumerated an impressive list of questions which the jurists of the time could not answer so long as they remained in their own realm, viz., the realm of positive law.[7] He mentioned the questions concerning the foundation of criminal law, the binding character of agreements, liability with respect to indemnity suits, the juridical ground on which the private ownership of modern means of production is based, the binding power of the law itself, and many others.[8] Positive law itself became the occasion for asking questions that could not be answered by the same positive sciences of law. In this way it became necessary to appeal again to the philosophy of law.

The same happened again but on a larger scale after World War II,

---

[5] Welzel, "Naturrecht und Rechtspositivismus," *Festschrift für Hans Niedermeyer,* p. 279.

[6] The same year saw the foundation of a vigorous special society for the study of the philosophy of law. Cf. W. Duynstee, *Geschiedenis van het natuurrecht en de wijsbegeerte van het recht in Nederland,* Amsterdam, 1956, p. 87.

[7] R. Kranenburg, "De rechtsphilosophie en de juridische vakwetenschappen," *Handelingen v.d. Vereniging v.d. Wijsbegeerte des Rechts,* 1921, pp. 5-25.

[8] Kranenburg, *art. cit.,* pp. 7-11.

particularly in Germany.[9]   In times of peace and internal tranquillity it can happen that the legal order enjoys a prestige that seems to be beyond question.   It is in the interest of almost everyone that the legal norms be regarded as indubitable and definitive.   Only to the underprivileged and the oppressed does that legal order appear questionable.   They look upon that order as the product of the arbitrary rules established by those who are powerful.   The law prohibits to beg at the door of the churches, to steal bread or to sleep under bridges.   All that is forbidden to both the rich . . . and the poor.[10]

After World War II no one regarded the legal order as simply inviolable.   It was realized that this order had been corrupted by the arbitrariness of the powerful.[11]   That corruption had to be eliminated. Thus, there arose a legal vacuum in various realms.   It became necessary to establish new regulations.   But what should be the basis on which these new rules should be established?   This question gave rise to renewed interest in the natural law, the central problem of the philosophy of law.[12]

Absolutism in the Value Attached to Positive Law.   The above-described situation meant a revolution in the then current mentality of legal positivism.   Bergbohm may perhaps be named as one of the most eloquent representatives of that mentality.[13]   Nearly his entire work is devoted to a struggle against the natural law, which he ridicules without mercy and rejects without qualification.[14]   By "natural law" he means

---

[9] G. E. Langemeyer, "De huidige betekenis van het natuurrecht," *loc. cit.* in footnote 7, vol. XXXXIII (1958), pp. 26-51.

[10] Fechner, *op. cit.,* pp. 9-10.

[11] G. Radbruch, "Die Erneuerung des Rechts," *Die Wandlung,* vol. II (1947), pp. 8-16.

[12] "In large realms there arose a legal vacuum requiring a fundamentally new order.   But the very norms of law needed for this had been destroyed, disfigured or forgotten.   This situation led to a call for the natural law, which like a phoenix rose from the ashes of positivism and experienced a hitherto unexpected 'rebirth.'   Through this rebirth, the philosophy of law—whose core is the theory of the natural law—gained renewed importance."   Fechner, *op. cit.,* p. 3.

[13] K. Bergbohm, *Jurisprudenz und Rechtsphilosophie,* vol. I, Leipzig, 1892.

[14] "In other words, the 'weed' of natural law, no matter in what form and disguise it occurs, whether openly or camouflaged, must be eradicated without mercy, down to its very roots. . . .   Any thought that something can be right (*Recht*) without positive law or be concerned with right without being affirmed in 'real law,' most definitely must be kept far from any (doctrine) that calls itself jurisprudence, theory of law or philosophy of law and wants to lay claim to being scientific."   Bergbohm, *op. cit.,* p. 118.

any form of right that claims to be independent of man's "positing" expression,[15] normative with respect to positive law,[16] and binding independently of positive law or even against this law.[17] People sometimes claim, says Bergbohm, that the natural law has been overcome, but as a matter of fact it continues to live a clandestine life both in the theory and in the practice of law.[18] Yet this natural law must be completely eradicated. The only form of right is the positive law,[19] and anything else is nothing but "subjectivism elevated to a principle."[20] For the natural law has nothing that makes it of any importance for the legal order. It is not the product of any historical event; it did not arise from an objectifying will; it did not result from any deed. It seems to be simply there.[21] Thus, Bergbohm argues, anyone can claim whatever he fancies in the name of the natural law.[22] Proponents of the natural law are people who present subjective fancies and ideas as "right" and assign to them a normative value independently of, and even against, positive law.[23]

The most actual form of legal positivism is the "pure theory of law" proposed by Kelsen.[24] His theory, says Kelsen, is "pure" because it has been stripped of all possible philosophical speculations about the natural law,[25] and as a theory of positive legal norms *as* positive legal norms remains aloof from investigations concerning man's actual behavior which is governed by causal laws[26] and constitutes the object of other

[15] Bergbohm, *op. cit.*, pp. 130-131.
[16] Bergbohm, *op. cit.*, p. 140.
[17] Bergbohm, *op. cit.*, p. 131.
[18] Bergbohm, *op. cit.*, pp. 109-122.
[19] "We want to and are able to recognize as rights only positive rights." Bergbohm, *op. cit.*, p. 546.
[20] Bergbohm, *op. cit.*, p. 133.
[21] Bergbohm, *op. cit.*, p. 132.
[22] "By their very essence 'ideal' and 'theoretical' rights (*Recht*) lack any element of contact with anything outside the individual proposing them." Bergbohm, *op. cit.*, p. 532.
[23] Bergbohm, *op. cit.*, pp. 140-141.
[24] Kelsen, *Reine Rechtslehre,* 2nd ed., 1960.
[25] Kelsen, "Was ist die Reine Rechtslehre?", *Demokratie und Rechtsstaat. Festgabe zum 60. Geburtstag von Zaccaria Giacometti,* Zürich, 1953, pp. 145-146, 154-155.
[26] "The postulate of purity intends only to make the scientific jurist aware that the specific method of his knowledge is different from that of causal social science; hence the frequent attempts to give 'sociological' answers to questions of right and law either are based on self-deception or aim at luring others away from the given law." Kelsen, *art. cit.*, p. 148.

sciences such as sociology and social psychology.[27]   On the basis of comparative studies of the norms that are termed legal norms, it is possible to understand the essence of the legal norm independently of the changing content of the various norms admitted at different times and in diverse places.[28]

Such a comparison clearly shows the difference between the laws of physical science and those of the sciences of law.   In a physical law two facts are connected as condition and effect by means of the principle of causality.   But in a law pertaining to the positive sciences of law two facts are connected as condition and effect by means of the principle of imputation.[29]   Because of this imputation, the principle of every legal order is: if an injustice is done, an action ought to occur as the effect of this injustice.[30]   If, for example, a legal order posits the right to life, this simply means that, in case someone kills a person, force ought to be exercised against the killer.   Accordingly, physical science formulates laws concerning "being," while the science of law formulates laws concerning an "ought."[31]   The "pure theory of law" is a normative science of society[32] and nothing else.

According to Kelsen, we must make a clear distinction between, on the one hand, *science* of law as the tendency toward knowledge of positive law and, on the other, legal *policy* as the tendency to establish justice.[33] Kelsen demands that the science of law be apolitical.   Politics is, of course, a necessity and requires the creation of a legal order as a necessary instrument.   Subjective value judgments are inevitable in this matter.   But it would be intolerable if the theory of positive law did anything else than describe positive law, analyze its structure and define the concepts used in positive law.   The theory of positive law must be "pure"; and this implies that this theory must rigorously abstain from all value judgments.[34]   The "pure theory of law" is not concerned with

---

[27] Kelsen, *art. cit.,* p. 147.

[28] Kelsen, *art. cit.,* p. 143.

[29] Kelsen, *art. cit.,* p. 144.

[30] "Hence the pure theory of law formulates the basic schema of the law as follows: if an injustice is done, an effect of injustice (a sanction) ought to occur." Kelsen, *art. cit.,* p. 145.

[31] Kelsen, *art. cit.,* pp. 145-146.

[32] Kelsen, *art. cit.,* p. 147.

[33] Kelsen, *art. cit.,* pp. 152-153.

[34] "But the pure theory of law does not want to be and cannot be a theory of the right or just law, for it does not pretend to answer the question of what is just." Kelsen, *art. cit.,* p. 143.

justice. As doctrine of positive law, the pure theory of law is the theory of *actual* right and does not ask itself whether this real, positive right is just or unjust, good or bad.[35] Any positive right can be called just from one particular standpoint and decried as unjust from another.[36] The "pure theory of law" explicitly hopes to keep aloof from such emotional and subjective value judgments. In other words, the legal order of Soviet Russia is just as much a legal order as that of fascist Italy or that of capitalistic-democratic France. The "pure theory of law" wholly abstracts from the question whether those legal orders are just or unjust and whether one is more just than another.

This is also the reason why the "pure theory of law" wants to have nothing to do with the natural law, for an appeal to the natural law and the justice corresponding to it is nothing but an appeal to a political ideology. Any ideology lives by virtue of its political intentions to gain control of power.[37] But the "purity" of the "pure theory of law" consists precisely in the fact that it is a science and not a politics.[38]

The way in which the theorists of the natural law contradict one another when they appeal to the natural law and its justice makes it easy, says Kelsen, to reject the natural law in favor of the "pure theory of law." One theorist of the natural law deduces from the nature of man the absolute necessity of private property and democracy, while another theorist, on the same basis, affirms the absolute justice of collective ownership and the dictatorship of the proletariat. As anyone can see, this appeal to the natural law and justice simply serves to camouflage the purely political intentions of those theorists. The "pure theory of law" wants no part of this farce;[39] it accepts nothing but positive law; it is legal positivism and the theory of legal positivism.[40]

Because for Kelsen right is identical with positive law and because

---

[35] "As a science of positive law, it is a doctrine of actual (*wirklich*) rights, of rights and duties as they have actually been created by custom, legislation and the administration of justice and are at work in social reality, regardless of whether such positive law is considered good or bad, just or unjust, from any value-standpoint, that is, from any political standpoint." Kelsen, *art. cit.*, p. 153.

[36] Kelsen, *art. cit.*, p. 153.

[37] Kelsen, *art. cit.*, p. 154.

[38] "For its purity lies essentially in the fact that it wants to be only a science and not politics." Kelsen, *art. cit.*, p. 161.

[39] Kelsen, *art. cit.*, p. 157.

[40] "The pure theory of law is legal positivism; it is precisely the theory of *legal positivism*, and legal positivism goes hand in hand with *relativism*." Kelsen, *art. cit.*, p. 153.

positive law has to be posited, it stands to reason that for him there exists no distinction between the legal order and the order of the state.[41] The legal order, the state order and the order of force are absolutely identical. This identity, of course, will have ramifications in the ultimate foundation of the normative character proper to the rules of law if we wish to preserve the "purity" of the theory of law.

The answer to the question why a norm is valid, i.e., why man *ought* to behave in accordance with a certain norm, cannot be found in a reference to what *de facto is*. From the fact that something *is* it does not follow that it *ought* to be.[42] The basis of a norm's validity can only be found in the validity of another, higher norm.[43] It merely *seems* that a fact of being can be the foundation of a norm's validity. For instance, people are inclined to base the validity of the Ten Commandments on the fact that God gave these Commandments on Mount Sina. In reality, however, their validity is not based on the fact that they were given by God but upon the norm that one must obey God's commandments.[44]

The search for a higher norm as the foundation of a lower norm cannot be pursued to infinity. Ultimately, one must arrive at a norm that is supposed to be the highest and last. As the highest norm, it cannot have been "posited" (*gesetzt*) by an authority, for such an authority can be called a *competent* authority only on the basis of a higher norm. The highest norm is not "posited" (*gesetzt*) but "presupposed" (*vorausgesetzt*).[45] Kelsen calls such a highest norm a "fundamental norm." It gives unity to the plurality of norms because it is the foundation on which all norms pertaining to a given legal order are valid.

According to Kelsen a legal norm is not valid because of its content but because it has been established in a way that is determined by a presupposed fundamental norm.[46] For this reason any arbitrary content can be given to a legal norm. There is no human behavior which by its very nature cannot become the content of a legal norm. The validity of

---

[41] Kelsen, *art. cit.*, p. 155.

[42] Kelsen, *Reine Rechtlehre,* p. 196.

[43] Kelsen, *op. cit.*, p. 196.

[44] Kelsen, *op. cit.*, pp. 196-197.

[45] "As highest norm, it must be *presupposed,* for it cannot have been *posited* by any authority, whose competency would have to be based on a still higher norm." Kelsen, *op. cit.*, p. 197.

[46] Kelsen, *op. cit.*, pp. 200-201.

such a norm can never be denied, not even if its content goes against a norm that does not belong to the legal order.[47]

Within a given legal order all norms are legalized by the constitution. The constitution is not, however, what Kelsen calls the fundamental norm. Not even the constitution that was historically first was the fundamental norm of a legal order. Every constitution is "posited," but every norm ultimately derives its normative validity from a norm that is not "posited" but "presupposed," in order that the entire legal order can be normative. One is forced to admit this presupposed norm if one rejects every "meta-legal authority,"[48] and this rejection is demanded by the requirement that the theory of law be "pure." The "purity" of the legal order is negated as soon as one attends to the content of this order, asks whether the order is just or unjust, or judges it important that the legal order safeguard a condition of relative security in a society. The "presupposition" of the fundamental norm, however, has nothing to do with the affirmation of values transcending positive law.[49] This fundamental norm has no other function than to serve as the foundation of the objective validity of a positive legal order.[50] This fundamental norm is: "One must behave as is prescribed by the author of the legal order."[51]

The Strength of Legal Positivism. The fact that positive law itself provokes questions which cannot be answered by any positive science of law shows how untenable legal positivism is. Its adherents have not failed to notice those questions but they have always tried to get rid of them, for, within the attitude of questions and answers proper to the positive sciences of law, there is no room for problems concerned with the entire realm of positive law as such. Legal positivism is precisely a form

---

[47] "Hence any content whatsoever can be (contained in a) legal (norm) (*Recht*). There is no human relationship that as such, by virtue of its content, would be excluded from being the content of a legal norm. Its validity cannot be denied on the ground that this content contradicts that of another norm which does not belong to the legal order." Kelsen, *op. cit.,* p. 201.

[48] Kelsen, *op. cit.,* p. 203.

[49] "What content this constitution and the state's legal system based on it have, whether this system is just or unjust, is a question that is irrelevant. So also is the question whether this legal system does indeed guarantee a condition of relative peace in the society constituted by it. In the presupposition of the fundamental norm there is no affirmation of any value transcending positive law." Kelsen, *op. cit.,* p. 204.

[50] Kelsen, *op. cit.,* p. 205.

[51] Kelsen, *op. cit.,* p. 204.

of positivism because it claims that those problems are therefore problems for which there is no room anywhere; they are mere pseudo-problems. However, life itself has already shown that such a standpoint is untenable.

All this, however, does not mean that legal positivism is an unimportant phenomenon in the history of the philosophy of law. The contrary is true. Legal positivism rejects the philosophy of law, but it presents itself as *the* philosophy of law. It identifies right with the legal order, that is, with the rules laid down by laws, legal customs and jurisprudence,[52] and with the institutions established in the course of history. Although legal positivism is untenable, it occupies a strong position. We cannot at once show here why it is so strong, but we want to mention it because we have to speak here about the "untenability" of legal positivism and do not wish anyone to think that it is void of any worth-while truth. Anyone should be sensitive to the view that a society is worth what the relationship of man to man is worth in that society; anyone should be able to see the importance the *deed* of establishing a legal order has in the actual humanization of those relationships.[53] Such a one will readily understand that it is not possible even to speak of right, in the provisional and vague sense of being-human, unless the legal order is explicitated as an essential aspect of right and justice in human society.[54]

However, the deed of establishing a legal order presupposes a certain

---

[52] *Wezen en grondslagen van het recht,* Nederlands gesprekscentrum, no. 15, 1957, pp. 8-10.

[53] "The most noble 'consciousness' and the most beautiful 'idea' as such do not contribute a single line to the growth, change or even the origin of the law (*des Rechts*). Unless they become 'deeds' they are nothing. . . . Without this process no legal order (*Recht*) has ever arisen, does ever arise or is able to arise." Bergbohm, *op. cit.,* pp. 544-545.

[54] "Although 'positivism' is a serious sign of the decay affecting the ethics of the law and is the expression of a hybrid belief in the power of the (national) state to create justice (*Recht*), positivism must not be judged only in this respect. True, 'legal security' (*Rechtssicherheit*) as the *only* legal value (*Rechtswert*) of the idea of the natural law, it seems, must be denied very strongly; for 'legal security' omits 'justice,' i.e. the 'differentia specifica' between 'justitia' and 'utilitas.' Nevertheless, even in the 'positivity' of the law there is something 'natural,' something belonging to the 'nature of the matter.' The basis for this is that ultimately all rights want to be 'there' (*da*), to be 'valid,' to 'realize' themselves, to 'embody themselves in time.' This is implied in the 'reality' (*Wirklichkeit*) which the law (*Recht*) has by necessity of nature, in its 'praxis' as a regime of peace." Erik Wolf, *Das Problem der Naturrechtslehre,* Karlsruhe, 1955, pp. 95-96.

power, viz., the power to enforce decisions and regulations. One who has a clear understanding of the demands made by the ideal of humanity but does not have the power to impose certain decisions and regulations does not really accomplish anything. He can demand humanity but cannot build human conditions; he can hope for peace but cannot establish it. Considering that there is no humanity without a legal order, that there is no legal order not established by power, and that generally speaking this power actually resides in the state, one can understand that the legal positivist simply identifies right with the commandments of the state. Right, in the provisionally vague sense of humanity, supposes order. But there exists no order, no real humanity reigns, unless it is established, imposed by someone who has the power to do so. Barbarism, the struggle of all against all, is more effectively combated by a primitive emergency measure than by an ideal of justice.[55]

Nevertheless, as history has taught us in a hard lesson, all this cannot be the last word. As late as 1932 Radbruch, in the third edition of his *Rechtsphilosophie,* wrote that he who has the power to impose legal regulations thereby shows that he is called to posit legal regulations. The judge then has the professional duty to make the law's will to validity become *de facto* validity. He has merely to ask himself what legally ought to be done and not what is just or unjust. The judge must disregard his own sense of justice and obey the law's command. If a priest or a minister preaches something counter to his conviction he is a despicable man, but for a judge it is praiseworthy that he does not let himself be influenced by his sense of justice.[56]

Thus instructed, says Hans Welzel, the German jurists entered the Third *Reich.* Theoretically, it had already been established that they could not resist any command to kill all children with blue eyes, provided the commanding authority had the power to execute its orders. This theoretical powerlessness to resist showed itself to be practical also. When the Third *Reich* had gone under in disaster, legal positivism was an hypothesis wrecked by the gruesome reality of history. The same Radbruch who had made the German jurists powerless before Hitler's

---

[55] "An order theoretically most ideal that does not possess this power to influence reality is not a legal order (*Recht*), but the most imperfect emergency measure that shows itself endowed with this power to influence reality fulfills the essential function of the law (*Recht*)." Welzel, "Naturrecht und Rechtspositivismus," *Festschrift für Hans Niedermeyer,* pp. 286-287.

[56] Welzel, *art. cit.,* p. 279.

system wrote in 1947 that the legal sciences should again reflect upon the age-old wisdom that there is a higher right than the law, a natural right, a divine right, a right of reason, and that injustice remains injustice as measured by this right, even if that injustice is given the form of a law.[57]

One who identifies right with the legal order scores a *near* miss, just as one who identifies right with power. But it is a miss, nevertheless, and not a hit!

2. *The Untenability of Legal Positivism*

Despite the power of legal positivism, its identification of right with the legal order is untenable. First of all, the legal rules which jurists use have been *made*. The legal rules that existed formerly, exists now or will exist in the future, are the work of men. Legal rules are made; they are not discovered somewhere as a traveller discovers a mountain. Why do men make those rules? Obviously, in order that there be justice, and not in order that there be rules of law. The fact that rules of law are made in order that there be justice means that the aim pursued by the making of those rules is the establishment of rights, in the provisionally very vague sense of humanity. If this is true, then right and legal rules can no longer be identified.

Secondly, man constantly revises the legal rules. The reason lies in his conviction that there are injustices in the system of his laws. Anyone who knows something about the law realizes how true that conviction is. The fact that the body of legal rules contains injustices does not mean that among the rules of law there are some which go counter to the rules of law, but that they go against justice, against human rights, against humanity. Man must constantly revise the rules of law in order that

---

[57] "The traditional conception of the law, the *positivism* that for decades unopposedly dominated the German jurists, and its teaching that 'the law is the law' were defenseless and powerless in the face of such an injustice clothed in the form of the law. The followers of this conception were forced to recognize as 'just' (*Recht*) even that iniquitous law. The science of the law must again reflect upon the milennial common wisdom of Antiquity, the Christian Middle Ages and the Age of the Illumination that there exists a higher justice (*Recht*) than the law, a natural law, a divine law, a law of reason—briefly, a justice (*Recht*) that transcends the law. As measured by this higher justice, injustice (*Unrecht*) remains injustice, even when it is given the form of a law. Before this higher justice also the judgment pronounced on the basis of such an unjust law is not the administration of justice but rather injustice." Radbruch, "Die Erneuerung des Rechts," *Die Wandlung,* vol. II (1947), pp. 9-10.

there may be less and less injustice, i.e., in order that the legal rules correspond better to justice.[58] But if this is true, then it is again impossible to identify right and the rules of law.

Finally, it is possible to manipulate the complex of legal rules in such a way that the greatest injustice can be perpetrated efficiently and with impunity. As a matter of fact, this is sometimes done. But if justice and legal rules are identical, then such a possibility could not exist. The fact that it does exist and does happen shows that the identity of the two cannot be maintained.

We realize, of course, that all this is an abomination in the eyes of a man like Kelsen, who spent his entire life in "purifying" the philosophy of law from these kinds of questions. On the basis of the "purity" of the theory of law, he refuses to call a legal order good or bad, just or unjust. One who occupies himself with those kinds of questions makes value judgments, pursues politics and falls into subjectivism. The theory of law can be an "objective science" only by abstaining from such questions.[59]

The American jurist Roscoe Pound counters this position by pointing out that if the philosophy of law must, for the sake of the "purity" of legal theory, reject every value judgment, then it actually gives up everything which make having a philosophy of law worth while.[60] The same point keeps coming back all the time: the philosophical attitude of questioning is not the same as that of a positive science; *therefore,* says the positivist, there can be no question of "objectivity" and "being scientific" in philosophy. The only valid conclusion, however, would be that in philosophy "objectivity" and "being scientific" cannot be of the same kind as in a positive science. But this "otherness" cannot be a ground for rejecting something simply because it differs from what is accepted within a particular positive science.

There would be few, if any, objections to Kelsen's view of the "purity" of the theory of law if he had simply wanted to stress that

---

[58] "One can and, in a sense, one must even appeal from inferior laws and institutions to more perfect laws and institutions, and, against the justice that exists and is defined by customs, practices, institutions and laws, work at the establishment of a better justice." G. Madinier, *Conscience et amour, Essai sur le "Nous,"* Paris, 1947, pp. 54-55.

[59] Kelsen, "Was ist die Reine Rechtslehre?", *Demokratie und Rechtsstaat,* pp. 152-153.

[60] Roscoe Pound, *An Introduction to the Philosophy of Law,* New Haven, 1955 (revised ed.), pp. 23-24.

asking philosophical questions does not pertain to the task of a jurist as such.[61] Within the attitude of questioning proper to the positive sciences of law the question of whether a positive law and the legal order are just or unjust does not arise. The position is very much the same as that of bacteriology, within which the question regarding the ethical position of bacteriological warfare does not arise and cannot arise. But Kelsen goes much farther. He considers it a fatal form of presumption for a "pure theory of law" to ask any questions concerning the justice or injustice of a legal order.

Undoubtedly, it is true that the positive science of law cannot ask this question. However, one who, like Kelsen, reflects upon positive law and the positive sciences of law does not pursue a positive science of law but philosophizes about the law. He imposes on the philosophy of law the same demands as on the positive sciences of law and refuses to let this philosophy ask certain questions *because* the positive sciences of law are unable to raise these questions. Thus, in order that the theory of law be "pure," he demands that the philosophy of law be a science of law. But how can this demand be justified on a ground of positive science of law? One who holds such a position must logically accept the consequence that any arbitrary content can be the content of a legal norm, for the positive sciences of law cannot show that this is not possible. But in that case, according to Kelsen, not even the philosophy of law may deny this consequence under pain of becoming "impure." All this can have only one meaning namely, that the philosophy of law cannot and may not be "pure" in the sense specified by Kelsen. In other words, the philosophy of law cannot be a kind of positivism.

This shows that even for those who dominate the positive sciences of law there remain fundamental questions which can never be answered by these sciences themselves. The first of these has already been mentioned above: what exactly is the principle or right that serves as an orientation point for the rules of law[62] and guides man to be just?

---

[61] "Positivism is the *practical* pursuit of the law itself. It is fully encompassed by this task and sticks to the word of the poet: 'The artist shapes, he does not reason.'" Welzel, *art. cit.,* p. 282.

[62] "This conceptual determination, then, . . . is not juridical but prejuridical, i.e. with respect to the science of law it is of an *a priori* nature. The concept of right (*Recht*) is not an ordinary and contingent concept but a necessary universal concept; hence the legal order (*das Recht*) is not right (*Recht*) because the individual forms of law (*Recht*) can be incorporated in it. Rather the reverse is true: the individual forms of law are manifestations of 'right' only because the concept of right encompasses them." Radbruch, *Rechtsphilosphie,* 4th ed. prepared by Erik Wolf, Stuttgart, 1950, p. 129.

The Normative Character of the Legal Order. All jurists are convinced that the rules of law *ought* to be observed. This conviction, however, inevitably gives rise to certain crucial questions. Why must the legal rules be obeyed? Is it because there is a rule of law that prescribes this obedience? Such an answer merely evades the question, for one can ask at once why the rule of law prescribing obedience to legal rules must be obeyed. It is the task and the duty of the positive sciences of law to pay attention to all kinds of details and shades of meaning with respect to the obligatory character of various positive regulations. But the most fundamental question, viz., the ground on which the obligatory character of the entire legal order as such is based, cannot be answered by a reference to any positive regulation of law. Legal positivism, which identifies right and legal order, leaves the entire legal order without a foundation. Although the positive sciences of law can be specific with respect to all kinds of particular obligations, the obligatory character of the entire legal order as such cannot be given a foundation by referring to any particular obligation.

The same idea can also be expressed in a different way. This way has the advantage of clearly showing the relationship between the following two questions: What is right in contradistinction to the legal order? and, What is the foundation of the "ought" contained in the legal order?

Within the context of a constituted legal order the statement that man ought to be *just* means that he ought to obey the rules of law. In this context, therefore, justice must be described as man's willingness to conform to the demands of the legal order. This willingness presupposes man as *subject,* and the "ought" ascribed to justice implies that the willingness in question is not something that can be left to the subject's arbitrary decision, but must be an *obligatory* attitude. If, then, the subject *himself* is not obliged, more clearly, if being a subject *itself* does not imply a certain obligation, it remains fundamentally unexplained that the legal order has an obligatory character. If the subject *himself* cannot be explicitated as an "obligation," one can endlessly keep repeating that the legal order is obligatory, but all those repeated assertions do not really say anything. A certain "ought" must be inherent, not to the legal order, but to the subject: he *ought* to be just.[63]

---

[63] "As soon as we ask *who* ought and recognize man as the 'addressee' of the 'ought' and his relationship to the world as the reality measured by this criterion, we are at once forced to ask, over and beyond all the self-assured prescriptions of *what* he ought, about the basis of the fact which we accept so unquestioningly that he ought 'by law' (*Recht*). What is the meaning of such an ought? What

Legal positivism did not fail to realize the importance of this question. However, the legal positivist admits nothing but the legal order; hence he is not open to any "ought" that is not identical with the normative character of the legal rules. But it is precisely the total legal order as such whose normative character is at stake. Kelsen tried to explain its normative character without appealing to the subject. For him a norm is a norm because it has been "posited" by a competent authority. But an authority cannot be called competent unless it is made legitimate by a higher norm.[64] Since one cannot go on to infinity in the search of higher norms legitimating lower norms, we must accept a "fundamental norm." This fundamental norm is not "posited," of course, for otherwise it would need again a higher legitimating norm. The fundamental norm is "presupposed" and has to be "presupposed" if certain deeds are to be seen as creating or applying norms of right.[65]

One should realize what is implied in all this. With respect to the question of the basis on which the entire legal order is normative, Kelsen refuses to refer to a certain "ought" in the subject. Nevertheless, the question must be asked, for there must be a reason why certain deeds create or apply norms of right and are not mere tyranny or barbarism. Evidently, the positive sciences of law *as such* cannot answer this question. For Kelsen this means that the philosophy of law cannot answer it either without surrendering its "purity." "Pure" philosophy of law must "presuppose" a fundamental norm, and this presupposition must be the foundation on which the normative character of the entire legal order is based. In other words, his answer to the question why the total legal order is normative is: it is *presupposed* to be normative. The big question, however, is on what ground one can make this presupposition. If the subject himself is not a certain "ought," then no objective rule can be said to be normative.

---

is the purpose of the entire world of law? What does this world matter to you, a human being whose existence in this world did not begin 'by law'?" Werner Maihofer, *Recht und Sein, Prolegomena zu einer Rechtsontologie,* Frankfurt a.M., 1954, p. 37.

[64] "The fact that someone somewhere issues an order is not a ground on which the order can be regarded as valid, that is, as a binding norm for the one to whom it is addressed. Only a competent authority can posit valid norms, and such competence can be based upon a norm giving power to posit norms. The authority enpowered to posit norms is just as much subject to this norm as the individuals are obliged to obey the norms posited by this authority." Kelsen, *Reine Rechtslehre,* p. 197.

[65] Kelsen, *op. cit.,* p. 203.

Kelsen's view will not be surprising if it is looked at in the light of an authentic philosophy of law. Such a philosophy affirms that the jurist *as* jurist presupposes the normative character of the legal order. *As* jurist he need not concern himself with this point. Kelsen's demand that the theory of law be, above all, "pure" implies that the philosophy of law must be positivistic. But in such a perspective the philosopher of law also sees nothing but what is seen by the jurist *as* jurist, viz., the legal order with its *presupposition* of being normative. However, one who reduces the normative character of the legal order to the *presupposition* that the legal order is normative empties this character to such an extent that the theory is no longer in agreement with reality.

It is precisely this elimination of everything pertaining to right and justice that makes Kelsen's positivism unacceptable. His views about the nature of the legal norm are particularly instructive in this respect. In a rule of positive law, he says, two facts are connected with each other by the principle of imputability;[66] hence the basic scheme of any legal order is: if an injustice is committed, then an action ought to occur as the effect of that injustice.[67] If, for instance, a legal norm asserts the right to bodily integrity, this means simply that the power of the state will react when someone violates the bodily integrity of a person. Obviously, we do not want to deny that in a society possessing a measure of legal organization the power of the state will react against any violation of its members' bodily integrity. The question, however, is what does it mean that there exists a norm asserting one's right to bodily integrity? Does it mean *nothing but* that the state will react when this bodily integrity is violated? Does such an existential point as the right to life mean *nothing but* that the state will proceed with force against anyone who does not respect the other's life?

Kelsen's reply to this question is unhesitatingly in the affirmative. On the side of the subject, then, who has the right, there is nothing.[68] My right to life *is* nothing but the fact that the state will react if someone kills me. The so-called subjective right of the one is nothing but the

---

[66] Kelsen, *art. cit.* (footnote 59), p. 144.

[67] Kelsen, *art. cit.* (footnote 59), p. 145.

[68] "But this relationship (*Sachverhalt*) called the 'right' or 'title' of an individual is nothing but the obligation of the others. If in such a case one speaks of a subjective right or title of the individual as if this right or title were something different from the obligation of the others, then one produces the semblance of two relationships of right (*rechtlich*) where there is only one." Kelsen, *Reine Rechtslehre,* p. 132.

obligation of the other, and this obligation is nothing but the fact that the power of the state has attached a sanction to a certain form of behavior.[69]   Kelsen does not object to the use of the term "subjective right" as an auxiliary concept, provided one keeps in mind that this subjective right is nothing but a kind of "reflex right."[70]   Strictly speaking, then, this right is nothing.   This conclusion follows for Kelsen from the fact that one would have to ascribe subjective rights also to plants, animals and things if the reflex of someone's obligation were conceived as something *real* in the legal order.   For the law specifies that certain flowers may not be plucked at certain times, certain animals may not be killed in certain seasons, and it is prohibited to demolish certain buildings.[71]   He who violates those laws will be struck by the sanctions of the legal norms; hence he has an obligation.   Nevertheless, no one will, on the basis of this obligation, ascribe subjective rights to flowers, animals and buildings.[72]   Consequently, man likewise has no right if the sanction of the legal norm obliges the others to a certain type of behavior toward him.[73]

Did Pound go too far when he claimed that Kelsen's "pure" theory of law is stripped of anything making it worth-while to have a philosophy of law?   Kelsen's idea about subjective right show that Pound was right. Kelsen first explicitates the legal norm as the mere fact that a sanction is attached to a certain form of behavior.   This alone is enough to make the normative character of the norm an enigma.   Kelsen then realizes that the norm as the duty of the one is correlated to the right of the other.   However, his way of thinking about the norm forces him to ascribe rights to plants, animals and monuments as well.   The fact that no one wants to claim such rights for these nonhuman beings does not make Kelsen change his theory about the legal norm but induces him to deny also the subjective rights of man.   That a subject has a right to

---

[69] "The fact that an individual is obliged to a certain conduct means that in case he conducts himself differently a sanction ought to follow. His obligation is the norm prescribing this conduct insofar as this norm attaches a sanction to opposite conduct."   Kelsen, *op. cit.,* p. 132.

[70] Kelsen, *op. cit.,* p. 133.

[71] *Ibid.*

[72] "But 'reflex rights' of animals, plants and lifeless objects, the direct opposites of which those duties are, are not accepted."   Kelsen, *ibid.*

[73] "Because the 'reflex right' is identical with the duty to observe this right (*Rechtspflicht*), the individual in reference to whom this duty exists is rightly not considered the 'subject' because he is not the subject of this duty."   Kelsen, *op. cit.,* p. 134.

something actually does not mean anything *for this subject;* for, in Kelsen's eyes, the norm is *everything.* Everything that brings the meaning of the subject to mind is in Kelsen's view a reminder of the "natural law";[74] and for the sake of positivism this natural law must be eradicated.

We can now approach the second fundamental question of the philosophy of law. The first question asked about the essence of the principle, or the right by which the legal order is orientated. The second is concerned with the essence of the "ought" of justice, understood as a being-obliged to what is right. The legal order is not identical with what is right; sometimes it even goes counter to it. In such a case justice makes it a duty for man to reject the legal order or to reform it. Man "ought" to be just. This "ought" remains unexplained within legal positivism, which cannot even justify the normative character of the legal order and is helpless before arbitrary and inhuman laws. Radbruch, especially, has shown this very clearly since World War II.[75]

3. Marx on the Legal Order and Justice

The Marxist theory of the legal order reveals with great clarity how inevitable the questions are which occupy the attention of the philosophy of law. It therefore deserves to be considered here in greater detail.

The Meaning of the Means of Production. According to Marx the character of the means of production unambiguously indicates the level reached by a particular phase of history.[76] This view is based on the conviction that man from his origin is not simply man just as a rain squall is wet or a lily white, but has slowly to rise to being authentically man through his productive labor.[77] For this reason the various phases of history show also different phases of authenticity and these phases, says Marx, are determined by the situation in the realm of the means of production.

---

[74] *Ibid.*

[75] "Positivism with its conviction that 'the law is the law' did indeed make the German jurists powerless with respect to laws of an arbitrary and criminal nature. Moreover, positivism is not at all able to assign, by virtue of its own power, a foundation to the validity of laws." Radbruch, "Gesetzliches Unrecht und übergesetzliches Recht," *Rechtsphilosophie,* Stuttgart, 4th. ed., 1958, p. 352.

[76] Karl Marx, *Das Kapital,* Berlin, 1957, p. 185.

[77] "By working through this motion on nature outside himself and changing it, he changes at the same time also his own nature." Marx, *ibid.*

The character of the *means* of production also determines the character of the *relationships* of production. The fact that a society uses a particular type of productive means has as a consequence the fact that the producing men enter into relation with one another in a particular way. Where wool is produced on a spinning wheel people do not relate in the same way as in modern textile mills. In juridical terms the relationships of production are called ownership relations.[78]

There exists, of course, no objection to the fact that in a certain phase of economic life everybody is occupied with the production of wool and owns his own spinning wheel. But in a subsequent phase of economic development *all* these wheels are replaced by one machine. Or in general terms, the modern means of production make all primitive productive means economically valueless. Just as the spinning wheels were, however, these modern means of production will, at least at first, be privately owned. And this, says Marx, is objectionable, for these modern means of production are by their very nature social. Because the primitive means have become economically valueless, those who earned their living through them have now to depend on working for hire in the service of owners of modern productive means. In this way the private ownership of these means gives the possessor absolute power over the have-nots;[79] the owner becomes an exploiter and the have-nots are his victims.

The Will of the Ruling Class. The legal order, says Marx, is to be understood on the basis of the actually existing ownership relations. For this order is nothing but the will of the ruling class elevated to law. The content of this will is implied in the material living conditions of the ruling class.[80]

When society reaches a certain level of development, there arises a need to establish a common regulation for the daily recurrent actions of production, distribution and exchange, in order to prevent each individual from going his own way in this production, distribution and exchange. Such a regulation is called a "law." As the development of

[78] Marx, "Zur Kritik der politische Oeconomie, Vorwort," Karl Marx and Friedrich Engels, *Ausgewählte Schriften in zwei Bänden* (hereafter quoted as MEAS), Berlin, 1952, vol. I, p. 338.

[79] "At a certain stage of their development society's material forces of production came into contradiction with the existing relationships of production within which they had moved. From being developmental forms of these productive forces these relationships changed into chains." Marx, *ibid.*

[80] Marx-Engels, "Manifest der Kommunistischen Partei," MEAS, vol. I, p. 39.

society progresses, the law becomes more or less elaborate and slowly man forgets that these laws are an expression of the economic living conditions. The rule that stealing is prohibited thus actually and exclusively comes to mean that the owners who are exploiters must be allowed to have their way. The legal order, then, begins to lead a kind of independent existence. This independence gives rise to professional jurists and, at the same time, to the science of law. The professional jurists compare the legal systems of the various peoples, not as expressions of economic conditions but as independent and self-sufficient systems. This comparison shows that there are certain similarities, and these similarities the jurists call the "natural law," [81] the object of "justice." Once the jurists have reached this point, the development of the law consists for them in the effort to bring the relationship between men closer to "eternal justice." But even this so-called "eternal justice" is nothing but the ideological, "heavenly" expression of economic relationships.[82] The jurists imagine that they are dealing with *a priori* theses, while in reality they are working with reflexes of economic conditions.[83]

Organs are needed to maintain the law; they are the state and its power. The state is nothing but the organized power of the possessing class, the large land-owners and capitalists, over the exploited class, over farmers and laborers.[84] As long as society is composed of classes, there has to be a state, for the ruling class must use every means to oppress the exploited class. The state considers itself the official representative of the entire society, but in reality it represents only the economic interests of the ruling class.[85] Thus the laborer does not have a country, a fatherland.

The state establishes public power. This power is not the armed power of the organized people, for the people is divided into classes. The slaves also belong to the people of a state, but they are kept in

---

[81] "The comparison presupposes something common. The jurists find this common element by compiling what is more or less common to all those legal systems into natural law." Engels, "Zur Wohnungsfrage," MEAS, vol. I, p. 592.

[82] Engels, *art. cit.*, MEAS, vol. I, pp. 592-593.

[83] Engels, "Brief an Schmidt," MEAS, vol. I, p. 464.

[84] "The state is nothing but the organized common power of the possessing classes, the landowners and the capitalists, against the exploited classes, the peasants and the workers." Engels, *art. cit.* (footnote 81), p. 573.

[85] Engels, "Die Entwicklung des Sozialismus von der Utopie zur Wissenschaft," MEAS, vol. II, p. 139.

submission by the state's public power. Justice is a class justice. The state and public power are reflexes of economic interests.[86]

Right or Power? The Marxist theories of law and justice very clearly show how inevitable the questions are with which the philosophy of law is concerned. The present-day situation adds a dramatic accent to these questions. One who understands the Marxist position with respect to the existing legal order of the West must arrive at the conclusion that, for the Marxist, this legal order is identical with injustice and that justice must be defined as the willingness to overthrow that order.

The firmness with which the opposition to Marxism organized itself against the possible consequences of Marx' ideas was at first purely political. Its opponents tried to establish a power system to prevent the Marxists from putting into effect their intention to overthrow the legal order and the state. The theoretical foundation of this political firmness, however, was far from being as solid as that firm attitude seemed to suggest. In the era of liberalistic capitalism it was almost impossible to offer a theoretical defense against the Marxist identification of legal order and injustice and against the definition of justice as willingness to overthrow that legal order and the state.

The realization of this impossibility led the progressive countries of the West to a fundamental revision of their legal order. Marx's Communist Manifesto enumerated ten points of the program for social reform to be realized at once *after* the revolution. But they were introduced practically in their entirety by the progressive nations of the West *without* the revolution desired by Marx.[87] The result was that the state also acquired a meaning that differed radically from that existing in Marx's time.

Generally speaking, the progressive nations of the West have realized the economic, social and political liberation of man in a more effective and more comprehensive way than the countries in which Marxism was given a chance to do so. Nevertheless, the Marxists continue to maintain the Marxist view of law and justice in spite of all the evidence to

---

[86] Engels, "Der Ursprung der Familie, des Privateigentums und des Staats," MEAS, vol. II, pp. 296-297.

[87] W. Banning, *Om mens en menselijkheid in maatschappij en politiek,* Amsterdam, 1960, pp. 92-93.

the contrary.[88] The firmness with which they turn against the progressive nations of the West reveals itself to be of a purely political nature. This means that by means of a naked power system they try to overthrow the legal order of countries which have achieved more for the liberation of man than has been done by countries in which Marxism was given a chance, and all this *in order that there be justice!*

Thus the question that imposes itself with renewed urgency is: What, then, exactly is "right"? What is justice? One thing should be clear, viz., that justice cannot be defined as the willingness either to obey and preserve the legal order or to overthrow this order. The legal order is identical with neither justice nor injustice. What justice or injustice is cannot be decided by power.

4. *Rules of Law, Authority and Power*

Our inquiry into the specific questions of the philosophy of law has actually led us to a critical reflection upon legal positivism. This is not surprising because the philosophy of law's question about the essence of right is given an unequivocal answer by legal positivism: it simply identifies right and the legal order. We indicated above why this identification must be rejected.

Meanwhile, however, it has also become evident that the philosophy of law investigates not only the essence of right and justice but must reflect also upon the essence of the legal order, understood as the complex of rules of law and legal institutions. For, granted that it is impossible to identify right and the legal order, nonetheless these two are so intimately connected that it is simply impossible to speak of right without speaking of the legal order. The question about right evokes the question about the legal order, and the answer to this question is not of a juridical nature but belongs to the philosophy of law. Thus it cannot belong to the task of the jurist *as* jurist to reflect upon the nature of the legal order.

---

[88] "The definition of right (*Recht*) developed by Wyschinsky . . . expresses that the existence of right is connected with the split of human society into classes; secondly, that the norms reflect the needs of their former foundation, laid down in the will of the economically and politically ruling class which they represent; and finally that the legal norms are destined to play a role in the service of the interests of the former ruling class in the system of the superstructure." H. Klenner, *Der Marxismus-Leninismus über das Wesen des Rechts,* Berlin, 1954, p. 10.

An Illustration. This statement should not be misunderstood. We do not want to say that jurists should not reflect upon the legal order. Of course, they should, but the question is whether or not they can do so as jurists. *As* jurists they know and handle the legal order,[89] they know and handle the rules of law and the legal institutions, just as physicists *as* physicists know and handle the quantitative world. This comparison can throw some light on the question occupying us here, provided one keeps in mind that we speak here of physicists *as* physicists. *As* physicists they have a specific task. Inspired by a specific *cogito,* they try to express the quantitative aspect of reality. The result of their investigations is always a statement such as: "it is of such and such a size, such and such a weight, such and such a velocity," although those statements are constantly more and more refined. The specific *cogito* of the physicist always results in a measuring number and *nothing else.*

Thus for the physicist as physicist nothing is beautiful, imposing, full of love or hatred, or created. As soon as this statement is made, the difficulties begin, for we are at once misunderstood when we say that for the physicist *as* physicist the beautiful, the imposing, the lovable, the hateful, and the created do not exist. Many physicists rise in protest because they have overcome the scientism for which only that is real which can be approached by the methods of science in the narrow sense of the term. They loudly proclaim that they too recognize the beautiful and the lovable. They unambiguously testify that they realize the limitations of the specific *cogito* used by the physical sciences and thus have opened the road to the recognition of things other than those revealed by these sciences.

There is every reason to rejoice over the fact that so many scientists have overcome the tendency to scientism. Nevertheless, it remains important to preserve the necessary distinctions. When physicists claim that they recognize non-quantitative realities, we must ask whether or not this recognition arises from the specific *cogito* of the physical sciences, from the way physical science approaches everything. The answer is obviously in the negative, and for this reason we said above that the beautiful, the imposing, the lovable, the hateful and the created do not

---

[89] "This 'range of the law' (*Raum des Rechts*), however, is somehow also for the jurist something 'obvious' and, precisely because of its 'obviousness,' he cannot offer any explanation of it 'as jurist.' For his juridical problems and questions begin only later, viz. *within* this range or realm that remains unquestioned but is very much subject to question." Maihofer, *Recht und Sein,* p. 67.

exist for the physicist *as* physicist. If, then, a particular physicist claims that those meanings do exist for him, he expresses the fact that he does not identify his being a physicist with the whole of his being man. He gives expression to the insight that his subjectivity-as-*cogito* is involved in the world by means of many attitudes and that the specific attitude of physical science is only one of these many. But this insight does not entitle him to claim that non-quantitative realities can be recognized by the mind of the physicist *as* physicist. For this reason we said above that the physicist's specific *cogito* always results in a measuring number and never in anything else.

The objection is sometimes made that man should not be divided into many parts as we seem to do here. Man is a totality, a *Gestalt* of many attitudes. We fully agree with this statement and recognize that it is not possible to separate the many attitudes of the subject as *cogito*. On the other hand, they need to be distinguished, for one attitude is not the other. If their distinction is neglected and one claims, for example, that the specific *cogito* of the physicist as such can disclose the beautiful or the created, one fails to recognize the specific nature of being beautiful and being created.

Positive Science of Law and Philosophy of Law. Let us apply these ideas now to the distinction between knowledge pertaining to positive law and knowledge pertaining to the philosophy of law. From what was said above, it should be clear that it is not the task of the physicist *as* physicist to reflect upon the nature of his own science and upon that of the specific region of being connected with the specific *cogito* of physical science. The physicist *as* physicist does not have the duty to define the essence of the knowledge given by physical science and of the physical, in the sense of that which is attained by physical science. Obviously, however, he can attempt to do so anyhow, but in that case he should realize that he abandons the typical attitude of questioning and answering of the physicist and becomes a philosopher.

The same line of thought applies also to the jurist. *As* jurist he does not have the task of defining the nature of his work and its object, the legal order. This kind of reflection does not belong to the positive legal thinking in which the jurist *ex professo* engages.[90] We do not mean, of

---

[90] "Just as electricians handle wires and do not know what electric current is, so, jurists do not really know what right (*Recht*) is. The question of what right is constitutes the central question of the philosophy of law or also of the problem

course, that in our eyes the jurist must *per se* be what some have called the "dehydrated" jurist,[91] and that he is insensitive to philosophical considerations of the law.[92]   On the contrary, the philosophy of law should preferably be pursued by jurists, and only philosophical reflection upon the law can prevent the jurist from becoming "dehydrated."   The question, however, is whether the jurist *as* jurist can ask philosophical questions about the law.   The answer is in the negative.   Jurists who ask philosophical questions about the law abandon the typical attitude of positive legal science, and if they think that they can raise the philosophical questions about the law from the standpoint that is proper to them as jurists, they can only cause the greatest confusion both for themselves and for others.   It happens, for example, that philosophical considerations lead the jurist to the recognition of the natural law.   But then it happens not infrequently that he quickly rejects this natural law again because he realizes that this law cannot be handled in the same way as he can handle the legal order.   He assumes that it *should* be possible to handle both in the same way.

Accordingly, our view does not imply that we "cut man into separate fragments."   We recognize in man a *Gestalt* of many attitudes of being in the world; man is a total "melody of meaning."   This recognition, however, does not take away the necessity of making distinctions, and neglecting them can only cause confusion.

The philosophical question concerning the essence of the legal order, i.e., the essence of the rules of law and legal institutions, is raised by the philosophical question about the nature of right and about the "ought" of justice.   As we have emphasized already, it is not possible to speak about right and justice without mentioning the meaning of rules of law and legal institutions.   The intimate bond between right and legal order leads positivism to identify these two.

Through this identification, however, positivism clothes itself in a strange garment when one considers that a legal order is not a legal order unless it is "posited."   A legal order becomes a legal order only when it is posited by someone with authority and power.   If we abstract from the juridical regulations pertaining to smaller groups, it is obvious

---

of the natural law."   Fechner, "Naturrecht und Existenzphilosophie," *Archiv für Rechts- und Sozialphilosophie,* vol. XLI (1954-55), pp. 311-312.

[91] Thus W. Pompe on the occasion of the discussion about "Phaenomenologie van het recht," *Annalen v.h. Thijmgenootschap,* vol. 48 (1960), p. 101.

[92] Thus G. Hoefnagels, *ibid.,* p. 104.

that the state functions as the "positing" authority and power. The legal order supposes the authority and the power of the state.

Positivism and State Absolutism. The fact that the legal order supposes the authority and the power of the state implies that state absolutism is *per se* inherent in the absolutism of positive law. For legal positivism the question of the justice or injustice of the legal order is simply meaningless nonsense. The legal order is posited by the state; it is not what it is without the authority and the power of the state. But if that question is meaningless nonsense, then it is also nonsense to ask whether that which the state posits is just or unjust. What else is this if not state absolutism?

In time of peace and domestic tranquillity it can happen that this consequence of legal positivism does not clearly manifest itself. But twentieth century man has gone through such bitter experiences that he no longer accepts the proposition: "Right is that which the state posits." Even if the theoretical arguments against legal positivism would not appeal to him, the disastrous consequences of state absolutism would suffice to open his eyes. The mechanized death of millions of human beings has stripped legal positivism of its armor. Its arguments were strong but collapsed under the weight of legalized mass murder. But the misery of legal positivism and the state absolutism inherent in it cannot be prevented unless man has the courage to ask himself whether the legal order is just. Courage is needed to ask this question. The philosophy of law, it is said, spoils the "good" jurist because it takes away his security and certainty and burdens him with scruples and useless thoughts in his work. The philosophy of law, it is alleged, gives the jurist a "bad conscience." Philosophy offers no apologies against these accusations.[93] It does not make things easier but, rather, more difficult. But the rejection of philosophy is also a philosophy—the worst possible type. Philosophizing is not a tranquilizer; philosophy is not a hospital (Merleau-Ponty).

Brief History. The strength and the weakness of legal positivism are mirrored, as it were, in the history of the struggle between legal positiv-

---

[93] "The old story is: the philosophy of law spoils the 'good' jurist; it disturbs his tranquillity and security and overloads the self-complacency of the acquired practices of his trade with 'scruples' and 'useless' thoughts; it gives him a 'bad conscience' for his profession. This reproach strikes not merely at the philosophy of the law, for all philosophy, by its very nature, makes things not easier but more difficult." Maihofer, *Recht und Sein*, pp. 40-41.

ism and the theory of the natural law. This struggle can be traced back from our time to far into antiquity. The positivism of the Third *Reich* was followed after World War II by a strong revival of the natural law in Germany. In the second half of the nineteenth century legal positivism was greatly stimulated by the developments occurring in the sciences, but the Thomistic theory of the natural law managed to maintain itself. In the first half of the same century the positivism of the Historical School battled against the remnants of the rationalistic conception of the natural law dating from the era of the Enlightenment. In the period of the bloom of rationalism the theory of the natural law faced the positivistic concept of right and justice resulting from a "social contract." In the Middle Ages Thomas Aquinas conceived the natural law as an eternal order of being which originated in God's intellect. Nominalism, guided by William of Ockham denied this eternal order of being and sought the basis of right and justice in the will of God. In antiquity the positivism of the Sophists came into conflict with the theory of the natural law defended by Plato and Aristotle.[94]

The struggle between positivism and the natural law imposes itself as an existential dilemma on all those who are concerned with humanity. No humanity is possible without positive law, but positive law itself can be an incarnation of inhumanity. Hence positive law must be supported by a foundation and subject to a critical norm. It is the merit of the defenders of the natural law that they saw this necessity.

---

[94] Fechner, *op. cit.* (footnote 90), p. 313.

CHAPTER TWO

THEORIES ABOUT THE NATURE OF MAN'S CONSCIOUSNESS OF RIGHT AS THE SOURCE OF THE LEGAL ORDER

Anyone is aware of the fact that the legal order is man-made. Thus the question about the origin of the legal order can be answered, it seems, rather easily. Unless, however, one holds that man can "make" a legal order in a wholly arbitrary way, the question about the source of this order still remains. Man makes a legal order in accordance with his "consciousness of right." It is always a certain conviction about what is just that induces man to establish a particular legal order. Thus the question about the origin of the legal order is really a question about the nature of man's "consciousness of right."

Instead of the term "consciousness of right" we would prefer to use the expression "existence as projecting right." The use of this expression, however, assumes that one is familiar with the idea of human consciousness as an "existent" consciousness, and this idea has not yet been mentioned. Moreover, the term does not fit into the context of this chapter, which will present a survey of the various theories about the origin of the legal order. The reader who is familiar with existential phenomenology will not fail to notice that these theories always start from the implicit conviction that man's consciousness is not an "existent" but an isolated consciousness. Provisionally, therefore, we will use the old terminology and speak of the consciousness of right.

The consciousness of right, the implicit or explicit conviction of what is just, is, we said, the source of the legal order. In this way the question about the origin of the legal order becomes the more profound question about the nature of man's consciousness of right.   In the existing studies of the philosophy of law a distinction between the consciousness of right and the legal order is not always made, not even by those who refuse to identify man's consciousness of right with the regulations of the legal order, as is done by legal positivism.   Treatises about the nature of man's consciousness of right as the origin of the legal order are often presented as if they were theories about the origin of "the" law; yet the authors of these treatises do not necessarily identify right and the legal order.   To avoid misunderstandings that could arise from such a terminology, we will refer to those theories as theories about the nature of man's consciousness of right as the origin of the legal order.

The number of theories about the nature of man's consciousness of right is discouragingly large.[1]   However, it is not difficult to discern a certain order in this seeming chaos if one keeps in mind that in the past man's consciousness was conceived as isolated from that which is not this consciousness itself.   (We will use the provisionally vague term "worldly meaning" to refer to that which is not consciousness itself.)   With respect to man's consciousness there are two possibilities of emphasis: one can stress its activity, spontaneity and inspirational significance and neglect the proper "weight" of the "wordly meaning," or one can stress the significance and influence of the worldly meaning.   This twofold possibility exists not merely in theory within the Cartesian trend of philosophizing, it has also been put into practice, with all the consequences flowing from it for the philosophy of law.   Erich Fechner distinguishes two groups in those explanatory theories: realistic views and idealistic views.[2]   The same distinction could be expressed also by referring to objectivistic and subjectivistic theories, provided those terms are understood correctly.   Objectivistic theories are those which try to explain the consciousness of right "from below," i.e., from the weight of worldly meaning.   Subjectivistic theories pay great attention to the subject's spontaneity and inspiration in his consciousness of right; hence then try to explain the legal order "from above."[3]

---

[1] Cf. Hommes, *Een nieuwe herleving van het natuurrecht,* Zwolle, 1961.

[2] Fechner, *Rechtsphilosophie,* pp. 21-51.

[3] "The replies . . . can be put . . . into two groups: those who, in a sense, build up the legal order of rights and duties (*das Recht*) from below, on the basis of the real, though changeable, data of life and of social facts; and those who derive it 'from above,' from absolute norms of justice (*Recht*) determined by the 'mind.' " Fechner, *op. cit.,* p. 21.

1. Objectivistic Explanations of the Origin of Man's Consciousness of Right

What do the objectivistic theories about the origin of man's consciousness refer to when they exclusively emphasize the weight of worldly meaning? The answer is not far to seek; they refer to the actually existing relationships among men. The proponents of those objectivistic theories show themselves particularly sensitive to the undeniable fact that an existing legal order also contains the facticity of a society. In any legal order one can also see, at least to a certain extent, how the relations actually are between men. True, the legal order states how the members of a society ought to behave toward one another and toward society, but, at the same time, this order also shows, at least to a certain extent, what kind of relations actually exist in that society. The legal order reveals whether a society is organized in a patriarchal or matriarchal way; it shows that the society is actually composed of men and women, married and single people, adults and children, employers and employees, farmers, technicians, officials and teachers, dwellers in houses or trailers and hoboes, white and colored people, colonists and natives; and if a legal order prohibits unfair competition or the formation of trusts, it shows also to some extent what the actual conditions are with respect to industrial production.

It would be unthinkable that a legal order would reveal nothing at all of the actual conditions existing in a particular society. For, if the legal order primarily tries to determine what those conditions ought to be in order to be just, all its regulations concerning this "ought" would be in a vacuum unless they endeavor to regulate existing conditions. A legal order is wholly meaningless if it does not come to grip with actual conditions. Hence these conditions manifest themselves in that order.

Objectivistic theories about the origin of man's consciousness of right are not only especially sensitive to the weight of the actually existing conditions, but they also exaggerate this weight to such an extent that they see in this consciousness of right nothing but a *passive* mirroring of those actual conditions. The legal order, they hold, is made in accordance with this passive mirror image of those conditions.

Various Types of Objectivism. It stands to reason that this description of objectivism does not do justice to the variations existing within those theories. For the actually existing relations among men are what they are only on the basis of certain conditions. According as one or the other of these conditions is more emphasized, objectivism appears in a different light.

Some theories about the origin of man's consciousness of right pay attention only to conditions of a biological nature. They defend a kind of legal biologism, in which the consciousness of right is conceived as a reflection of actual biological conditions. The fact that the legal order contains certain rules about sexual intercourse means, in the eyes of the legal biologist, nothing but that the fact of man's sexuality and the fact of sexual relations mirror themselves passively in the consciousness of those who establish the legal order. The fact that the legal order imposes certain obligation upon the parents of the newborn child means nothing but that the relationship existing between parents and the child, based on the parent's procreative action and the child's helplessness, is mirrored in the consciousness of those who are charged with the legal order. In Hitler's Germany the Jews were deprived of all human rights by the "legal order" because they were biologically Jews; in other countries Negroes are prevented from developing themselves according to their capacities because they are biologically Negroes. Such regulations were or are "justified" with an appeal to legal biologism.[4]

For others again the actual conditions are determined exclusively by economic factors. The situation with respect to the means of production implies that the members of a certain producing society are related to one another in a certain way. These relations are mirrored in man's consciousness, so that in the legal order also one finds nothing but these actually existing economic relations. This idea is the central thought of legal economism, which, according to Marxism, is embodied in the liberalistic-capitalistic society.[5]

Finally there is a view about the origin of man's consciousness of right that is based upon power politics. In this view, consciousness of right is nothing but the expression and reflection of the *de facto* existing political power relationship. The greater power a particular group in a society has, the less restrained it will be in imposing its will upon the other groups. But the powerful group cannot impose its will permanently upon the others unless it is backed by a legal order. Because the legal

---

[4] Fechner, *op. cit.*, pp. 22-25.

[5] Klenner, *Der Marxismus-Leninismus über das Wesen des Rechts*, Berlin, 1954.

order makes it possible to exert force with respect to the actions it prescribes, this order becomes the means *par excellence* by which those who actually hold power impose their will upon the others. Thus the legal order is simply the expression of the existing power relations. Machiavelli and Hobbes are the most prominent representatives of this theory of right.[6]

Objectivism as a Form of Sociologism. Accordingly, it is always and exclusively the *de facto* existing relationships that are viewed as the origin of man's consciousness of right by the proponents of legal objectivism. Hence it is not surprising that in the elaboration of its explanatory theories legal objectivism appeals to sociology, for it is precisely the task of positive sociology to describe the actual conditions existing in a particular society. Objectivism, moreover, as we saw, holds that in the formation of man's consciousness of right there are no other factors whatsoever present save those spoken of by sociology. For this reason this objectivism, as an overemphasis upon the role of sociology, may also be called sociologism.

We realize, of course, that the above-mentioned description of the objectivistic explanatory theories regarding the origin of man's consciousness of right fails to pay attention to the many differences existing among the authors defending those theories. This failure, however, could be remedied only by writing an extensive history of the philosophy of law, which is beyond our intention. Let us add a few words, nonetheless, to show that many such differences are possible. The views defended by the so-called "Historical School" may be mentioned as an illustration.

These views, of which von Savigny and Puchta are the principal protagonists, must be called a form of objectivism. In keeping with its orientation to the history of the growth of law,[7] the Historical School is almost exclusively interested in the rise of "law" among primitive groups of men. These groups are not communities of persons in the authentic sense of the term but groups constituted by a kind of biological-affective union of their members, driven by quasi-instinctive, almost unconscious and quasi-animal forces and impulses of a gregarious nature. From those forces and impulses there "grows" almost spontaneously a kind of

---

[6] Fechner, *op. cit.*, pp. 29-32.

[7] Von Savigny, "Über den Zweck dieser Zietschrift," *Zeitschrift für geschichtliche Rechtswissenschaft,* vol. I (1815), pp. 1, 17.

order and equilibrium within the group, which its members observe as a
necessity of life. According to the Historical School, this order is a kind
of "sediment" from the forces resulting from the "unreflecting spirit of
the people" (*Volksgeist*).[8] Only in a later and higher phase of culture
was this quasi-unconscious creation of the "people's spirit" developed in a
technical-juridical way by jurists.[9]

These views of the Historical School show that objectivism as an
attempt to explain "from below" man's consciousness of right can assume
many forms. But the characteristic feature of all forms of objectivism is
that the subject's spontaneity, inspiration and activity receives hardly any
attention. True, the subject is not absent from the objectivistic explanations, for it is obvious that the legal order is "made" and that this
"making" is done by a subject. The legal order does not grow as a tree
develops twigs and leaves. However, the subject's making ultimately is,
in the eyes of objectivism, only a kind of "being driven" by the actually
existing conditions. Ultimately the legal order is nothing but a mirror
image of those conditions in a passive subject.[10]

All this became rather crude when sociologistic objectivism fell under
the influence of the ideal of science which in the nineteenth century was
propagated by Comte and almost unanimously accepted. For Comte
sociology was a kind of physical science. Many sociologists treated
sociological facts as if they were facts of physical science and, consequently, endeavored to cast man's social life in the same molds in which
the physicists tried to compress the events of nature. In this way they

---

[8] Carlos Gits, *Recht, persoon en gemeenschap*, Louvain, 1949, pp. 355-375.

[9] "Thus the legal order of rights and duties (*das Recht*) grows with the
people, develops with the people, and finally dies when the people loses its
proper character. . . . As culture increases . . . all activities of the people
become more particularized, and what formerly was done in common now
belongs to individual classes. The jurists also appear now as such a separate
class." Von Savigny, *Vom Beruf unsrer Zeit für Gesetzgebung und Rechtswissenschaft,* Freiburg i.Br., 1829, p. 7.

[10] "There arises a regularity in man's way of acting toward his kind or, which
is the same, society assumes a certain form, a fixed order. In this way there
arises the matter from which the legal order (*het recht*) is built, for man's mind
becomes aware of this regularity. From all the particular actions he perceives,
he formulates the rule that is immanent in them. Consciousness of this rule we
call 'ethical consciousness' or, if it is attained through deliberate inquiry, 'ethical
conviction.' " H. J. Hamaker, "Dogmatische en empirische rechtsbeschouwing,"
Verspreide Geschriften, vol. VII, Haarlem, 1913, pp. 15-16. Cf. *ibid.,* pp. 19-
133, "Het recht en de maatschappij."

conceived the influence of the actually existing social conditions on the subject constituting the legal order as a unilateral and deterministic causal influence, as a process in the same sense in which the physicist speaks of a process. The subject's passivity under the pressure of the existing conditions was overemphasized to such an extent that *de facto* there remained nothing worthy of the name of the subject as subject. Under the influence of scientism, objectivism degenerated into a vulgar kind of physicalistic materialism.[11]

The Strength and Weakness of Objectivism. Generally speaking, a philosophy fails not so much by what it says as by what it neglects to say. The philosopher is tempted to this neglect because he absolutizes what he sees and expresses, so that there remains no room for anything else.

This general principle makes us conclude that objectivism is likely to remain always alive in the philosophy of law. Whatever objections one can raise against objectivism, they can never obliterate the fact that the objectivistic theories about the origin of the legal order contain a hard core of truth. The objectivist recognizes the fact that the legal order is made by the subject. While this truth is rather trivial, another truth which is not at all trivial is stressed very strongly and convincingly in objectivism, viz., the idea that there can be no question of the development of legal rights unless the subject is involved in actual relationships and shows himself sensitive to these relations.[12] As result, no matter what legal order one studies, this study will also give an idea of the actually existing relations. If, for example, someone will study one hundred years from now the Civil Rights Act of 1964 in America, he will learn not only what according to this law the relationship between white and colored *ought* to be but also what the relationship actually was in 1964.

All forms of social legislation determine the relationship between "master" and "servant" or whatever other terms may be used to express a similar relationship; they express what this relationship ought to be.

---

[11] "It stands to reason that in this view the singularly exceptional position which, according to the other view, man occupies in nature disappears. . . . He is a part of matter and, although this part is peculiarly organized and very powerful in its effects, its activity is not specifically different from that of all other matter. . . . In its eternal motion matter has also assumed the form of man." Hamaker, "Het recht en de maatschappij," *ibid.*, p. 121.

[12] Gits, *op. cit.*, pp. 267-274.

But in these laws one can also see what those relations *de facto* are or were. The *actual* power of organized colored people, the *actual* power of organized labor is reflected by the legal order. This fact induces objectivism to see in the legal order *nothing but* a mirror image of actual conditions. Objectivism is *almost* right. That which objectivism "sees" is beyond dispute: it is impossible that the subject alone be self-sufficient in the creation of a legal order. If the subject were not involved in actually existing relations among men and were not sensitive to those relations, his creation of a legal order would be a vain attempt to establish order in a vacuum.

This idea is strongly supported by the fact that man's consciousness of right and the corresponding legal order are constantly changing. One who tries to understand this undoubtedly sees in it *also* a reference to changing actual conditions.[13] That the legal order "changes" means, of course, that it is changed by the intervention of the subject. Nevertheless, the changing actual conditions occasion the change of the legal order. If the subject were not sensitive to those changes, he would be resigned to see the legal order become constantly more estranged from reality and relegated to governing a vacuum; life would become unbearable if its efforts to find a solution were made impossible by the coercive power of an antiquated legal order.[14] In the tragic conflicts between some countries and their old colonies, there were people who could not or did not want to see the former relationships changed. They defended a consciousness of right and a legal order flowing from this consciousness in which the weight of the actually changed conditions was disregarded. Their attitude, which they called "standing on principles," was in reality a position in a vacuum. It is utterly impossible for the subject to be self-sufficient in constituting a legal order. Objectivism has the merit of emphasizing this point.

Objectivism, however, absolutizes its strong side, and this is its weakness. We will omit here the objections which the various forms of objectivism raise against one another. The legal biologist, for example, reproaches the legal economist for disregarding the importance of biological conditions; and the legal economist complains that the representative of the political power theory of right does not do justice to the weight of

---

[13] "The mutability of the real relationships entails of necessity the mutability of the law (*Recht*), insofar as the law depends on these real relationships." Fechner, *op. cit.*, p. 142.

[14] Fechner, *op. cit.*, p. 143.

economic conditions. But these kinds of objections remains on a purely sociological level[15] and do not touch the specifically philosophical critique of objectivism.

Before we present this critique, it may be useful to point to the consequences of legal objectivism. If man's consciousness of right is nothing but a consciousness of actually existing conditions, then the conviction and the corresponding legal regulation stating that married people ought to be faithful to each other would mean nothing but that the actual faithfulness of husbands and wives is mirrored in that consciousness. If such faithfulness did not *de facto* and regularly exist, then it would also be highly unjust for man and wife to be faithful to each other. The same can be said with respect to theft and murder. The fact that man's consciousness of right and, therefore, also the legal order do not accept murder and stealing means, in the eyes of objectivism, simply that something other than murder and theft are mirrored in our consciousness. But if murder and stealing were to occur regularly, then they could no longer be called unjust.[16] Starting from this consequence of legal objectivism, it is easy to formulate its philosophical critique.

Philosophically speaking, from the standpoint of objectivism it is not possible to take a position against the actually existing conditions among men.[17] The objectivist can observe that certain conditions are actual conditions. But what would be the use of doing that? Within the perspective of objectivism no one can claim that certain actually existing conditions are just or unjust. But, we must ask, can not those conditions be just or unjust? Because the objectivist sees the legal order as nothing but the reflection of actual conditions and because he is unable to say that certain actually existing conditions are just or unjust, he is bound to accept the conclusion that he is unable to assert whether the legal order is just or unjust. The point, however, is whether this order can be just or unjust and whether man can make a judgment concerning this matter.

Critically speaking, we must say that the objectivistic theories about

---

[15] Fechner, *op. cit.*, pp. 53-63.

[16] Cf. H. G. Rambonnet, "Opvattingen van Nederlandsche juristen over recht en rechtswetenschap," *Tijdschrift v. Philosophie*, vol. IX (1949), pp. 333-337.

[17] "However, he does not have any possibility of 'taking a position' with respect to these relationships. He can observe that a certain positive system of law no longer harmonizes with the actually existing conditions because the changed relationships press toward a new arrangement. But he cannot say whether the existing system of laws, aside from this correspondence, is the 'best' possible or the 'correct' system of law." Fechner, *op. cit.*, p. 163.

the origin of man's consciousness of right and the legal order do not say anything at all about the *proper* meaning of these concepts. On the other hand, the objectivist intends to say everything that can be said with respect to this consciousness of right and the legal order based on it. He is sensitive to the importance of the actually existing relationships among men with respect to their consciousness of right and the establishment of a legal order. But he does not at all explain why this consciousness is called a consciousness of *right* and why the legal order is an expression of such *rights*.

The same difficulty arises with respect to the attempt to find an explanation for the normative character ascribed to man's consciousness of right and the corresponding legal order.[18] Why should anyone observe the rules prescribed by the legal order if this order is nothing but a mirror image of actually existing conditions? This question cannot be answered with a reference to actual facts. Moreover, it is evident that the actually existing conditions are often precisely not what they ought to be. In terms of objectivism this statement is nonsense, but is it *really* nonsensical?

Because the objectivist certainly does not disregard the fact that the legal order is a *made* order, he will answer to the above-mentioned questions by referring us to the "positing" of this order by authority. The mirror image of the actual conditions acquires juridical meaning, he holds, because the act of an authority makes that which at first was merely a question of facts into something that ought to be. We ask, however, on what grounds must we accept the thesis that this "positing" act is more than a mere *fact?* And if it is a mere fact, how can this new fact make actual relationships become relationships of rights? How can that which is a fact be changed into that which ought to be by a new fact? The possibility of taking a stand against actually existing conditions is open only to one who sees more in the human subject than mere passivity. To take a stand is clearly something done by an active subject. This point is emphasized, but to the exclusion of everything else, by subjectivism.

2. SUBJECTIVE EXPLANATIONS OF THE ORIGIN OF MAN'S CONSCIOUSNESS OF RIGHT

Objectivism, as we saw, is in every respect an explanation "from below" of man's consciousness of right and is insensitive to any "higher"

---

[18] Gits, *op. cit.,* pp. 274-275.

viewpoints. Subjectivism, on the other hand, limits its attention practically in an exclusive fashion to those "higher" viewpoints with respect to the nature of man's consciousness of right and the establishment of the legal order. This means that in subjectivism the full burden of explanation lies on the subject's spontaneity and inspiration and that hardly any attention is given to the importance of the conditions actually existing in a given society. In a certain sense one can understand why subjectivism pays so much attention to the subject, for the neglect of the subject is the weak side of objectivism. The latter cannot explain the normative character of man's consciousness of right and therefore leaves us with the puzzle of why a particular legal order should be regarded as an expression of human rights. Norms suppose a subject that "ought" to. . . . One who repeats a hundred times that a legal norm ought to be observed and never refers to the subject that ought to observe does not really say anything. If the legal order is to be called normative, one will have to justify that "I" ought, that "you" ought, that "we" ought—briefly, that being-a-subject implies a certain "ought." This is the starting point of subjectivism. Subjectivism points to the subject as the bearer of the *idea* of right, the *sense* of justice, and as such the origin of the legal order.

Various Trends of Subjectivism. Rationalism is the trend of thought which defends most vigorously that the origin of the legal order must be sought in the idea of right. For the rationalist genuine knowledge is knowledge through necessary and universal ideas. The fact that our senses sometimes deceive us induces him to deny his confidence in sense knowledge. If the senses deceive us sometimes, it could very well be that they deceive us all the time. The rationalist attaches value only to man's thinking reason and its necessary and universal ideas. He accepts dogmatically that that which reason can think in a coherent way also exists in reality. Hence necessary and universal ideas have automatically an ontological value. Accordingly, for the rationalist it is certain that, if we start from an indubitable principle, the results of all logical deductions will be in agreement with reality. He accepts unqualifiedly that the ontological order is built according to the same laws as the order of knowledge. It stands to reason that mathematics is always considered *the* model in this type of philosophy.

With respect to the philosophy of law this means that the rationalist holds it possible to deduce a complete set of legal rules from a few very general principles. With a timeless validity, an idea of right open to human understanding dwells in the interiority of consciousness, where it rules over the events of history while it itself transcends the contingency of the concrete.[19] The rationalist was convinced that this idea of right contained in principle a complete system of legal norms which lacked only juridical expression. Thus the origin of the legal order was to be found solely in the idea of right, and this idea would develop solely through the internal impulse of thought itself.

This description of rationalism in the philosophy of law applies only to its most extreme forms. The latter are known as the "theories of natural right" and were defended, e.g., by Pufendorf, Thomasius and Wolff. More moderate forms of rationalism are possible; for instance, those of Kant and Stammler, who do not hold that a complete system of legal rules can be deduced from the idea of right. All forms of rationalism, however, put the main emphasis on the idea of right itself; they either neglect or de-emphasize the importance of the actual conditions.

The same applies also to the views about philosophy of law implied in the value philosophies of Max Scheler and Nicolai Hartmann. A fundamental conviction of these value philosophies maintains that values exist as independent entities in an autonomous ideal realm; these values are accessible to man in an act of emotional intuition; they present and impose themselves directly in a hierarchical order as values.[20] In grasping values, man goes beyond experience. Grasping values is more than the experience that the good gives delight and reward and that evil leads to displeasure and punishment. Grasping values, however, is not the work of man's reasoning power, but is done by a "sense of value" (*Wertgefühl*) or "intuition of value" (*Wertschau*),[21] in which man is sensitive to the ideal "self-existence" of the values.[22] Man lets his gaze

---

[19] Fechner, *op. cit.,* pp. 37-41.

[20] "The fundamental idea of value philosophy lies in the conviction that there are (*gibt*) 'values' as autonomous essences in an ideal world existing in itself. Man can intuitively grasp and experience these values, and their valuable character is immediately clear and convincing to him." Fechner, op. cit., p. 43.

[21] Nicolai Hartmann, *Ethik,* Berlin, 3rd ed., 1949, p. 149.

[22] "The proper mode of being of values is obviously that of an ideal being-in-itself. They are original structures of an ethically ideal sphere, of a realm with its own structures, its own laws, its own order. This sphere is organically connected with the theoretically ideal spheres, the logical and mathematical spheres of being, as well as those of pure essences. It is the continuation of those spheres. No matter how different the ideal structures of being in those realms may be from values, nevertheless, they share with them the fundamental modal character of ideal being-in-itself." Hartmann, *op. cit.,* p. 151.

wander over an autonomous realm of ideal values. For this reason it seems as if all values are merely relative, but in reality this relativity applies only to man's consciousness of those values.

This kind of theory has exercised influence also on the philosophy of law. For within the leading ideas of this trend of thought it must be considered possible to establish ideal, but nonetheless objective and fixed norms for the organization of society. There exists a *sense* of justice through which man intuitively and emotionally feels what in given conditions is right or not right. This feeling is the source of the legal order. According to Hommes, the philosophies of law defended by Coing and Hubmann are typical examples of legal philosophies derived from a philosophy of value.[23]

Strong and Weak Points of Subjectivism. Precisely the point where objectivism always meets with difficulties in its attempts to justify the normative character of the legal order is the place where subjectivism encounters no resistance. If the legal order is the product of the idea of right or the sense of justice in man's consciousness, then the legal order can be called normative on the basis of the normative meaning of this idea or this sense. The legal order participates in the subject's "ought" through the intermediary of the idea of right or the sense of justice. One who claims that the legal order arises solely from the actually existing conditions can only say that the subject is a *de facto* image of the actually existing conditions. Thus he eliminates any form of "ought." Subjectivism, in a sense, owes its success to the failure of objectivism. It explicitates the subject himself as "ought" and as such considers him the origin of the legal order. On the basis of the idea of right or the sense of justice it is possible to take a stand against actual conditions, which is not possible in the objectivistic views.

Under the influence of Comte, objectivism sometimes degenerated into a crude kind of physicalistic materialism. Subjectivism has suffered a similar fate: it has succumbed to psychologism. According to Krabbe, one of the most militant protagonists of the priority of right over authority, all fundamental questions of the philosophy of law must be considered to be psychological issues.[24] Krabbe objects to the idea that the legal order has a normative value simply because it has been "pos-

---

[23] Hommes, *op. cit.* (footnote 1), pp. 126-135.

[24] "This leads us to the realm of psychology. It is from this science that the doctrine of the law's sovereignty takes over the idea that the legal order has a primordial character." H. Krabbe, *Het rechtsgezag,* The Hague, 1917, p. 28.

ited" by authority. He knows, of course, that the defenders of authority
tried to find a title of justification for this authority. Some of them had
recourse to God's will, while others claimed that it was "natural" for the
strong to rule the weak. But all this does not impress Krabbe. He
recognizes no other authority than that of right, whose title lies in the
sense of justice that is at work in man's consciousness.[25] It is the task of
the psychologist to investigate the working of this sense, for man's
consciousness of right is, according to Krabbe, an irreducible psychological fact. Certain contents of consciousness simply happen to be
normative, and this is the last word that can be said about the origin of
the legal order.[26] The entire legal order can be reduced to the working
of man's sense of justice.[27] Since only the psychologist is qualified to
speak about this sense, the philosophy of law, according to Krabbe, is an
integral part of psychology.

This and other similar views show how simple it is for the subjectivist
to explain the normative character of the legal order. This order can be
called normative only in reference to the subject. Subjectivism, however, explains the totality of the legal order exclusively in terms of the
subject. Through the intermediary of a normative idea or feeling, the
entire legal order is permeated with normative power.

On the other hand, subjectivism does scant justice to the reality of the
actually existing conditions which also are embodied in the legal order.
Any system of legal rules wants to put order in the actual conditions.
But how would a system of norms really be able to put order in the
actual conditions if the latter do not influence those norms? And how
could those conditions have any importance for the legal order if this
order arises exclusively from an idea or a feeling in the subject's interiority? Are we supposed to accept that ideas or feelings "automatically"
guarantee a grasp of the reality of the actual conditions that are to be
regulated by the legal order? How could there ever be question of
effectively regulating the actual conditions if man's normative con-

---

[25] Krabbe, *op. cit.*, p. 2.

[26] "My starting point, on the other hand, is . . . that among the emotions filling
our consciousness there are some endowed with a normative character, i.e., they
reveal themselves as a power 'binding' us to judge, think and act in accordance
with the orientation expressed in such a consciousness. Hence man's consciousness of right is a psychological fact, but one of a peculiar nature, as are
aesthetic feelings, ethical consciousness, consciousness of truth and religious
emotion." Krabbe, *op. cit.*, p. 21.

[27] Krabbe, *op. cit.*, p. 28.

sciousness of right were not sensitive to the meaning of those conditions? For instance, how could there be question of a "right to emigrate" if the subject were not sensitive to what it means to live in an overpopulated country?

In the preceding pages we presented very succinctly both the strong and the weak points of objectivism as well as subjectivism. Both trends of thought are important because they assign weight to certain undeniable factors with respect to the origin of man's consciousness of right and the legal order. But it is not difficult to see that those theories are influenced by Cartesianism. The objections that can be raised against both types of theory are, strictly speaking, identical with those provoked by any form of Cartesianism. It is impossible to separate subject and meaning. Theories that endeavor to explain the origin of the legal order exclusively "from above" or "from below" fail precisely because of their exclusivism. This exclusivism is overcome in existential phenomenology. Before we examine what existential phenomenology can contribute to the philosophy of law, whoever, we want to devote first some attention to a very special form of explanation "from above."

CHAPTER THREE

THEORIES REGARDING THE RELIGIOUS ORIGIN OF MAN'S CONSCIOUSNESS OF RIGHT AND THE LEGAL ORDER

The violation of rights is often called a flouting of "sacred" rights. This way of speaking is typical of those who see in man's consciousness of right and in the legal order a relationship to God's will and His dispositions.[1] In the course of history this relationship has been affirmed in several ways.

1. Direct and Indirect Relationship Between the Legal Order and God

The view that affirms a direct relationship between a particular legal order and God is very old. Already Hammurabi called himself "King of Justice" because he received the legal order of his kingdom from the hands of Shamash.[2] Moses spoke with Jahweh, who wrote the law of the Jews on stone tablets. In both cases there is clearly question of a system of laws and legal institutions that was judged to come directly from God.

Sometimes, however, only a part of the legal order was considered directly willed by God—namely the authority of the ruler. The right to give binding orders, attributed to certain rulers, was derived from a

---

[1] "The sacredness of the law (*Recht*), of which we are accustomed to speak, has no real meaning without the existence of a personal God." J. Messner, *Das Naturrecht*, Innsbruck, 2nd ed., 1950, p. 154.

[2] Fechner, *Rechtsphilosophie*, p. 48.

disposition of God's will. The Eastern potentates who were defeated by Alexander the Great attributed their power and authority to the will of the gods, and in line with this Alexander himself was proclaimed the son of Zeus after his victory. The Roman emperors also wanted to be given divine honors.[3]

It stands to reason that the entire legal order or at least the authority and the power of the rulers receive an absolute, inviolable and sacred character if they are seen as directly related to God's will. The same holds if the relationship is indirect. There are several ways in which there can be question of an indirect relationship. Sometimes an appeal is made to history to show that a particular situation is willed by God's providence. In Holland, for example, De Savornin Lohman held that the House of Orange had been called to the royal throne by Him who guided both that House and the nation and joined them together by a firm bond.[4] In other cases the indirect relationship of the legal order or of the ruling authority to God's will is affirmed through an appeal to the natural law.

2. *An Invincible Nostalgia: the Natural Law*

Whoever uses the term "natural law" can expect trouble. How can one use this term meaningfully without being obliged to mention a few hundred names and an equal number of definitions? Does it make sense to speak of *the* natural law?

On the basis of an historical survey listing the various Western concepts of the natural law till the nineteenth century, Hommes has tried to describe a "traditional" concept of the natural law.[5] The main object he had in mind was the possibility of dividing the modern conceptions of the natural law according as they lie or do not lie in line with the great Western tradition of the natural law. In this way it would be possible, he hoped, to end the confusing divergency of senses in which the term "natural law" is used today.[6]

---

[3] R. Kranenburg, *Positief recht en rechtsbewustzijn,* Groningen, 1928, p. 10.

[4] Kranenburg, *op. cit.,* p. 11.

[5] "The natural law in the traditional sense is a complex of 'supra-positive' (i.e., not established by a declaration of man's will to form a legal order), immutable, universal and *per se* valid norms of law and, eventually, subjective natural rights with their correlative duties, which are based upon a natural order that is or is not derived from a divine source and which are *a priori* deduced from that natural order by man through the use of his natural reason." Hommes, *op. cit.,* p. 55.

[6] Hommes, *op. cit.,* p. 9.

It stands to reason that such a methodic attempt to reach clarity has both advantages and disadvantages. It establishes order, which is one of the advantages. A disadvantage, however, is that certain representatives of legal philosophy whose way of thinking has always been called "natural law philosophy" are banished from the sphere of "traditional thinking in terms of the natural law" because of the description of the "traditional concept of the natural law" given by one author. Spinoza, for example, is excluded from that tradition according to Hommes[7] and, what is even worse, so are all those who in our time have made magnificent efforts to give new vigor to the concept "natural law." Is it to be excluded that these thinkers give expression to a *more* authentic idea of the natrual law than others whose thoughts remain in line with a "traditional" concept of the natural law? To use a comparison, if one were to bundle the concepts of "experience" till the nineteenth century in order to put an end to the confusing divergency of meanings given to this term, then the idea which contemporary phenomenology has of experience would certainly lie outside the "traditional concept of experience." Yet all phenomenologists would insist that their concept of experience must be called more authentic than other views that remain in line with a "traditional concept of experience."

Those who are sensitive to the objections raised above in connection with Hommes' methodic attempt to find unity have to face the confusion caused by the multiplicity of meanings given to the term "natural law." This situation is the reason why legal positivists see any type of natural law theory as nothing but subjectivism, romanticism, arbitrariness, politics, ethics or plain skulduggery. In their eyes there exists only the legal order together with the jurists who handle this order.

On the opposite side, however, those who are given short shrift by the legal order look at this order as nothing but deceit and tyranny. They, too, find it easy to point out "the confusing multiplicity of meanings" resulting from positive legal regulations that have vanished in the history of mankind. The disappearance of those regulations meant freedom for some and slavery for others. One who understands this point cannot remain a legal positivist.

In both the establishment of a legal order and its abolition it is as if man tries to regain a lost paradise. In reality there has never been such a paradise; nevertheless, man wants to dream of it. A paradise of

---

[7] Hommes, *op. cit.*, p. 55.

humanity—is it merely a dream or is it also an imperative, an existential demand imposing itself, within the co-existence of human beings, on all those who have become human at least to some extent? The answer is in the affirmative.[8] The actuality of this imperative is the actuality of the natural law.

Speaking about legal positivism, we have shown that right cannot be identified with the legal order and that justice is not to be equated with the willingness to execute the regulations of that order. The questions of what right and justice essentially are, we said, constitute *the* questions of the philosophy of law. For one who is familiar with the history of the natural law it is evident that the philosophical question about the essence of right and justice is identical with history's search for the essence of the natural law. We will not hesitate to face this question again. However, we will not let ourselves be guided by a more or less artificially limited "traditional concept of the natural law" but by the living and thinking "inspiration" which finds expression in man's struggle to make the legal order become human. In this perspective the struggle for the natural law can be conceived as a search for a justifying ground and a critical norm of the legal order.[9] This way of formulating the question has the added advantage of not driving into the arms of positivism all those who, not being positivists, cannot accept a rigidly circumscribed "traditional concept of the natural law."[10]

Opinions. The present chapter discusses the theories regarding the religious origin of man's consciousness of right and the legal order. As already mentioned, sometimes a direct relation to God, either of the entire legal order or of the ruler's authority, was or is affirmed. In other

---

[8] "Somewhere in us the 'born jurist of the natural law' (Bergbohm) always and everywhere fights for the natural law, whether we believe and trust in him or doubt and criticize him. In all the confusion of emotions for or against the natural law, it remains certainly true that we have a feeling regarding this word; it does not leave us indifferent, but invites us to take a position." Erik Wolf, *Das Problem der Naturrechtslehre,* Karlsruhe, 1955, p. 1.

[9] "In all these possibilities of such a problematic and doubtful character . . . the same need expresses itself. We would like to give a justifying ground and a critical norm to the legal norms, legal institutions and legal views with their contingent validity, their frequent contradictions and their changes, in order to distinguish the essential ('existentiel' natural law) from the arbitrary, the permanent ('institutional' natural law) from the perishable in all law (*Recht*)." Wolf, *op. cit.,* p. 5.

[10] Langemeyer, "De huidige betekenis van het natuurrecht," *Handelingen v.d. Vereniging v. wijsbegeerte des rechts,* vol. XXXXIII (1958), pp. 50-51.

cases this relationship is or was affirmed through the intermediary of the natural law.

In what follows here about the natural law, we have to plead guilty of a minor irregularity in systematics. For, as we will see, there are also conceptions of the natural law whose representatives explicitly deny the relation to God, i.e., the religious origin of man's consciousness of right and the legal order. Even though it is, *in general,* true that the indirect relationship to God of man's consciousness of right and the legal order is affirmed through the intermediary of the natural law, this does not mean that *every* conception of the natural law implies that man's consciousness of right and the legal order has an indirect relationship to a religious origin.

In our time we witness the fact that legal positivism is constantly losing ground. Nevertheless, there continues to be a violent opposition to the natural law. With respect to this opposition, however, it should be kept in mind that very often only a *particular* conception of the natural law is rejected. If, then, in the eyes of the opponent this particular conception is regarded as *the* theory of the natural law and this particular conception is indeed untenable, then one can understand how it is possible to agree fully with this opponent without at the same time precluding the recognition of a natural law.

As we mentioned, there exists innumerable and very divergent opinions about the natural law. We need not describe them here, for others have done so very competently. But in connection with the contemporary "struggle about the natural law" we want to present a brief description of those "types" of natural law conceptions which today's opponents of *the* natural law reject. For, surveying the objections to *the* natural law, one comes to the conclusion that they are widely divergent. This divergence is not surprising if one is familiar with the fact that the conceptions of the natural law are similarly widely divergent.

Nature and Natural Law. The history of the philosophy of law knows one conception of the natural law in which the term "nature," in its most current sense, is regarded as the origin of norms for human relations. This conception is very lucidly explained by J. Loeff[11] who, basing himself on the investigations of G. van der Leeuw[12] and Mircea

---

[11] J. J. Loeff, "De huidige betekenis van het natuurrecht," *ibid.,* pp. 3-25.
[12] G. van der Leeuw, *De primitieve mens en de religie,* Groningen, 1952.

Eliade,[13] explores what it meant for primitive man to live in a society whose norms were, as it were, dictated by nature. There was a time when nature imposed itself so imperatively on man that it fully controlled all his actions.

"Nature," we said, should be understood here in its most current sense—more or less the sense in which one is said to "go back to nature." But we should keep in mind that for primitive man nature had a numinous and sacral meaning.[14] The natural was the original, the new, the powerful but, at the same time, the sacred. Primitive man saw all this in the rising sun, the new moon, the flooding river bringing fertility, spring chasing winter, and in the soil which each summer again brought a new crop to maturity.[15] Primitive man desired to share in the life of nature, to be initiated into its life, in order to participate in this way in a higher life.

Because nature's life spoke to primitive man of the numinous and the sacred, he tried, as it were, to integrate his own life into that of nature.[16] For the natural, conceived as the numinous and the sacred, imposed respect on primitive man and thus became the source of all kinds of norms for his behavior. The necessity he experienced to submit to the laws of nature and of his bodily existence imposed on primitive man norms regarding his agriculture, fishing, hunting, his primitive technique, mating, giving birth, growing up, illness, dying and burial.[17] On this basis one could speak here of a "natural law," in the sense that there was a complex of norms derived from nature which, as such, shared in the numinous and sacral character of nature and which, with the same "natural necessity" as existed in nature, controlled primitive society. In this sense we have here a "natural law of divine origin."

Obviously, when in connection with the above-mentioned "type" of natural law conception the term "law" is used, this term should be understood as referring to an existing complex of norms, i.e., a legal

---

[13] Mircea Eliade, *The Sacred and the Profane,* Chicago, 1959.

[14] "For primitive man nature is never merely 'natural'; it is for him always filled with religious meaning." Loeff, *art. cit.,* p. 7.

[15] Loeff, *art. cit.,* p. 6.

[16] "The unity and sacredness of life stand in the foreground here. Nature and culture have, as it were, spontaneously a religious meaning. Not only birth and death, sexual relations and sickness, but also work, politics, morality, traffic, science, economy—everything has a religious foundation." van der Leeuw, *op. cit.,* p. 163.

[17] Loeff, *art. cit.,* pp. 7-9.

order. Secondly, the term "nature" is evidently understood as referring to "thinglike" reality. Mountains, rivers, the harvest, rain, the sun and the moon, spring, summer, autumn and winter, in a word, nature imposes itself on man; and with the same "thinglike" necessity as there exists in nature, man's behavior toward nature and toward his fellow-men "originates" in accordance with the "natural" norms. Those norms are conceived as "just being there" in the same way as the mountains, the sun, the moon and the rain just happen to "be there."

Such a view can manage to survive only as long as man is forced to submit to nature. As soon as he decides to resist nature's overpowering influence and to control nature, the latter is no longer the origin of norms imposing themselves on man and human society with a necessity of nature. The natural law in a primitive society is simply the repercussion of nature's overpowering hold on man and the primitive group. As soon as that power is broken, there is no longer any room for that natural law, so that society finds itself in a "juridical vacuum." Moreover, nature loses its numinous and sacral character as soon as man decides to subdue nature. Because primitive man was powerless against nature and had to submit to it in every respect, nature was called sacred and divine. The law, as a repercussion of nature, was considered to participate in the sacred and the divine. But this conviction, too, undergoes a crisis as soon as man manages to break through his dependence upon nature. The natural law is then no longer sacred.

A natural law, in the sense spoken of here, can no longer be defended in our time. It is typical of "modern" man, as opposed to "primitive" man, that he refuses precisely to submit to the overpowering control of nature. The man who is at least to some extent authentically a human being imposes his will upon nature and forces it into subservience. Thus there no longer can be question of a complex of norms which nature imposes upon man with the same natural necessity which exists in the realm of things. One can no longer say that the natural law "is just there," as nature itself "is just there," for to modern man nature itself no longer appears as that which "is just there" but as "the place where the possibilities of human power become reality." [18] Natural law, in the

---

[18] "The primitive is a part of a living world from which he does not distinguish himself. . . . The primitive knows himself as one force among many other forces." van der Leeuw, *op. cit.,* p. 26. And: "Here lie the roots of all culture: man who undertakes something with nature, who makes something of nature." *Ibid.,* p. 161.

above-explained sense, can rule only where man has not yet become an authentic subject.

It is in this light that we must understand and evaluate certain—but not all—objections raised today against *the* natural law. "Nature" and "right" or "law" are unrelated, and therefore the "natural law" is a contradiction in terms. Natural law is meaningless today. As J. von Schmid says, "today's philosophy of law can no longer be a natural law philosophy."[19]

The conviction behind this objection is that whoever today uses the term "right" refers to the domain of the subject with his autonomy and freedom with respect to nature. The ontological priority of the subject over "thinglike" nature can certainly not be disregarded, and one would fail to do justice to the subject's authenticity by considering the subject governed by norms imposed on him with the same necessity that rules "thinglike" nature. "Right," "law" and "subject" belong together, but not "right," "law" and "nature." By "nature" there is no more "right" than there are by "nature" language, art, economy or culture.[20]

The above objection is often proposed as an objection against *the* natural law. That claim, however, goes too far. It holds good only in reference to a particular conception of the natural law. Only a "thing-like," "processlike" natural law contradicts the human subject's authenticity. But there are also other ways of conceiving a natural law.[21]

Reason and the Natural Law. How divergent the concepts can be that are indicated by the same term becomes evident when one compares the above-described naturalistic conception of the natural law with the rationalistic view. We shall be brief about this view because it has been mentioned already in connection with the "ideal conceptions" of the origin of man's consciousness of right. Fascinated by the power of thinking in terms of necessary and universal ideas, the seventeenth and

---

[19] See Loeff, *art. cit.*, p. 6.

[20] "What as a 'crisis of law' (*Recht*) comes so lethally to our attention today is the insight that 'by nature' there exists just as little law (*Recht*) as there exist a language, an art, an economy or, generally, a culture." Adolf Arndt, "Die Krise des Rechts," *Die Wandlung*, vol. III (1948), p. 432.

[21] "The theory of the natural law of the European tradition, whether that of Aristotle, of the Stoics, the Church Fathers, the Scholastics, the Reformers or that of the Rationalists, is not naturalistic but anti-naturalistic. The concept of 'nature' on which it is based is always a theological, religious and moral concept of a norm, and the underlying concept of the *lex naturae* has nothing to do with what today is called 'natural law.'" Emil Brunner, *Gerechtigkeit, Eine Lehre von den Grundgesetzen der Gesellschaftsordnung*, Zürich, 1943, pp. 102-103.

eighteenth centuries representatives of the rationalistic view of the natural law considered it possible to derive from a few very general and self-evident principles a system of juridical norms that would be in principle complete. They called this system "the natural law," and even thought that this natural law, because of the completeness and detailed character of its norms, could at least be favorably compared with positive law. Sometimes they even estimated it as superior and better than positive law because it did not come forth from the will of a lawgiver and therefore was valid for all times and places for all human beings.

As was mentioned above, *generally speaking,* the religious origin of man's consciousness of right and the legal order was or is affirmed through the intermediary of the natural law. Above we saw how it was done in the naturalistic conception of the natural law and we will still see how it is done in the Thomistic conception. In the rationalistic conception, however, man's consciousness of right and the legal order is not brought into relationship with God.

The difficulties that are raised with respect to the rationalistic view of the natural law are totally different from those put forward against the naturalistic conception. One cannot object that the rationalistic view fails to do justice to the subject's authenticity. On the contrary, this view overemphasizes the subject-as-*cogito*. The defenders of the rationalistic view stress the power of man's discursive reason beyond any acceptable limits.

One who knows how demanding a task it is to create positive rules of law easily understands that jurists vigorously reject the rationalistic conception of the natural law. How would the discursive reason on its own be able to formulate a system of legal norms which in its completeness and its detailed character can be compared with positive law when the creation of a single rule of positive law sometimes demands months and even years of strenuous work? How can reason alone be able to excogitate a system of norms valid for all people at all times and all places when it is certain that no two times, no two places and no two people are alike? How can a system of norms be unchangeable if times, places and people change? In the light of the strenuous work jurists must perform in order to precisely take account of the concrete and changing times, places and people, the rationalistic view of the natural law presents itself as an intolerable pretention. This pretention, however, was exposed and wrecked by the legal positivism of the nineteenth century. The rationalistic view of the natural law has disappeared from the scene.

Essence and Natural Law. Above we interpreted the nostalgia for the natural law in today's legal philosophy as the search for a justifying ground and a critical norm of the positive legal order.[22] This search is not something new in history, but was already performed by all those for whom it stands to reason that an authority, in making rules and taking steps to secure their observance, cannot arbitrarily raise any fancy to the dignity of a legal norm. The legal order as a whole must have a foundation, and this foundation itself cannot have a purely positive-juridical character.

Many philosophers have tried to base the positive legal order on the nature of man. In this connection the term "nature" does not mean a "thing of nature," it does not imply a naturalistic view of man, but it means solely "essence," conceived as "that by which a being is what it is." Thus it is to be expected that, insofar as the legal order is based on man's essence, there will be as many different views about the natural law as there are different anthropologies. Even the rationalistic conception of the natural law is based on a view of man. The reason why we considered that conception separately was the striking form it had assumed in the history of philosophy and the special objections raised against it.

The strongest view of the natural law on an anthropological basis is the Thomistic view which continues to find supporters even today.[23] We will discuss this view in detail. First, however, we want to consider two other views of the natural law that are likewise founded on an anthropological basis, namely, the views of Hobbes and Spinoza. This consideration can be very useful, for these views show how easily the search for a justifying ground and a critical norm of the positive legal order can degenerate into the exact opposite, viz., a theory of absolute power.

Hobbes. In his theory of law and the state, Hobbes starts from the natural condition in which man was supposed to have lived before he formed a system of laws and a state. In this natural condition nature gave everyone a right to everything. Everyone could do what he liked,

---

[22] "The struggle for the natural law, which began as soon as mankind reached the age of reason, has continued in various ways until our time. In a certain sense one can say that this struggle is destined to know no end as long as injustices are committed on earth and as long as the lawgivers themselves make mistakes." G. del Vecchio, "Over het natuurrecht," *Rechtsgeleerd magazijn Themis,* 1957, p. 81.

[23] Langemeyer, *loc. cit.* (footnote 10), p. 37.

possess what he wanted, use and enjoy whatever he wanted to use or enjoy.[24] Usefulness was the norm of right. But it was to no avail that nature gave everyone the right to everything. The effect of such a right was the same as no right at all,[25] for it amounts to the war of all against all,[26] in order to acquire safety, gain or glory. It is easy to see that the everlasting war of all against all is hardly suitable to safeguard the tendency to self-preservation of the human race and of the individual man.[27] In the natural condition of war of all against all, violence and deceit are the principal virtues.[28] But nothing can develop that makes life worth living.[29]

In his natural condition man let himself be fully guided by his egoism. There simply could be no question of genuine sympathy with one's fellowmen, of love and unselfishness. Even when men are not together, they cannot leave one another in peace, but spend their time in talking evil of the absent.[30] Because in the natural condition everyone has a right to everything, even to the other's body, and because there cannot be any mutual love in that condition, life is dominated by the paralyzing fear of death. It is fear of one another that drives men to seek peace.[31] The search of peace is prescribed by the natural law. For the natural law, understood as a *dictamen rectae rationis*,[32] prescribes in a binding way that which is necessary for man's self-preservation.[33] In a condition

---

[24] "Nature gave everyone a *right to everything;* that is, in the purely natural state or before men bound themselves by any pacts, anyone was permitted to do whatever he wanted and to whomever he wanted, to possess, use and enjoy everything he wanted and was able to." Hobbes, *De cive,* c.I, 10.

[25] Hobbes, *op. cit.,* c.I, 11.

[26] Hobbes, *op. cit.,* c.I, 12.

[27] Hobbes, *op. cit.,* c.I, 13.

[28] Hobbes, *Leviathan,* ed. Michael Oakeshott, Oxford, 1946, p. 82.

[29] "In such condition, there is no place for industry; because the fruit thereof is uncertain; and consequently no culture of the earth; no navigation, nor use of the commodities that may be imported by sea; no commodious building; no instruments of moving, and removing, such things as require much force; no knowledge of the face of the earth; no account of time; no arts, no letters; no society; and which is worse of all, continual fear, and danger of violent death; and the life of man, solitary, poor, nasty, brutish, and short." Hobbes, *ibid.*

[30] Hobbes, *De cive,* c.I, 2.

[31] "The passions that incline man to peace, are fear of death." Hobbes, *Leviathan,* p. 84.

[32] Hobbes, *De cive,* c.I, 15.

[33] "To define the natural law, it is a dictate of right reason concerning that which is to be done or not done with respect to the longest possible preservation of life and limbs." Hobbes, *De cive,* c.II, 1.

in which war of all against all prevails, the search of peace is a primary prescription, for otherwise man cannot safeguard his self-preservation.

From this first natural law a second law can be derived, viz., that, for the sake of peace and self-defense, man must be willing to give up his right to everything and be satisfied with having as much freedom toward the others as he is ready to accord others toward himself.[34] Such a social contract gives rise to society, to the state. Thus it is not mutual benevolence but mutual fear that gives rise to the state.[35] This state, arising from mutual fear, is the only means to safeguard man's self-preservation. But for this purpose it is not sufficient that only a handful of people unite themselves. Their number must be so large that enemies cannot hope to overcome them with ease.[36] Moreover, there must be unanimity among those who formed a league. For this purpose they must subject their wills to that of a prince or council, so that what these decide is regarded as the will of all.[37] By this subjection they oblige themselves by treaty not to resist the will of their prince or council,[38] and those who do not want to become part of the league must be considered enemies. The citizens, however, may demand that they be given security and that there no longer be any reason to fear others so long as they themselves do not commit any injustice.[39] For security is the only reason why people subject themselves to someone. If they do not receive that security, then they cannot be regarded as having subjected themselves to someone else or as having lost the right to defend themselves.[40] To safeguard this security, the state must decree penalties for the violation

---

[34] "From this fundamental law of nature . . . is derived this second law; that a man be willing, when others are so too, as far-forth, as for peace, and defence of himself he shall think it necessary, to lay down this right to all things; and be contented with so much liberty against other men, as he would allow other men against himself." Hobbes, *Leviathan,* p. 85.

[35] Hobbes, *De cive,* c.I, 2.

[36] Hobbes, *De cive,* c.V, 3.

[37] "It is required that there be but *one will.* But this cannot happen unless everyone submits his will to the *one* of someone else, i.e., of one *man* or of one *council,* in such a way that whatever this one wants in matters required for common peace must be considered to be the will of all and of each one." Hobbes, *De cive,* c.V, 6.

[38] Hobbes, *ibid.,* c.V, 7.

[39] Hobbes, *ibid.,* c.VI, 3.

[40] "For security is the reason why men subject themselves to others. And if no security is had, no one is understood to have subjected himself to others or to have lost the right to defend himself at his own discretion." Hobbes, *De cive,* c.VI, 3.

of the citizens' security, and these penalties must be so severe that the advantage of violating the security is outweighed by the disadvantage of the punishment. For by natural necessity men choose what is obviously good for them.[41]

Against external attackers also the authorities must wield the sword. Every citizen has by treaty yielded to them the right to decide over war and peace. Thus in wielding the sword, whether against evildoers in the state or against external enemies, the state authority itself judges and makes the decision. For otherwise the bearer of that authority would be the servant of someone else and therefore he would not *really* wield the sword and not *really* guarantee security.[42] This is also the reason why the ruler can proclaim laws wholly and entirely by his own power and cannot leave it to the sentiments of his subjects to judge whether something is just or unjust, advantageous or disadvantageous, honest or dishonest, good or evil. For the sentiments of the subjects about such matters can only cause disunity and altercations, which endanger the citizens' security.[43]

Accordingly, the power of the state's ruler is by right an absolute power. The ruler is not bound by the laws of the state, for he makes those laws. He cannot be punished, for he is the one who punishes. No one can claim any rights against the ruler, for all rights are derived from him. The ruler may and must demand absolute obedience from his subjects. Sometimes, however, the latter have the right to refuse obedience. If, for example, the ruler orders his subjects to kill him, they have the right to refuse, for such an act does not belong to the contract on which the state society is based. Similarly, the subject may refuse to commit suicide or patricide, even if his father is guilty, for the authorities can always find someone else willing to perform the execution.[44] In spite of everything, however, the authorities retain the right to kill those who refuse to obey.[45]

This, finally, is also the reason why the head of the state has the right to control the "sentiments" and "dogmas" held by his subjects. He

---

[41] Hobbes, *ibid.*, c.VI, 4.
[42] Hobbes, *ibid.*, c.VI, 7-8.
[43] Hobbes, *ibid.*, c.VI, 9-11.
[44] Hobbes, *ibid.*, c.VI, 13-15.
[45] "For he does not in any case lose the right to kill those who will refuse obedience." Hobbes, *ibid.*, c.VI, 13.

cannot countenance the teaching that someone else—e.g., the Pope of the Roman Church or certain bishops outside that Church—has a right to greater obedience. For many civil wars have arisen from such a position. Since, then, the authorities of the state must protect its peace and security, they must also possess supreme and decisive power in matters of faith.[46]

Hobbes's amazing logical power is almost irresistible to anyone who expects *at least* that the legal order will bring peace and security. After reading him, one is convinced that there can be no lasting peace and security without positive law and without power. If there is no legal order and no exercise of power, barbarism prevails. Anyone who wants to see "humanity rule" must be tempted to give his allegiance to legal positivism and to the absolutism of power.[47] Hobbes "justifies" this positivism and absolutism with an appeal to the natural law. Paradoxically expressed, he is not so much concerned with justice as with the security of the law, in the conviction that taking care of this security is the only possible form of justice since only the legal order and the exercise of power can overcome barbarism.

Nevertheless, despite the clarity of his ideas and the logical power of his thought, Hobbes overlooks precisely the points that are at issue. Is it really impossible, we must ask, that the legal order *itself* and the exercise of power *itself* imply and even *are* a negation of peace and security? As history shows, this can happen. But, are not peace and security the reason why the legal order and power have been established? As soon as one realizes that this order and power can be the negation of peace and security, the *real* problems impose themselves, and with respect to these problems Hobbes' powerful logic is helpless because his thought pays no attention to those issues. Only on one occasion he accords them a perfunctory footnote to "settle" them.

In this footnote, Hobbes asks himself whether the citizens living under the absolute rule of a prince are not leading a most wretched existence.[48] Does their happiness not simply mean that they have *not yet* been

---

[46] Hobbes, *ibid.*, c.VI, 11.

[47] "The entire system of Hobbes is permeated with the idea that the law (*Recht*) is essentially an order shaping *reality* and that any theory of the law must serve only to justify and strengthen the power of positive law to shape reality." Welzel, "Naturrecht und Rechtspositivismus," *Festschrift für Hans Niedermeyer,* p. 287.

[48] Hobbes, *De cive,* c.VI, 13 note.

plundered and murdered? Hobbes tries to put the citizens at ease by asking: – "Why would the prince plunder and murder them?" Certainly not because he has the power to do it, but he will do it only if he wants. And he will not want to rob the many for the sake of the few. He can do it without violating the legal order but he cannot do it in "justice," i.e., without violating the natural law and the law of God. Hence the citizens' security is heightened if the prince swears an oath. Of course, one cannot deny that the prince is sometimes inclined to evil and can even violate his oath. But, says Hobbes, let us assume that for this reason we do not give him absolute but only relative power. This power would still have to be so great that it would protect the citizens against one another, thereby safeguarding peace and security. But in that case such a relative power would be just as much to fear as an absolute power, for one who has enough power to protect all has also sufficient power to oppress all. The inconvenience, then, attached to absolute power is merely a special instance of the general inconvenience characterizing everything human.[49] Moreover, there is no reason to address to the state the reproach that its absolute power has inconveniences; for if the citizens were able to live peacefully of their own accord, there would be no need for a state as an instrument of restraint.

All this shows that Hobbes was not a cynic who had no interest in humanity. The very purpose of his system is precisely victory over barbarism because nothing human can flourish when barbarism rules. To overcome barbarism, absolute power is needed. Hobbes recognizes the existence of a moral law, founded in God, to which both the authorities of the state and the citizens are subject. But he wants to stress that this law does not become effective, cannot cope with the individual's passions, unless the power of the state compels the citizens to observe the moral law.[50] The question, however, is, who will compel the state authorities to observe the moral law? The citizens have the right

---

[49] "There is no hardship here, save that human affairs cannot be without a certain inconvenience." Hobbes, *ibid.*

[50] "The customary labelling of Hobbes' ethic as wholly political and relativist is not strictly correct. What he does say is that the moral laws are so contrary to our passions that we cannot bring ourselves to follow them except under fear of an external coercive power, and when we are sure that our neighbours are under the same reliable control. The precise formulation of Hobbes' ethic is, then, that the moral laws are objective, perpetually valid, and divine in origin, but can only become operative or effective in a State." T. E. Jessop, *Thomas Hobbes*, London, 1960, p. 25.

to refuse obedience if the ruler's commands are against the law of God,[51] but the ruler has the right to put to death anyone who refuses to obey. What power, however, will force the ruler to observe God's law?

It appears impossible, then, to avoid contradictions in replying to questions that impose themselves while one is unwilling to raise them. But if those questions cannot be altogether ignored, the proper procedure is to raise them in an explicit fashion.

Spinoza. It is an unmistakable fact that all men, whether civilized or not, always enter into relationship with one another and establish a kind of state. This fact induced Spinoza to investigate the foundation of this tendency in the nature common to all men.[52] Human nature is found among other natures. The power and force through which everything in nature exists and operates is, according to Spinoza, nothing but the power and force of God. God's power, however, is unlimited and therefore God has a right to everything. Now, since whatever is in nature exists and operates by virtue of God's power and since God's absolute power is God's absolute right, it follows that the right of whatever is in nature is in direct ratio to the power it has to exist and operate.[53] This right of everything that exists in nature is the natural law, and the natural law extends as far as the power of nature and of everything that exists in nature.[54] Applied to man, this means that man's right to what exists in nature extends as far as his power over nature.[55]

If, then, man lived according to his reason, if he let reason guide his existence and the exercise of his power over other beings, man's natural rights would be determined by the power of his reason. But man does not live according to his reason; he is driven by passions and desires. This does not mean, however, that the power displayed by passionate and desirous man is not his right. His right extends as far as his power. His nature as power gives him this right, whether he lets himself be

---

[51] "Subjects owe to sovereigns, simple obedience, in all things wherein their obedience is not repugnant to the laws of God." Hobbes, *Leviathan*, p. 232.

[52] Baruch Spinoza, *Tractatus politicus*, c.I, 7.

[53] Spinoza, *op. cit.*, c.II, 3.

[54] "By right of nature, then, I understand the very laws or rules of nature according to which everything happens, i.e. the power itself of nature. Hence the natural right of nature and, consequently, of every individual extends as far as its or his power." Spinoza, *op. cit.*, c.II, 4.

[55] Spinoza, *ibid.*

guided by reason or by his passions.[56] The foolish ones, then, do not at all disturb the order of nature,[57] for the natural law forbids man only that which no one can do or wants to do.[58]

Everyone is by right his own master as long as he can resist all violence and avenge the wrongs inflicted upon him; in other words, as long as he has the power to do his own will.[59] Giving one's word does not entail any obligation, but remains valid only as long as he who gives his word does not change his mind. But he should, of course, have the power to break his word.[60]

Because people let themselves be swayed by their passions and desires, they are naturally one another's enemies. Man must fear his fellow-man—the more so because men are more resourceful and more ruthless than the other animals. However, since in the natural condition each one is his own master only as long as he is able to resist the others' violence, it follows that man's rights, *strictly speaking,* are not really rights. No single man can, all by himself, exercise power over all others; and the more numerous the people who join forces, the more power they are able to exercise. The rights given by the natural law acquire a real existence only within the society of the state.[61] Thus it follows that every member of the state has less right in direct ratio to the greater power the others together have.[62] Hence he has only as much right as positive law grants him, and he is obliged to execute the orders given by positive law. The law even has every right to force him to do so.[63]

Spinoza calls society's power, that is, right, its "authority." This authority is in the hands of those who by common consent are charged with the common good.[64] Once the natural condition is transformed into an orderly society, so-called "sin" becomes possible. Sin is that which is forbidden by the state's positive law; obedience is the willing-

[56] Spinoza, *op. cit.,* c.II, 5.

[57] Spinoza, *op. cit.,* c.II, 6.

[58] "From this it follows that the law and institutions of nature, under which all men are born and live for the most part, forbid nothing except that which no one wants and no one is able to do." Spinoza, *op. cit.,* c.II, 8.

[59] Spinoza, *op. cit.,* c.II, 9.

[60] Spinoza, *op. cit.,* c.II, 12.

[61] Spinoza, *op. cit.,* c.II, 13-15.

[62] "Where men have common rights and all are, as it were, of one mind, it is certain that each one's right is less according as the power of the others together is greater." Spinoza, *op. cit.,* c.II, 16.

[63] Spinoza, *ibid.*

[64] Spinoza, *op. cit.,* c.II, 17.

ness to do as prescribed by positive law. Sin and obedience, justice and injustice are possible only within the framework of the state.[65]

If the state would give one or the other individual person the right, and therefore the power, to live as he fancies, it would automatically diminish the right and the power of the state itself. By giving this right to two persons, the state would introduce divisiveness into society. And by according that right to everyone, the state would destroy itself and cease to exist as a state. Thus it follows that the state can never give anyone the right to live as he fancies. In consequence of this, the natural law ceases to exist in an orderly society.[66] Accordingly, the individual citizens do not have the right to give their own interpretation of the authority's decisions, for otherwise they would again begin to live as they fancy.[67]

Thus every citizen is wholly dependent upon the state. Whatever the state commands he must unreservedly execute, even if he thinks that certain orders are against reason. For, by executing them, he does not act against reason since reason itself teaches man that he must first of all seek peace and security. Unless the orders of the state's authorities are unreservedly executed, that peace and security become simply impossible. Moreover, the society of the state has been established to eliminate man's fear of his fellow-men and to overcome chaos. Man in his natural condition must recognize this aim precisely as a demand of reason even though it can never be realized in that natural condition. The importance of the state with respect to the elimination of fear and putting order in the natural chaos is an ample compensation for the inconvenience attached to obeying a command against reason. Finally, it is in accordance with reason to choose the lesser of two evils.[68]

Nevertheless, the leaders of the state themselves must try to be reasonable. For obviously that state is most powerful that is based upon reason and guided by reason. The power of a state is determined by the

---

[65] "Accordingly, just as sin and submission in the strict sense, so also justice and injustice can be conceived only within the state (*imperio*). For there is nothing in nature that can justly be said to belong to this one and not to that one, but everything belongs to all who have the power to claim it. But in the state, where a common law determines what belongs to each one, he is called just who has the constant will to give everyone his due and, on the contrary, unjust he who tries to appropriate that which belongs to someone else." Spinoza, *op. cit.,* c.II, 23.

[66] Spinoza, *op. cit.,* c.III, 3.

[67] Spinoza, *op. cit.,* c.III, 4.

[68] Spinoza *op. cit.,* c.III, 5-6.

harmony reigning among its people, and this harmony becomes impossible if the state does not desire and prescribe what reason demands. Secondly, the members of a state are subject to it only to the extent that they fear the state's power and punishments. That which no one can be induced to do by either promises or threats does not lie within the competence of the state. If the authorities persist in acting against reason, the citizens will conspire against the state. But since the rights of the state are determined by the united power of the people, it is evident that these rights and the state's power will be undermined to the extent that the state itself provokes people to conspire against it. Even the state has reason to fear. The more it has to fear, the less independent it is and the fewer rights it has—just as the individual citizen living in his natural condition.[69]

All this shows also unambiguously what right a state can claim with respect to other states. Two states are related to each other as two human beings in the natural condition: they are natural enemies. A state has the right to exist insofar as it can take care of itself and is able to resist the violence of another state. A state also has the right to wage war against another state; it merely has to will war. However, it is better for two states to enter into a peace treaty, for together they are more powerful than alone.[70] Such a treaty is valid only as long as there is a reason for it, viz., the hope of gain or the fear of loss.[71] If one of the two ceases to fear, he has the natural right to cancel the treaty, and the other should not complain that he has been deceived. For, first of all, both states made the same proviso when they arranged the treaty and, secondly, the state that feels disillusioned can only accuse itself of being foolish enough to entrust its welfare to another state, while knowing that this other state must obviously put its own welfare above everything else.[72]

The more numerous the states that bind themselves by treaty, the less

---

[69] "Because the right of a state is defined by the common power of the many, it is certain that the power and the right of the state decrease according as the state itself provokes many to conspire (against it). Certainly, the state has reasons to fear. And just as any citizen, any man in the natural condition, so also the state is less autonomous according as it has greater reason to be afraid." Spinoza, *op. cit.* c.III, 9.

[70] Spinoza, *op. cit.,* c.III, 12-13.

[71] "This treaty remains valid (*fixum*) as long as the cause giving rise to it, viz. fear of loss or hope of gain, continue to exist." Spinoza, *op. cit.,* c.III, 14.

[72] Spinoza, *ibid.*

dangerous any one of them is for the others, the more dependent it becomes on those others and the more obliged therefore to observe the conditions of the treaty.[73]

It is evident, so it appears, that Spinoza's theory of natural law is representative of what above we called conceptions of the natural law having an anthropological foundation. Spinoza thought that he could deduce his theory of the natural law from man's nature.[74] Let us add that Spinoza's view is rather strange: in his eyes, the natural law has the function of legitimating legal positivism and degenerates into a kind of "power mechanics."

3. *Protestant Theological Views*

Because this chapter is primarily devoted to the religious origin of man's consciousness of right and the legal order, it will be appropriate to mention briefly a few Protestant theological views of this origin. Some of these, in particular that of Emil Brunner, have drawn much attention in the past few decades.

In his book *Gerechtigkeit* (*Justice*), written during World War II,[75] Brunner very clearly and convincingly showed the inner connection existing between legal positivism and state absolutism.[76] It is especially this absolutism to which it logically leads that demonstrates how untenable legal positivism is. For Brunner, the rejection of legal positivism implies that there must be a justifying ground and a critical norm of positive law,[77] but he himself does not like to use the term "natural law."[78] He realizes very clearly that the disputes around the natural law all suffer from the defect that this term has so many different meanings; hence by being simply for or against *the* natural law one

---

[73] Spinoza, *op. cit.,* c.III, 16.

[74] "I want to draw attention to the fact that I have demonstrated all this from what is necessary in human nature, no matter how it is considered, that is, from the universal tendency of all men to self-preservation. This tendency exists in all men, whether they be ignorant or wise." Spinoza, *op. cit.,* c.III, 18.

[75] Brunner, *Gerechtigkeit.* Zürich, 1943.

[76] "The whole state is nothing but legal positivism changed into political praxis." Brunner, *op. cit.,* p. 7.

[77] The natural law of the Reformers "conceives itself as a norm that is to be adapted to historical reality. Its main importance lies therefore in its being the element of justice in positive law, for which it serves both as source and as norm in the formation of the legal order." Brunner, *op. cit.,* p. 320, note.

[78] Brunner, *op. cit.,* p. 110.

merely adds to the confusion unless one's standpoint is elaborated in great detail.[79] But when such details are presented, Brunner adds, one realizes that jurists and theologians still show themselves unable to avoid "thinglike," naturalistic interpretations with respect to the use of this term.[80] Although it may be possible to avoid the term "natural law," it is nevertheless impossible to escape from that which Christian thinking endeavored to express by this term.[81]

Brunner conceives justice as the disposition to respect in one's actions an order transcending man, an "order of belonging" (*Ordnung des Gehören*), that should be the norm of man's law-making (*Setzen*).[82] Man forms part of a structure, he occupies a particular place in a framework, and therefore his entire life is encompassed by a certain order. For, by the fact that I am integrated into a structure, a framework, certain things are orientated toward me, "belong" to me, while others are orientated toward someone else. Justice gives each one his due in accordance with this "belonging" and "being orientated."[83]

For Brunner, the idea of justice and the divine law of justice are one and the same,[84] because Christian faith teaches us that the "order of belonging" in which man is integrated is the "order of the Creator." [85] In the light of Scriptural revelation the order of nature appears as the product of God's will. "God spoke: 'Let it be,' and it became."[86] The law of justice, then, does not express merely what *ought* to be but what is. In creating, God assigned to every creature its domain of life, its freedom and its limits. He gives every creature not only its being and being this or that but also the law governing its being and its being this or that.[87] God determines what belongs to every creature. The expression *suum cuique* (to everyone his due), in which the demands of justice

---

[79] Brunner, *op. cit.*, pp. 100-101.

[80] Brunner, *op. cit.*, p. 103.

[81] "The concept of natural law imposes itself irresistibly on Christian thought with respect to its content (*sachlich*), even when the term itself can be avoided." Brunner, *op. cit.*, p. 104.

[82] Brunner, *op. cit.*, p. 22.

[83] Brunner, *op. cit.*, pp. 22-23.

[84] "The idea of justice and the thought of a divine law of justice are one and the same." Brunner, *op. cit.*, p. 54.

[85] Brunner, *op. cit.*, p. 57.

[86] Brunner, *ibid*.

[87] "God the Creator gives every creature, together with its being and being-this-or-that, the law of its being and of its being-this-or-that." Brunner, *op. cit.*, pp. 57-58.

can be summarized, has its ground in God's will expressing itself in creation. "Creation is original allotment,"[88] and therefore the law of justice is of divine origin. Every creature must respect every other creature as a being willed by God and in the way it is willed by Him. The fact that man can claim rights and ought to respect rights in others has its ultimate basis in what God Himself has willed in this matter.[89]

From a perspective on the order of creation Brunner thinks it possible to enumerate a list of divine demands of justice.[90] These demands are for him legal principles that lie beyond man's arbitrariness and which must receive their necessary concrete specification in positive law. This necessity implies that every concrete legal order will always be a compromise between the truly just and the concretely possible.[91]

What is the above-mentioned "perspective on the order of creation"? According to Brunner, it is a believing perspective, one that presupposes the revelation of the Bible and "standing" in this revelation, i.e., Christian faith. A doctrine of justice, then, is theological and presupposes Christian faith. But this does not mean for Brunner that the "natural man" has no perspective on the order of creation and does not see any demands of justice. Aristotle has said things about justice that are and remain beyond dispute even though he did not "stand" in the Christian revelation. Because the orders contained in creation are "orders of nature," man is bound to become aware of them at least to certain extent, even if he does not know the Creator.[92] The stars move according to the Creator's will without knowing it; the order of creation has its effect in their motions. But also in man this order has its effect, and for this reason the idea of justice is "something common to all men,"[93] even though many are unable to affirm the divine origin of this idea.

However, the universality of the idea of justice does not mean that the demands of justice can be understood without divine revelation. In

---

[88] Brunner, *op. cit.,* p. 58.

[89] "Creation itself is the ground on which man not only ought to do something but also has a claim and rights to something which others must respect. Something is due to him." Brunner, *ibid.*

[90] Brunner, *op. cit.,* pp. 64-76.

[91] "Any positive order of justice is a compromise between the genuinely just and the possible. But it must be kept in mind that the best solution is not an abstract similarity with what is good in itself but that adaptation which, in the given conditions, corresponds best to the demands of justice." Brunner, *op. cit.,* p. 120.

[92] Brunner, *op. cit.,* p. 106.

[93] Brunner, *op. cit.,* p. 107.

opposition to the medieval Catholic thinkers' ideas about natural law, the reformational theologians have always emphasized that "a certain and clear knowledge" of the Creator and His will of creation is needed for a "certain and clear knowledge" of the foundations and demands of justice.[94] What Aristotle has said about justice offers a lasting foundation to the doctrine of justice, but it does not suffice for a "basic and clear understanding" of what justice really is. Only the biblical idea of creation offers man access to a solution of the problems that Aristotle had to leave unsolved.[95] For this reason Brunner declares his adherence to the reformational conception of justice.[96]

We do not want to consider here whether or not Brunner is right in describing his view as reformational,[97] for that question lies beyond the scope of this book. But it is a fact that many reformational thinkers about justice and the natural law go far beyond Brunner with respect to the necessity of scriptural revelation for a correct understanding of the natural law. Brunner rejects the term "natural law," but not the idea of justice that is founded on the "orders contained in nature."[98] For other reformational theologians, however, nature is *per se* "corrupt nature," so that for them it becomes impossible to consider the natural law as the justifying ground, the critical norm and the source of positive law. For this reason they avoid the natural law and try to find another approach to the foundation of positive law.[99]

An example of such an approach is provided by Helmut Thielicke.[100] He correctly holds that the natural law evidently presupposes an image of man. But abstracting from the God—man relationship, this image is never constant. Thus it becomes impossible to derive from it evident, constant and universally valid norms; yet this is precisely what every

---

[94] Brunner, *op. cit.*, p. 108.

[95] "What Aristotle, the Master of the old theory of justice, said is lastingly valid and constitutes for all times the foundation of the theory of justice. However, as we saw, the Aristotelian doctrine is far from sufficient to grasp the essence of justice in a profound and clear fashion. Only on the basis of the biblical idea of creation can we gain access to the solution of the problems which Aristotle had to leave unsolved." Brunner, *ibid.*

[96] Brunner, *ibid.*

[97] We are convinced that this is not true.

[98] Brunner, *op. cit.*, p. 106.

[99] Welzel, *Naturrecht und materiale Gerechtigkeit*, pp. 182-183.

[100] H. Thielicke, *Theologische Ethik, vol. I, Dogmatische philosophische und kontroverstheologische Grundlegung*, Tübingen, 1951.

theory of natural law claims to do.[101]   On the other hand, the relationship between God and man is not open to anyone outside the perspective of faith.   But what is "known" about this relationship in and through faith cannot be called "natural law knowledge," for this kind of knowledge claims—or at least should claim—to be knowledge-without-faith.[102] Natural knowledge cannot speak about the essence of man as a relationship of God and man; and everything else it alleges to know about man's essence is nothing but things that are posited on the basis of a particular historical, changeable and fortuitous situation.[103]   Thielicke tries to prove this point by showing that the principle *suum cuique* has constantly been interpreted in a different way throughout history[104] and remains even now subject to varying interpretations.   Nothing can be deduced from it, for it clearly has only an apparent constancy.[105]

Similar ideas are expressed by Walther Schönfeld.[106]   One who takes man's fall into sin seriously must regard not only the "temporal law" but also the "natural law" as corrupt mirrors of the "eternal law."   The latter reveals itself solely in the "law of Christ."[107]   In the light of faith both the theory of the natural law and legal positivism are "equally condemned";[108] the theory of the natural law because it holds that the juridical phenomena can be saved by a reflection on the natural law; and legal positivism because it thinks that man can save those phenomena if he is willing to establish the necessary order.   Both disregard man's fall into sin and the Cross of Christ.   In a Christian theory about the foundations of the law the person of Christ must be the first and the final

[101] "Is not every appeal to what is allegedly 'known by the natural law' illusory from the very moment when one takes the natural law in its proper point, viz. its universal validity and its evident character?" Thielicke, *op. cit.,* p. 691.

[102] "Thus we hold fast to this: the natural law depends on the presupposed view of man.   But this view is not constant if we abstract from the relationship between God and man.   This relationship itself, again, is not open to insight *extra fidem.*   Hence, there can never be a natural law that is constant, binding for 'all.' "   Thielicke, *op. cit.,* p. 677.

[103] "On the level of natural knowledge, i.e., if we abstract from the revelation of the one man Jesus Christ (*ecce homo*), there is no knowledge of man's essence. In support of this assertion we point out that man can be defined only as a relational unit.   Aside from this relation, whatever is presented as man's essence is determined by what is posited . . . by a momentary situation, in its contingency and mutability." Thielicke, *op. cit.,* p. 676.

[104] Thielicke, *op. cit.,* pp. 676-683.

[105] Thielicke, *op. cit.,* p. 677.

[106] W. Schönfeld, *Grundlegung der Rechtswissenschaft,* Stuttgart, 1951.

[107] Schönfeld, *op. cit.,* p. 229.

[108] Schönfeld, *op. cit.,* p. 231.

word.[109]   In line with this idea Erik Wolf also demands that "biblical ideas play a role in the elaboration of the law."[110]

An objection that readily presents itself against these Protestant theological views is the following. If in the Christian doctrine about the foundations of right and law the person of Christ must be the first and the final word, then it will not be possible to find a common ground on which Christians and non-Christians can meet in their efforts to organize their social relationships. Jacques Ellul does not hesitate to accept this consequence[111] and admits that the natural law cannot fulfill that function.[112]   In his view, the natural law has been invented to escape from the radical need to have recourse to revelation in order to know the true and the good. Thus the natural law has placed God outside the world which is the dwelling place of man. God was affirmed as an easy hypothesis to start the reasoning process, but this process actually proceeded as if the world functioned under its own power and as if the Incarnation had not upset all relationships.[113] The proponents of the natural law had the illusion that positive law depended upon the natural law, while in reality the natural law is nothing but the absolutizing of positive law.[114]   For Ellul it is certain that there exists no natural knowledge of justice and that the demands of justice only become accessible to man through revelation in Christ. "Right and justice are entirely Christocentric."[115]

---

[109] "In a Christian theory of law the person of *Jesus Christ* ought to be the first and the final word. Hence that theory should not begin with *Heraclitus, Plato* and *Cicero* and then end with *Christ,* as if they are on the same level. Moreover, such a procedure presupposes an agreement of the *lex aeterna* and the *lex naturalis* which, in the light of *Jesus Christ,* cannot at all exist and which leads to a confused view of the Christian legal order (*Recht*) and the Christian state. This confusion must be critically solved, for the corruption of nature through man's fall into sin forbids us to make that presupposition. Only the Ancients were able to make it because, in spite of their doctrine of 'the Golden Age,' they knew nothing about man's fall into sin." Schönfeld, *op. cit.*, p. 228.

[110] Erik Wolf, *Rechtsgedanke und biblische Weisung,* Tübingen, 1948, pp. 28-40.

[111] Jacques Ellul, *Le fondement théologique du droit,* Neuchâtel, 1946.

[112] "The natural law cannot in any way be a meeting ground between Christians and non-Christians. . . . The only possible meeting ground of men lies outside themselves, in the permanence of God's mercy toward all." Ellul, *op. cit.*, pp. 52-53.

[113] Ellul, *op. cit.*, p. 8.

[114] "It is an illusion to believe that our earthly legal order (*droit*) depends on the natural law, when the latter is nothing but the absolutizing of our earthly legal order." Ellul, *op. cit.*, p. 48.

[115] Ellul, *op. cit.*, p. 52.

These Protestant theological theories were mentioned here because they are concerned with the topic of this chapter, viz., the religious origin of man's consciousness of right, but we want to abstain, of course, from becoming involved in theological disputes. We agree with Brunner, however, when he claims that such views as those of Thielicke, Schönfeld and Ellul inevitably lead to a fanatical confusion of church and state, of the message of love and the doctrine of justice.[116]

---

[116] "The new direction . . . tries something entirely different, viz. it endeavors to deduce the order of the law and of the state from the 'event' of Christ, from the Cross of Christ. The fantastic character of this derivation is at once evident to any unprejudiced mind. Even jurists who place themselves deliberately on the basis of the biblical faith in Christ reject this derivation as wholly impossible. However, aside from this impossibility, . . . such a view is also very dangerous, for it must of necessity lead to a fanatical confusion of Church and state, of the message of love and the doctrine of justice." Brunner, *op. cit.,* p. 321.

CHAPTER FOUR

THE THOMISTIC DOCTRINE OF
THE NATURAL LAW

Thomism explicitly distinguishes the natural law and positive law. Positive law is conceived as the concrete expression or the more detailed formulation of the natural law that is given together with man's nature. The natural law is the foundation and the justification of positive law, but it can happen that the natural law will brand as unjust regulations imposed by positive law.

Nature as Teleology. The Thomistic concept of the natural law presupposes the Thomistic teleological view of man's nature.[1] Man is naturally orientated to certain ends. These ends lie on different levels, as is also the case of man's tendencies. That to which man is orientated as an end is, as the fulfilment of natural human tendencies, a good for man and is, by virtue of these tendencies, ordered to man. For this reason man may call "his" that which by virtue of his natural tendencies is ordered to him;[2] it is that to which he has a *right*. This right has an objective as well as a subjective aspect.[3] Subjectively, right entitles a man to possess something or to do something. For example, "man has a natural right to life, to self-reproduction, a right, very general and indefinite, to destine external goods to himself, a right to contact with other men, a right to truth, a right to act reasonably,"[4] and so on. The objective aspect of right is that to which these subjective titles refer.[5]

---

[1] W. Duynstee, *Over recht en rechtvaardigheid,* 's-Hertogenbosch, 1956, pp. 23-32.

[2] "Something is called 'his' with respect to someone when it is ordered to him." St. Thomas, *Summa theologica,* p. I, q. 21, a. 1, *ad* 3.

[3] Messner, *op. cit.,* p. 157.

[4] Duynstee, *op. cit.,* p. 28.

[5] We intentionally use the term "objective aspect of right" because among jurists the expression "objective right" is taken to refer to the complex of legal

In the Thomistic perspective of the natural law, justice must be defined as the willingness to give each one his due.[6] "One's due" must be conceived as that to which each one is ordered according to his natural tendencies toward perfection.[7] Thus "one's due" is not determined primarily by positive law but by the natural tendencies of human nature. If a positive legal order violates what is naturally due to man, then such an order is called unjust on the basis of the natural law.

In the Thomistic view the natural law owes its origin to God.[8] To see why, one must be acquainted with the Thomistic theory of order. This theory is a development of the doctrine of creation, according to which everything that is owes its *total* being to God and is preserved in its total being by God. All beings are ordered by Him to their natural ends, and whatever is needed for the attainment of these ends has been ordered by Him to the beings in question. This assertion applies to both rational and nonrational beings.

With respect to man, as we saw already, everything that by virtue of man's natural tendencies is ordered to man for the attainment of his ends must be called, as Thomism holds, "his," "his due." It constitutes the rights given together with human nature, the rights of natural law. The orientation to man, however, of everything he needs to attain his natural ends—his rights—has been given existence by God. God Himself, therefore, through His ordinance, is the origin of the natural law. "Even as God gave wings to swallows because He wants swallows to fly, as He gave to lions other animals as nourishment because He wants them to eat and stay alive, so also God gave all kinds of things to man. He assigned them to him as things due to him, because He wants man to live a good human life."[9] "Even as it cannot be true that God, as the wise Ruler of the universe, makes birds in that universe and wants them to fly and, at the same time, does not want them to have wings, so also it

---

rules. Cf. R. Kranenburg, *De grondslagen der rechtswetenschap,* 4th ed., Haarlem, 1952, p. 57.

[6] "Justice is the constant and lasting will to give each one his due." St. Thomas, *op. cit.,* p. II-II, q. 58, a. 1.

[7] "That every man is the bearer of a number of relationships by virtue of which various things are 'his' or are 'what belongs to him' has its basis in the fact that man is ordered to his own perfection as his end." L. Bender, *Het recht,* Bussum, 1948, p. 74.

[8] "It is the Creator who assigns these responsibilities to individual human beings and to societies by means of the ends laid down in their nature. Hence, ultimately rights find their origin in God." Messner, *op. cit.,* p. 154.

[9] Bender, *op. cit.,* p. 76.

cannot be true that God wills every man to attain through his efforts a certain good for which certain things are indispensable means and, at the same time, does not will that every man has these means at his disposal. Hence these means are due to him."[10]   Accordingly, the natural law is not invented or established by man, but "it has been made together with man's nature, and as a natural consequence of this nature, by God, the Creator and Ruler of the universe.   More simply expressed, it has been established and introduced in the life of man as this life was ordered by God."[11]

Just as positive laws formulate and assign particular rights, so also, Thomism holds, there are norms that formulate and assign those natural rights.   These norms are called norms of the natural law.   Unlike the norms of positive law, however, they are not promulgated by the authority of the state but are given together with human nature.[12]   For human nature is a *rational* nature, and it is precisely through his rationality that man knows of his natural orientations and their objects.   What God has ordered to man's natural tendencies and orientations as due to him, as his right, can be expressed in norms.   These norms, then, are initially given in man's nature but can be explicitly formulated because of man's rationality.   In other words, the natural law is promulgated by the rational character of human nature itself.[13]

Some French and German authors prefer to speak of "natural *right*" (*Droit naturel, Naturrecht*) instead of "natural *law*."   They do this because among jurists the terms *"droit"* and *"Recht"* refer to a complex of norms.[14]   Because norms are rules indicating how man as a striving being must act to attain his goal, norms must be distinguished according to the kind of tendency.[15]   Thus norms of natural "right" (*Recht; droit*) are those norms that are given to man's reason as rules of man's actions at the same time as man's *natural tendencies*.   As a rational being man merely has to *recognize* and formulate his natural tendencies as such.   The recognition and formulation of man's natural tendencies to their own ends *is* the natural-"right"(*Recht; droit*)-as-norm, i.e., the

---

[10] Bender, *op. cit.,* p. 75.

[11] Bender, *op. cit.,* p. 76.

[12] "Accordingly, the order of precepts of the natural law follows the order of natural inclinations." St. Thomas, *op. cit.,* p. I-II, q. 94, a. 2.

[13] "Promulgation, which is required for the validity of any law, takes place, with respect to the natural law, by human nature itself." Messner, *op. cit.,* p. 69.

[14] Duynstee, *op. cit.,* p. 1.

[15] Duynstee, *op. cit.,* p. 19.

natural law, of human action. These norms can also be called man's subjective rights, for the natural order of his natural tendencies to their own good as the end of these tendencies constitutes a ground prescribing how man *ought* to act and therefore entitles him to act accordingly. The object to which he is entitled in this way is "his due," the objective aspect of his right.[16]

Even if there is question of the natural *law*, understood as norm of the so-called natural "right" (*Recht, droit*), Thomism affirms that it owes its origin to God, for the natural law is a participation in the Eternal Law.[17] Because God is the Creator, all beings and all their actions are given existence and kept in existence by God. God's creative act is guided by His wisdom, i.e., it is done for a purpose. "This requires that there exists in God's intellect a plan expressing the order of all things to their end."[18] This plan is called the Eternal Law.[19] The Eternal Law orders everything created to its end.[20]

The implication is that everything created participates in the Eternal Law because, and to the extent that, everything created contains an orientation to its own end.[21] The creature's orientation to its own end is, as it were, the imprint of the Eternal Law on everything created. With respect to man, however, this "imprint" has a special meaning because of his rationality. In him the "imprint" of the Eternal Law possesses the eminent mode of being called the "natural law."[22] For the Eternal Law is God's design, by which he orientates the creature to its end. In irrational creatures this design is expressed in their actual, though unconscious, orientation to their end, but man, as a rational creature, is aware of his own orientation and of what is due to him as a right by virtue of that orientation. The norm known as the natural law

---

[16] Duynstee, *op. cit.*, pp. 21-23.

[17] "The natural law is nothing but a participation of the eternal law in a rational creature." St. Thomas, *op. cit.*, p. I-II, q. 91, a. 2.

[18] Bender, *op. cit.*, p. 27.

[19] "Hence the very plan of the government of things that exists in God as in the principle of the universe has the character of a law. Now, since the divine intellect does not conceive anything in time but has an eternal concept, . . . this law must be called eternal." St. Thomas, *op. cit.*, p. I-II, q. 93, a. 1.

[20] "The eternal law is nothing but God's wisdom insofar as it directs all actions and motions." St. Thomas, *op. cit.*, p. I-II, q. 91, a. 2.

[21] "All things participate to some extent in the eternal law, namely, insofar as, by virtue of an impression of this law, they have inclinations to their own acts and their own ends." St. Thomas, *op. cit.*, p. I-II, q. 91, a. 2.

[22] See footnote 17.

expresses this right.   Hence the natural law as norm is, on the basis of man's rationality, the revelation of the Eternal Law as norm,[23] insofar as the latter applies to man.   In the natural law the divine ordinance of the Eternal Law is accessible to rational man insofar as the Eternal Law applies to him.[24]   Accordingly, the natural law, as the norm of man's natural rights, derives its origin from God's Eternal Law.

Finally, Thomism also bases the authority of the rulers on God.   This authority comes from God.[25]   Thomism does not mean that the bearer of authority can appeal to a direct divine mandate or that, consequently, he is responsible only to God.   According to Thomism, authority has its origin indirectly in God, in the sense that human nature and the natural law, which have their origin in God, demand that there be authority. For man is naturally a "political and social animal";[26] he is by his very nature a being destined for society because he can lead a fully human life only in community with others.[27]   Now, a society or community is naturally an *orderly* form of living together, but there can be no order in a society unless there exists authority.   Thus, man's nature, as a social nature, demands that there be authority.   Since, then, man's nature and his natural orientations come from God, authority also is prescribed by the natural law and, as such, has its basis in God's Eternal Law.[28]

Thomism makes it impossible for rulers to appeal to God in order to assume absolute power. For its theory assigns to a ruler authority only to the extent that it has been granted by the natural law.   If he goes beyond his competence and tyrannizes the people, then, on the basis of the natural law, he has no longer any legitimate authority.[29]   According

---

[23] "Accordingly, the natural law is a revelation of the eternal Wisdom, giving being and order to creation. This eternal wisdom, which is identical with God's own 'law' of being and acting, *Augustine* calls *lex aeterna*." Messner, *op. cit.,* p. 69.

[24] "Hence we must say the eternal law as it is in itself cannot be known by anyone except God and the blessed who see God in His essence. But any rational creature knows this law by a stronger or weaker 'irradiation.'" St. Thomas, *op. cit.,* p. I-II, q. 93, a. 2.

[25] "Whence also in human affairs superiors move inferiors through their will by virtue of their divinely ordained authority." St. Thomas, *op. cit.,* p. II-II, q. 104, a. 1.

[26] St. Thomas, *Summa contra gentiles,* bk. III, ch. 85.

[27] St. Thomas, *De regimine principum,* bk. I, ch. 1.

[28] Messner, *op. cit.,* p. 476.

[29] "Thus every law posited by man has the character of a law to the extent that it is derived from the law of nature. But if in some point it disagrees with the law of nature, it will no longer be a law but a corruption of the law." St. Thomas, *Summa theologica,* p. I-II, q. 93, a. 2.

to Thomism, the rulers also are subject to the natural law;[30] hence it can happen that, on the basis of this law, his subjects must refuse obedience[31] or are even justified in starting a revolution.[32]

A Critical Look. The Thomistic theory of the natural law is deeply rooted in many parts of St. Thomas' all-encompassing philosophy. One who does not want to go to the trouble of tracing the numerous links and connections that this theory has with the entire philosophical system will be unable to understand this theory. However, there are today many non-Thomists who have made serious efforts to understand the very foundations of St. Thomas' theory of the natural law. Their studies have led them to realize that his theory is one of the most important attempts to defend the natural law.[33]

The fact that the Thomistic theory of the natural law has such a variety of profound roots in an all-encompassing system, however, has the disadvantage of making acceptance of this theory rather difficult for the non-Thomist. The theory cannot be detached from its links and bond with his system, for precisely these links give the natural law its solid foundation in God's Eternal Law, and it is this foundation which in the Thomist view gives the natural law the solidity and stability ascribed to it. Philosophically speaking, very much is demanded of the philosopher if he wishes to follow the chain of ideas woven by the Thomistic theory of the natureal law and give his adherence to it.

We do not want to avoid considering the ramifications of the theory, but we will connect their study with a discussion of the contemporary objections to the Thomistic theory of the natural law. A certain selection will, of course, have to be made. There are thinkers who point out against "the" natural law and therefore also against its Thomistic conception the difficulty that "nature" and "right" are disparate concepts because "nature" precisely implies the denial of the subjectivity that is contained in "right." Such thinkers obviously have in mind the primitive naturalistic view of the natural law, and without any further ado they identify it with the Thomistic idea of the natural law, of which they possess only the most rudimentary knowledge. Similarly, it does not make sense to reject "the" natural law, including its Thomistic conception, because one cannot bear the thought that a system of natural norms

---

[30] J. Loeff, *Verhouding staat en rechtsgemeenschap,* Leiden, 1955, pp. 6-7, 9-10.
[31] St. Thomas, *op. cit.,* p. I-II, q. 96, a. 4.
[32] F. Sassen, *Het recht tot opstand,* Nijmegen, 1936.
[33] Langemeyer, *art. cit.* (footnote 10 of Ch. 3), p. 37.

could present itself as a competitor in size and detail with positive law. This objection would be pertinent with respect to the rationalistic view of the natural law, but it is based on a lack of information about the Thomistic conception.[34]

Has the Thomistic View a Theological Foundation? We mentioned already that much is demanded of the thinker who wants to follow the chain of thought woven by the Thomistic theory of the natural law. Some critics think that Thomism demands not only very much but too much, that it demands the acceptance of a theological standpoint.

Erich Fechner is one of those who hold this view with respect to the Thomistic doctrine of the natural law. He does not hesitate to call it a "splendidly developed doctrine," acknowledges that it has withstood numerous onslaughts and realizes that it is now entering into a new period of bloom.[35] Nevertheless, he rejects the Thomistic theory of the natural law because a philosopher, he thinks, should not cover up the fact that he is caught in a philosophical *cul de sac* by seeking a theological exit. When the philosopher sees no way out, he must accept the tension resulting from the unsolved problems and try to overcome them by a courageous life. But revelation is not a source of philosophical knowledge; hence any appeal to incontrovertible religious truths means the end of philosophy.[36]

We need not quarrel with this standpoint. Philosophy is philosophy and not theology. The philosopher dwells in the wonder of all wonders, that there is something to see and something to say;[37] he expresses what he "sees" and not what he believes. However, Fechner is wrong when he thinks that *on this ground* the Thomistic theory of the natural law must be rejected: for the Thomist this theory is precisely something philosophical and not something theological.[38] Like others, Fechner thinks that the realm of theology is reached as soon as one speaks of God in any way whatsoever. But the Thomist disagrees and holds that as a

---

[34] J. Th. Beysens, *Ethiek,* vol. I, Leiden, 1913, pp. 650-651.

[35] Fechner, *op. cit.,* p. 48.

[36] "However, he who saves himself from the impasse of philosophical demonstration by having recourse to theological views, e.g., to a God-given order, and in this way stills his doubt, fails in the properly philosophical problem." Fechner, *op. cit.,* p. 82.

[37] "To philosophize is to seek, to imply that there are things to see and to say." Merleau-Ponty, *Eloge de la philosophie,* Paris, 12th ed., 1953, p. 57.

[38] Bender, *op. cit.,* pp. 14-16.

philosopher one can say something about God, and he specifically makes a distinction between a theology of law[39] and a philosophy of law.[40] Fechner could argue, of course, that the Thomistic doctrine of the natural law is a theology which mistakes itself for a philosophy. In that case one should be willing to examine the arguments to be adduced in favor of that mistaken self-interpretation. However, no such arguments are presented by Fechner. He rejects the Thomistic theory of the natural law *because* it is theology. On such a basis there is naturally no possibility of a genuine dialogue between Fechner and Thomism.

That is not all, however. Despite the Thomist's solemn assurance that his theory of the natural law is a philosophical theory, we can understand that others reject this assurance. The reason lies, we think, in the fact that the Thomist speaks with so much confidence about God and the natural order established by God that it is hardly surprising if many cannot escape the impression of being faced with something more than philosophy. It stands to reason, of course, that such an impression is also contingent on the explicit or implicit view one holds about the possibilities man has to speak philosophically of God.

Thus we are obliged to speak here about these possibilities, in spite of the fact that this discussion lies far from the realm of topics proper to the philosophy of law. But there is no escape from that obligation because Thomism bases man's natural rights on the order God has put into nature and considers the natural law a participation in God's Eternal Law. This view is loaded with grave consequences. On the basis of his theory of the natural law, the Thomist will sometimes claim that certain regulations of positive law are in accordance with or in disagreement with God's will. By doing this, the demand for obedience or resistance is given the absolute weight that must be ascribed to a divine affirmation.

Undoubtedly, it is true that the appeal to the natural law and therefore to God's will, as made by Thomism, was effective in the past

---

[39] Cf., e.g. J. Fuchs, *Lex naturae,* Düsseldorf, 1955.

[40] "When one speaks of God or brings God to bear on an argument, one does not necessarily speak as a theologian. For one can speak of God solely on the basis of principles and positions known and proved by man's natural reason. In that case one is purely a philosopher. One who speaks in this fashion about right and its ultimate causes and then shows that God and God's law are the ultimate cause of all rights, pursues pure philosophy of law, without any admixture of theology in general and of the theology of law in particular." Bender, *op. cit.,* pp. 16-17, footnote 2.

when resistance to totalitarian aspirations of the state had to be given a solid foundation.   Fechner also recognizes this point.[41]   That resistance was not infrequently invincible.   On the other hand, it has also happened quite often that demands for justice were disregarded or rejected with an appeal to the natural law, i.e., God's will.   Full of rancor as it is, a work of August Knoll presents us with an imposing and well-documented list of examples,[42] which one cannot simply disregard as irrelevant.   Thomas Aquinas defended slavery,[43] and considered it in keeping with the natural order that some human beings were slaves.[44] The slave is something belonging to his master, for he is the latter's instrument;[45] hence the slave does not form part of the people or the society.[46]   Let us realize what this means and keep in mind that, in the Thomistic view, the natural law is an expression of God's Eternal Law.

And there are more examples.   In the time of the Conquistadores, prominent professors of the natural law did not condemn the forced labor of the Indians in South America or the importation of Negro slaves from Africa.[47]   But they did enumerate the conditions to be observed before one could legitimately make Negroes slaves.   They also argued about the just price to be paid for slaves and wondered whether a small mirror, a piece of red cloth or a string of glass beads constituted sufficient payment.[48]   Similarly, in the time of Marx the actually existing economic, social and political situation was viewed as the natural order and, as such, was attached to the will of God.

These facts, however, in themselves do not answer the question whether and to what extent the natural law has its origin in God.   At

---

[41] Fechner, *op. cit.,* pp. 48-49, footnote 78.

[42] A. M. Knoll, *Katholische Kirche und scholastisches Recht,* Vienna, 1962.

[43] "We answer that to everyone is due what is his.   Now a thing is said to be his when it is ordered to him, as a slave is to his master." St. Thomas, *op. cit.,* p. I, q. 21, a. 1, *ad* 3.

[44] "Whence it is proved that some are slaves according to nature." St. Thomas, *De regimine principum,* bk. I, ch. 10.

[45] "The slave is something belonging to his master because he is his instrument." St. Thomas, *Summa theologica,* p. I, q. 97, a. 4.

[46] "Slaves do not form part of the people or of the state." St. Thomas, *op. cit.,* p. I-II, q. 98, a. 6, *ad* 2.

[47] "Although the leading Spanish Scholastics did not, as we said, leave us a judgment concerning the prebends, nevertheless, from their basic attitude we are permitted to conclude that they accepted this system of forced labor as well as slavery in their essential aspects." J. Höffner, *Christentum und Menschenwürde,* Trier, 1947, p. 280.

[48] Höffner, *op. cit.,* pp. 277-279.

most they can be called cases in which man spoke erroneously of the natural law and of God's will.   But, on the other hand, such facts demonstrate in a very clear fashion the consequences and risks involved in saying that concrete regulations are willed by God, thereby giving them the absolute weight that should be ascribed to God's own statements.   One who makes a mistake and ascribes a divine guarantee to his mistake when, on the basis of the natural law, he rejects unmistakable demands of justice, lapses into a subtle form of legal positivism that is almost beyond unmasking;[49] at the same time he is also the reason why his opponents are almost forced to reject his God together with his mistakes.   As a matter of fact, this is what happened in the case of Marxism.   For Marx, the critique of religion was the indispensable condition of all critique.[50]

However, let us return to the point under discussion.   We mentioned the effectiveness and the risk involved in any attempt to appeal to the natural law in order to assert that a particular positive legal ordinance is in harmony with God's plans, willed by God, or in agreement with His Eternal Law.   The question, however, was whether and to what extent the philosopher as philosopher can affirm the relationship of the natural law to the Eternal Law of God.   Against the allegation that it is always and exclusively done on theological grounds, the Thomist explicitly claims that he affirms this relationship on a purely philosophical basis. And if the others insist that, nonetheless, theology is implied in the Thomistic claim, they are implicitly or explicitly influenced by a certain view about man's possibility of speaking philosophically about God. They think that the confidence and self-assurance with which the Thomist speaks about God with respect to the problem of founding the natural law in God show that he at least overrates man's possibility of speaking philosophically about God.

Personally we think that the Thomist does indeed overrate this possibility.   But we do not at all consider it impossible to philosophize about God.[51]   The admission of this possibility, however, does not mean that we agree with every view regarding the possible philosophical affirmation

---

[49] "What is merely camouflaged positivism is then presented as taught by the natural law."   Erik Wolf, *Das Problem des Naturrechtslehre*, Karlsruhe, 1955, p. 10.

[50] "The critique of religion is the presupposition of all critique."   Marx, "Zur Kritik der Hegelschen Rechtsphilosophie," *Die heilige Familie*, Berlin, 1953, p. 11.

[51] William A. Luijpen, *Phenomenology and Atheism*, Pittsburgh, 1964, pp. 64-80.

of God's existence.   Especially with respect to the Thomistic affirmation of God as the origin of the natural law, we entertain serious reservations.

We are not convinced that the Thomist has a lively awareness of God's transcendence when he endeavors to base the natural law upon God's Eternal Law.   We are not yet referring here to what Thomism means by the natural law, but only to the affirmation of God and the so-called "names of God" that are mentioned in the attempt to affirm God as the origin of the natural law.

Thomism, of course, explicitly recognizes God's transcendence. However, as Thomistic thought about God develops, this awareness of God's transcendence simply disappears.   That God is transcendent means that He can never be put on a par with anything that is not God. One can affirm that an apple *is,* that a rock *is,* a conversation *is,* a football club *is,* that the state *is,* a professor *is* or a child *is.*   Metaphysically speaking, one must say that be-ing *is.*   But whoever accepts a transcendent God must also accept that we cannot affirm of this God that He *is, in the same way* as we affirm that an apple, a rock, a club or a child *is.*   Of a be-ing man can affirm that it *is,* but God is not a be-ing. Hence man cannot *unqualifiedly* say that God *is* and, if he does it anyhow, he lowers God to the level of a mere be-ing; he disregards His transcendence.

All this the metaphysician must keep in mind when his metaphysical reflection upon the implications of be-ing as be-ing forces him to "affirm" God as the Transcendent Origin of be-ings.   At the very moment when he realizes that he must "affirm" the Transcendent Being, he also realizes that it is impossible to execute that "affirmation" in the way he has hitherto made other affirmations.   He must at once add a "negation" to his "affirmation" to show that he does not want to "affirm" another be-ing belonging to the realm of be-ings.

The metaphysician's thinking and speaking about God is a thinking and speaking that does not reach God and dwell with Him *just as* his thinking and speaking about be-ings reaches these be-ings and dwells with them.   His thought and speech about God is an indirect thinking and speaking, one that uses concepts and terms which point to something other than themselves because be-ings point to something other than themselves.   Those concepts and terms are road signs pointing to a place to which they themselves do not go.   It would be blasphemous to say *unqualifiedly* that God *is.*

We become authentically aware of all this only when we *personally* become involved in the metaphysical search. When such a personal involvement is lacking, one does not realize how easily man's thinking about God can degenerate. The concepts and terms one uses begin to lead a kind of isolated existence, as the impersonal possession of a "community of speech." The necessary dialectics of affirmation and negation loses its tension, and there is no longer any control over the terms used in speaking of God. Ultimately one sincerely believes that he *knows exactly* what he is saying.[52]

If we look now at the way in which Thomism bases the natural law on God, we are struck by the reckless abandon with which the necessary terms are used. According to Bender, who is a Thomist, "God has given wings to swallows," He "wills that animals eat," He has "given all kinds of things to man";[53] God "made birds and wanted them to fly"; He has "inserted the natural law into man's life because He wanted man to have means at his disposal" to reach his ends;[54] "in God's mind there exists a plan that expresses the order of all things to their end";[55] and "all things tend to their own actions and ends through an imprint of God's Eternal Law."[56] When this author wants to state clearly that God orientates actions to an end but Himself is in no way oriented to anything else as His end, he says that God's purposive action is not "as the action of Peter who eats to remain healthy," but is "as the action of Peter who *makes* his horse eat in order that it remain healthy."[57]

Such a way of speaking about God is naive to the point of being scandalous. If one cannot *unqualifiedly* say that God "is," then likewise one cannot blandly assert that God "directs creatures and their actions to an end to be attained"[58] *just as* Peter directs his horse to the eating of its food. Lest we be misunderstood, we do not want to assert here that God is not the origin of man's natural rights. (We abstract here from the question whether these rights are correctly conceived by Thomism.) We do not make that assertion, just as we do not deny that God "is" when we say that we cannot unqualifiedly affirm that He "is." But the way in which Thomists affirm the connection of the natural law with

---

[52] Luijpen, *op. cit.*, pp. 314-319.
[53] Bender, *op. cit.*, pp. 75-76.
[54] Bender, *op. cit.*, p. 76.
[55] Bender, *op. cit.*, p. 27.
[56] St. Thomas, *op. cit.*, p. I-II, q. 91, a. 2.
[57] Bender, *op. cit.*, p. 26.
[58] Bender, *op. cit.*, pp. 26-27.

God has degenerated so much into a "spoken word" (*parole parlée*) that it is downright scandalous. The constant omission of the negative judgment that is required by any positive judgment concerning God makes itself felt here in a very painful way.

For this reason the Thomist's train of thought, in trying to base the natural law on God's Eternal Law, is wholly inaccessible to those who want to pursue philosophy as a "speaking word" (*parole parlante*). This inaccessibility makes some of them think that the Thomist offers them a theology instead of a philosophy. They are wrong in that matter, but one can understand their mistake.

What is "Nature" and "Natural"? The statement that the natural law has its origin in God is based, according to Thomism, on the relations a creature's natural orientations have to God. What nature assigns as a right or imposes as a duty Thomism affirms, on the basis of this relationship, as an implication of the ordinances of God's Eternal Law. In man, these natural orientations reveal themselves as a law[59] because of this creature's rationality. Thus the ordinances of the natural law are "imprints"[60] or "reflections"[61] of the ordinances of the Eternal Law.

Nature is the intermediary between the natural rights and duties, as expressed in the laws of nature, on the one hand, and God's Eternal Law, on the other. One who seeks the origin of these natural rights and duties in God's Eternal Law is obliged to have a clear notion regarding the meaning of the terms "nature" and "natural." When the Thomist says that certain ordinances or regulations of positive law agree with or violate nature, he asserts automatically that they are in harmony with or contrary to God's will. He thereby assigns them an absolute weight, with all the risks that implies.

Even without this appeal to God's Eternal Law, the risks run by the Thomist are very great. Man's natural orientations reveal his natural rights, expressed in the natural law. This natural law functions as the justifying ground and the critical norm of the legal order. But the appeal a Thomist makes to the natural law becomes actually a camouflaged form of legal positivism as soon as he is mistaken in his evaluation of a certain orientation as "natural," as the basis of a (natu-

---

[59] "To the natural law belongs all that to which man is inclined by his nature." St. Thomas, *op. cit.*, p. I-II, q. 94, a. 3.

[60] St. Thomas, *op. cit.*, p. I-II, q. 91, a. 2.

[61] St. Thomas, *op. cit.*, p. I-II, q. 93, a 2.

ral) right and a (natural) law, and makes his mistake serve as the justifying ground and the critical norm of the legal order.

In principle, however, it is clear what the terms "nature" and "natural" mean for the Thomist. In his theory of the natural law, "nature" simply means "essence"; and "natural" is whatever belongs to, harmonizes with, or is demanded by this essence. But the matter is not as simple as that! For, if we examine concretely what certain Thomists call "natural," we become rather confused. As we mentioned already, Thomas Aquinas himself considered it to be "according to nature" that some men are slaves,[62] and when he wanted to illustrate what it means to call something "one's own," he used the example of the slave who belongs to his master.[63] The "natural" character of slavery, however, is evidently different from the "naturalness" spoken of by the Thomist Duynstee when he says: "The infinite good is the most essential and necessary object of man's *natural* tendency."[64] With an appeal to the "natural" one Thomist justifies slavery while another demands the right to follow one's conscience in worshiping God.

It may be useful to add a few other examples. To prove that private property is a natural right of man, Boyer says: *"By nature* man takes care of what belongs to him and neglects the possessions belonging to society."[65] What, we may ask, does "nature" mean here? Is it against the natural law *not* to neglect common possessions? Of course not, but for Boyer nonetheless the right of private property is a demand of the natural law because "by nature" man neglects the goods belonging to the society. Sex deviates who murder their victims could appeal to such a "nature" to show that the "natural" law permits them to demand a legally recognized social status!

According to Thomas Aquinas, man is naked "according to the natural law" because nature has not clothed him.[66] Obviously, the term "nature" is taken here in a very special sense, for no one will claim that it is against nature to put on clothing. The term "nature" has again a different sense when one says that the marriage act is by its very nature orientated to the procreation of children and that therefore it is against

---

[62] St. Thomas, *De regimine principum,* bk. II, ch. 10.

[63] See footnote 43.

[64] Duynstee, *op. cit.* (footnote 1), p. 25.

[65] "It is natural for man to attend to his own affairs and to neglect that which is common." C. Boyer, *Cursus philosophiae,* vol. 2, Paris, n.d., p. 524.

[66] ". . . as we could say that man is naked by natural law because nature did not give him clothing. St. Thomas, *Summa theologica,* p. I-II, q. 94, a. 5, *ad* 3.

the natural law to deprive that act of its natural power.[67] Still a different sense is had when Duynstee says: "Whatever a man by nature can demand for himself that he must, also by nature, respect in all others."[68] To prove his point, Duynstee argues: "As a spiritual being, man is by his very nature not subject to any other created being; in his nature he is dependent only upon God. This is the reason why no created being may interfere with his nature, for that would be an interference in man's most fundamental natural relationships."[69] The term "nature" is used here again, but what does it mean? That man as a spiritual being is by his very nature not subject to any other created being apparently does not exclude that, as St. Thomas says, intellectually gifted men are "by nature" the leaders and rulers of the others.[70] What is meant here by "nature"? Or again, what does "nature" mean when Thomas says that in the family authority rests on the husband because the masculine is "by nature" better and the feminine is "by nature" worse; the man is "by nature" a leader and the woman is "by nature" a subject?[71]

These few examples suffice to show that the critics of the Thomistic natural law theory are certainly not to blame when they complain that the Thomists manipulate an uncontrollable concept of "nature." In principle there is no difficulty, for the natural law is based on "nature," i.e., on man's "essence" and his "essential" relationships. But in practice there exists the greatest confusion, so that in the past totalitarian aspirations could be both opposed and supported by an appeal to the natural law.

Ahistorical Individualism. A third group of objections against the Thomistic view of the natural law can be put together under the title "ahistorical individualism." These objections want to stress that in the description of "nature," conceived as "man's essence," the Thomist does

---

[67] "Since the marriage act is by its very nature destined to the procreation of offspring, those who, in performing that act, deprive it intentionally of this natural power and capacity act against nature." Pius XI, encyclical *Casti connubii.*

[68] Duynstee, *op. cit.,* p. 31.

[69] Duynstee, *op. cit.,* p. 31, note.

[70] "Men of superior intelligence are naturally the rulers and masters of others." St. Thomas, *In metaphysicam Aristotelis commentaria,* Prologus.

[71] "By nature the masculine is better and the feminine worse; and the male rules while the female is subject." St. Thomas, *In IV libros politicorum commentaria,* Lib. I, lect. 3, Parma ed., vol. IV, p. 377.

not, or at least not sufficiently, take into account that a man simply is not what he is without his fellowmen. Yet it is undeniably true that co-existence belongs to the essence of man.[72] This co-existence means that the others are present in what he is, viz., man. Differently expressed, the same idea could be stated by saying that history is present in the kind of man a human being is. It is utterly foreign to man's real essence to represent matters as if the man who lived half a million years ago was merely a primitive edition of the cultured man of the twentieth century. Today's civilized man is the result of a long intersubjective history, of which positive anthropology and ethnology show us the origin. A long history, which twentieth century man himself has not made, has placed this man on the level of authentic humanity on which it is evident to his rationality that it is against the natural law to sacrifice infants and to burn widows. But, was it also evident a hundred thousand years ago?

According to Thomism it is due to man's rationality that his natural orientations are not "blind" orientations. Through his reason man knows about his natural tendencies, and it is through his reason that they appear to him as norms. This rationality is a mysterious kind of "seeing," and this "seeing" *is* the "promulgation of the natural law." Never, however, does the Thomistic theory of the natural law emphasize that man's "seeing" is a historical "seeing." It fails to realize that the universality of this "seeing," which *now* is obvious at least in certain points, was made possible by the genius of a particular "seer" who at a datable moment of history was the first to "see" and thus originated a long history in which others began to participate in his "seeing." It is because of others, because of history, that *my* rationality promulgates the natural law for *me*. *My* "seeing" is a historical and social reality.[73]

Because the historical and social character of man's rationality is not emphasized in Thomism,[74] the properties traditionally ascribed to the natural law assume a very special form here. The natural law is said to have an absolutely general validity, to be eternal and immutable. For

---

[72] Remy C. Kwant, *Phenomenology of Social Existence,* Pittsburgh, 1965, pp. 67-104.

[73] Kwant, *De ontwikkeling van het sociale denken,* The Hague, 1960, p. 10.

[74] "On the contrary, we must say, I think, that man, personally and alone, is capable of learning the evident truths and their immediate conclusions, i.e. the *prima principia* and their first applications. For the situation is not such that man's reason cannot begin to operate without the aid of someone else." F. A. Weve, "Staat en algemeen welzijn by Aristoteles en St. Thomas," *Verslag v.d. 19e alg. verg. v.d. Vereniging v. Thomistische Wijsbegeerte,* Utrecht, 1954, p. 4.

the natural law is founded on man's nature; it even *is* this nature insofar as man's reason reveals human nature with its natural tendencies to man. But human nature, as that by which man is man, is found wherever there are human beings. Therefore, the natural law is valid for all men. As soon as man exists, the natural law also exists. Hence the natural law has been valid always and everywhere; it is valid and will be valid wherever man has existed, exists or will exist. This law cannot be changed by any circumstances, for the nature of man remains the same. Because circumstances are accidental, they cannot change the nature. The natural law is immutable.[75]

The Thomists, obviously, were not ignorant of the fact that certain primitive peoples had and have ways of thinking and acting which we today qualify as "against the natural law." For instance, the killing of infants, especially girls, and of the aged was and sometimes still is regarded as quite normal. The way in which Thomism met this difficulty permits us to penetrate more profoundly into its view of the natural law. But, at the same time, it raises new difficulties from the standpoint of contemporary thought. Let us see why.

Although the natural law is said to be universally valid, eternal and immutable, Thomism admits that certain peoples can begin to lose conscious knowledge of that law. They "begin" to lose that knowledge, says Duynstee,[76] thereby insinuating that the "conscious knowledge" in question was originally present. It is lost through corruption and evil habits.[77] But this "loss" is conceived by Thomism as a defect in man's *knowledge* of human nature and its natural orientations, and not as a different mode of being of that nature and its orientations. In other words, the natural law *is* already there; it exists independently of man and his knowledge. Whether man knows the natural law or not is irrelevant to the existence of this law as such.[78]

Contemporary man spontaneously feels called to protest against such a way of presenting matters. For the universality, eternity and immutability of the natural law is presented here with the rigid inflexibility of a divinized rock. Often, however, the critics lack the necessary epistemo-

---

[75] Duynstee, *op. cit.,* pp. 32-33.

[76] Duynstee, *op. cit.,* p. 32.

[77] "Nevertheless, it is not impossible that on rare occasions and because of the corruption of the will through malice or custom there occurs a variation." Boyer, *op. cit.,* vol. II, p. 494.

[78] Duynstee, *op. cit.,* pp. 32-33.

logical knowledge to formulate their objections very clearly. They then reproach the Thomistic standpoint for its "rigidity," meaning that this standpoint is unfamiliar with life. In more philosophical terms this "rigidity" can be called the objectivism or essentialism of the Thomistic conception of the natural law. We must discuss it here extensively.

Objectivism. In the Thomistic view the natural law as norm of man's actions "sees" and formulates the demands implied in man's nature. These demands are called "objective," by which Thomism rightly emphasizes that man may not think and speak about his nature in an arbitrary and fanciful way. Man's thinking and speaking is subject to bonds in this matter and he has simply to recognize this nature for what it *is*. For the specific case of the natural law, this idea formulates the general principle that our knowledge is authentic knowledge, and not an idle dream or fancy only when it expresses that which *is*. Such knowledge is called knowledge of "objectivity." Objectivity is not subject to man's arbitrariness.

To give sufficient emphasis to the fact that objectivity is beyond the knowing subject's arbitrariness, Thomism has gone to the extreme of making this objectivity entirely independent of the subject. It conceives objectivity in an objectivistic fashion. It stands to reason that objectivity is objective for a subject. If something can be called objective, there must be a subject for whom objectivity is objective. The subject is a kind of "light," and the objective is that which is "unconcealed" in and for this "light." In man's knowing, the subject and objectivity constitute a unity of reciprocal implication; we may even say that this unity *is* our knowing. To know, then, is to encounter, and in an encounter one cannot leave out or isolate any one of the two terms without destroying the encounter itself. In this sense, therefore, objectivity can never be made entirely independent of the subject, even though this objectivity lies beyond the subject's arbitrariness.

Thomism has failed to see this point. In Thomism objectivity was not seen as the term encountered by the knowing subject but as an "in itself," as a reality "isolated" from the subject. In "true" knowledge this "in itself" was thought to mirror itself accurately in the subject. This view is known as the representationalism, the objectivism or the essentialism of Thomism. This philosophy represented the objective and the real as a collection of essences accumulated in a land that did not even need to be discovered in order to be meaningful.

This view had its precursor in the philosophy of Plato. This Greek thinker was struck by the aspect of necessity and universality in man's knowledge but, burdened as he was by the heritage of Heraclitus, he was unable to find a basis of this necessity and universality in the world. He therefore claimed that there was a separate world of necessary and universal ideas, of pure essences that are the prototypes of all worldly realities. He conceived this world of ideas as the universal and necessary measure by which the worldly realities, as shadows of those ideas, could be measured and on the basis of which one could determine whether a particular being is a being having this or that essence. In this world of ideas there existed, according to Plato, the pure essence of the state, of the work of art, of man, virtues, and of the horse. The ideas functioned as the norm for the "truth" of things. Concrete living man has nothing to do but to realize his necessary, universal, immutable and eternal essence in changeable time.

The world of pure ideas was conceived by Plato as a world of pure "light." The pure idea is pure "light." The objectivity, reality and "meaning" spoken of by modern phenomenology is not pure "light." Meaning is a mixture of "light" and "darkness," of unconcealedness and concealedness for the subject. The meaning's unconcealedness presupposes that the subject-as-*cogito* lets the meaning be. The moment when the subject-as-*cogito* emerges is the "moment" (*Augen-blick*) when truth arises as unconcealedness. This moment is the beginning of a never-finished history of drawing from concealment, of dis-covery. Meaning is never *pure* "light."

The fact that phenomenology conceives meaning as the *chiaro-oscuro* of unconcealedness and concealedness makes it possible to call meaning the real term-of-encounter of man's knowledge. Such *real* terms are a mixture of "light" and "darkness." When Plato viewed meaning as pure idea, as pure "light," he no longer regarded meaning as a real *term of encounter*. The Platonic idea, conceived as pure "light," actually is the meaning whose "moment" of being dis-covered is "forgotten" and whose history of being drawn from concealedness is considered to be finished. But there is no room within knowledge as real *encounter* for such a finished result, for in a real encounter with meaning the latter discloses itself as the *chiaro-oscuro* of unconcealedness and concealedness and therefore as a never-ending invitation to dis-covery addressed to the subject-as-*cogito*. Thus Plato was practically forced to detach the meaning from the encounter and locate it as an "in itself" of a purely ideal type in a world of pure ideas.

Aristotle no longer conceived the essences as lying in an ideal world but in the real world. Plato had conceived the essences as the "in themselves" of an ideal kind but not as terms of encounter. Because Aristotle merely "realized" these essences, i.e., placed them in "reality," he implicitly conceived them also as "in themselves." He relocated these "in themselves" from the ideal world to the real world, but he did not restore them as terms of encounter. Just as the Platonic essences, the Aristotelian essences were conceived as an absolute "light," but of a real and not of an ideal type. Aristotle's essences also were presented as in themselves necessary, universal, immutable and eternally "true," for they functioned as an absolute real "light" that was the measure of the truth contained in man's judgments. In this way reality was pictured as a collection of essences accumulated in a land that was supposed to be an absolute "light," and no attention was paid to the history of the light's origin and growth.

This view underlies the realistic philosophy of order of the Schoolmen which assigns to each essence its own place in brute reality. Man also, together with his own essence, was supposed to occupy a particular place in the hierarchy of order,[79] a place below God but above animals, plants and mere things. The sacred outranked the beautiful, the beautiful was above the useful, the useful above the agreeable, the common good was higher than the individual good and the soul more noble than the body.[80] Even the essences of man's actions were located as so many rocks in the landscape of the "universe of reality" (*omnitudo realitatis*). In their essences these acts were supposed to be what they are, of necessity, universally, immutably and eternally "true" in themselves.

This view of reality led inevitably to a special standpoint with respect to the ethical aspect of man's actions. If it is granted that in the "universality of reality" immutable and eternal essences lie accumulated and that immutable and eternal relations between these essences constitute an immutable and eternal order, and if it is granted that man and his actions occupy an immutable and eternal place in this complex of

---

[79] "The source of the definition (of man) as *animal rationale* is surreptitiously but unmistakably governed by the radicalism of naturalistic objectivism, which, with a free glance, looks at the *omnitudo realitatis* and assigns to man his rank —albeit the first place—in the spectacle it offers. But it totally neglects to remember that the origin of that hierarchy resides in the legislative activity of that 'look' coming from the being that illuminates the spectacle and which 'constitutes' it as such." Alphonse de Waelhens, *La philosophie et les expériences naturelles,* The Hague, 1961, pp. 190-191.

[80] Max Müller, *Existenzphilosophie im geistigen Leben der Gegenwart,* Heidelberg, 1949, pp. 19-20.

"truths" in themselves, then it follows that for the concrete living man the ethical goodness of his actions consists in "reading" these essences and their essential order and conforming to this order.[81]   In this way man accomplishes the will of God.   For Thomism did not merely relocate the Platonic ideas in the real world but, at the same time, gave to them, as exemplars of the real essences, a place in the intellect of God, who through a command of His will gave reality to these exemplars in the act of creation.

Thomism, then, ascribed to the essences a "truth" in themselves, measured by and derived from their being "true" in God's intellect: "every being is true."[82]   To the extent that man in his true knowledge mirrors the essences' "truth" in themselves, he possesses God's view of things.   In this way the essentialism, objectivism and realism of Thomistic philosophy reaches its apex in the claim to speak about things in the name of God.[83]

It would be wrong, however, to think that representational realism is ever "officially," explicitly and deliberately defended by Thomists.   No one will ever "officially" claim to affirm, know or speak of the "in itself," that is, of reality that is not affirmed, not known or not spoken of. Representationalism always remains only an implicit conviction that is not recognized as such.   This conviction remains implied in standpoints which do not "officially" express representationalism but which nonetheless contain it of necessity.   Thus it is not surprising that representationalism is found even in thinkers who "officially" and explicitly reject the representational interpretation of realism.   For anyone who is conscious of the contradictory character of representationalism obviously will reject that interpretation.   Unfortunately, this does not mean that he does not continue to adhere to it implicitly.

As a matter of fact, that happens when one makes a distinction between "truth in itself" and "truth as a human possession."   "Truth in

---

[81] "For (your) actions there are no other maxims as these: observe the immutable order, protect this order where it is threatened, restore it where it is disrupted, bring it about where its opposite has been realized and where it has sunk to a mere possibility.   It belongs also to this order that you occupy the place belonging to you on the basis of your essence."   Müller, *op. cit.*, p. 20.

[82] Ludwig Landgrebe, *Philosophie der Gegenwart,* Bonn, 1952, p. 157.

[83] ". . . as if man's consciousness could somehow survey itself and its world and contemplate the universe from the standpoint of God."   Albert Dondeyne, "La différence ontologique chez M. Heidegger," *Revue philosophique de Louvain,* vol. 56 (1958), p. 57.

itself," it is said, does not change, but "truth as a human possession" can undergo changes. The reason is that man's grasp of truth is perspectivistic; he looks at the truth from a certain standpoint, so that every particular grasp of it is subject to growth and to being complemented. Man can never make definitive all-round statements. Only God could do so from His absolute "standpoint." No one has a monopoly on the truth. However, from the fact that man is aware of his perspectivism it follows that he transcends his perspectivistic approach. By approaching the truth through all kinds of different perspectives, he comes constantly closer to the one absolute reality.

Phenomenology, of course, does not deny that to a certain extent it is possible to transcend perspectivism. But when this undeniable possibility is expressed in the form of a distinction between "truth in itself" and "truth as a human possession," representational realism is reintroduced even if one "officially" rejects it. For, what could the term "truth in itself" possibly mean? It cannot refer to the truth of the judgment since the latter is not primary but based on the unconcealedness of reality. But if "truth" is to be understood as unconcealedness, then "truth in itself" would mean "unconcealedness in itself." However, what could this really mean? Within knowledge, conceived as the encounter with meaning, one does not find "unconcealedness in itself." Moreover, "unconcealedness in itself" is distinguished from "truth as a human possession," i.e., from "unconcealedness for man." The one is not the other; unconcealedness in itself is not unconcealedness for man. Unconcealedness in itself is, of course, never encountered anywhere really, for man *really* encounters only that which is unconcealed for man. This historical moment of dis-covery, through which every unconcealedness is unconcealedness, is "forgotten." The unconcealed in itself is distinguished from the unconcealed which through man's never finished, historical, perspectivistic grasping becomes a human possession. Thus, by positing unconcealedness in itself, one considers the history of discovery finished and presents truth in itself as an absolute "light" shining for no one.[84]

The preceding remarks were necessary to give a more specific content

---

[84] "What we refuse, because it would be to speak of a meaning before (there is) meaning, is to start, in an absolute way, with a truth in itself, a first truth, of things, to believe that the birth of the human race would come to ratify, modify or void this 'spectaculary' nature of the *omnitudo realitatis*." De Waelhens, *op. cit.*, p. 98.

to the vague critique that is now so often—and justly—addressed to the Thomistic conception of the natural law. This conception is accused of "rigidity," i.e., objectivism. The objective character of natural rights and duties is described by Thomism just as the objective character of hills and valleys lying in a land that has never been discovered would be described. Any *real* description of objective reality presupposes, of course, the discovery of this reality through the "light" of subjectivity. In principle, such a discovery is a datable event and an event which has a future. Such a statement remains incomprehensible to anyone who fails to see the subject's historicity. The subject and his history are "forgotten," and the objectivity of natural rights and duties is presented as an immutable and eternal "in itself." Even the natural *law,* as norm of these rights and duties, is conceived as "being there," as immutably and eternally "true" in itself.

It is not difficult to see that the essentialism, objectivism and representational realism of Thomism is a dangerous theory because it can easily jeopardize man as a seeker of truth. Thomistic objectivism does not sink into scepticism but raises itself to absolutism, the absolutism of "truth in itself." This absolute "truth in itself" is an absolute "light" for no one. Hence anyone can seize it and claim that the other who disposes of truth only as a human possession is wrong. And then "I piously kill my opponents."[85]

"Piously," says Merleau-Ponty. For the defense of the "truth in itself" becomes, as it were, an act of honoring God when one realizes that such truth is presented as a participation in the Truth Itself which God is: the natural law is an imprint and picture of God's Eternal Law. For "truth in itself" is measured by the exemplary ideas in God's intellect and is made real by a command of the divine will. Thus one who has the "truth in itself" at his disposal posssesses God's "view" of reality. He measures truth as a human possession with the truth-of-things-for-God. Who, then, would have the right to resist, who but those who dare to challenge God?

"To judge," says Merleau-Ponty, "I have only my own judgments at my disposal."[86] In a *real,* authentic, search and affirmation of the truth there is nothing but "truth as a human possession." The latter implies man's grasping for the truth, with all the risks which that involves.

---

85 Merleau-Ponty, *Sens et non-sens,* Paris, 1948, p. 190.

86 Merleau-Ponty, *op. cit.,* p. 189.

The existent subject-as-*cogito* himself stands in the truth as unconceal-edness, but the subject is not a pure *cogito*. He is also a *volo,* a willing subject, and therefore can throw all kinds of significations upon the things, while thinking that he "sees" them. How often has not man's "seeing" revealed itself later to be a purely proclaimed "seeing"! How often also, has not man rejected an authentic "seeing" as if it were merely a proclaimed "seeing"! All this, however, is inherent in the fact that for man in his search of truth nothing exists but "truth as a human possession."

The latter cannot be measured with "truth in itself." Authentic thinking can never display an "identity card," it can never adduce any external argument authorizing it to identify its results with reality.[87] There is always a possibility of error.[88] However, it would be wrong to hold, on the basis of this possibility of error, that man's thinking is left to the mercy of the subject's arbitrariness. The subject-as-*cogito* is a "responsive being."[89]

He who seeks the truth is involved in a dizzying search. Phenomenol-ogy does not hesitate to recognize this explicitly. This dizziness cannot be overcome, and he who fails to recognize it fails to do justice to man's thinking itself. This happens whenever one evaluates and measures man's "grasping" for the truth with the "truth in itself."[90]

Is there still hope for anyone who today dares to ask about the significance of natural rights? Many no longer "believe" in "the" natural law because certain views of this law fail to satisfy them. But is such an attitude justified? We meet here with a difficulty that con-stantly recurs in contemporary thought. Literally everything is sub-mitted to rethinking and all kinds of terms are given a different sense. This induces some thinkers to rejects all hitherto accepted terms, for they think that maintaining the traditional terms implies *per se* and of necessity the adherence to views that are no longer acceptable. To give

---

[87] "I am unable, and you do not want me, to supply an identity card, by means of which one can easily and at any time check whether what I have said is in agreement with 'reality.'" Heidegger, *Vorträge und Aufsätze,* pp. 184-185.

[88] Heidegger, *op. cit.,* p. 183.

[89] "The possibility of aberration is greatest in this way of thinking. It can never check itself as mathematical knowledge can. But it is just as little arbitrary, but bound to the essential 'mission' of being." Heidegger, *ibid.*

[90] "Among the strange experiences I have had with my lecture is that people ask whence my thinking receives its direction. As if this question is needed only with respect to my thinking!" Heidegger, *op. cit.,* p. 184.

an example, it is evident that the term "objective" can no longer be given the objectivistic sense attached to it by representational realism. This makes some philosophers claim that authentic knowledge is *not* "objective." They simply fasten the term to its most untenable sense and decree that anyone who uses that term has by the very fact lapsed into the form of thinking which they reject. Thus they make any form of dialogue impossible, even with those who adhere to the same trend of thought as they themselves. Moreover, they cannot avoid playing into the hands of their opponents. For by asserting, e.g., that knowledge is not objective, they readily lay themselves open to the reproach of being subjectivists. And since they have rejected unqualifiedly the term "objective" with respect to authentic knowledge, they have left themselves defenseless.[91]

Accordingly, it is nonsense to reject absolutely "the" natural law on the ground that one has identified the use of this term with views of the natural law which can no longer be defended. He who does so anyhow will hear himself accused, of course, of being a legal positivist, for with his absolute rejection of the natural law he has also rejected the search for a justifying ground and a critical norm of the legal order. And he is utterly without defense against this accusation.

A New Anthropology. The use of such terms as "natural rights" and "legal order" refers to man as subject and to intersubjectivity. Hence a philosophy of law is always a phase of a philosophical anthropology. In our time it is especially the implications of phenomenological anthropology that raise new expectations for the philosophy of law.

The title of this book speaks of a "phenomenology" of law. This can give rise to confusion because so many contemporary writers use a so-called "phenomenological approach," understanding this term according

---

[91] Modern philosophers who want to be radical in their rejection would no longer be able to use even the term "is." For whoever uses "is" as a "speaking word" implicitly affirms a metaphysics. Now, if one claims that the simple use of a term dating from the past implies *per se* a past way of thinking and extends this claim to the use of the term "is," then modern thinkers who object to a metaphysics of the past must avoid also the term "is." But thus they are unable to say anything at all. They cannot even ask any question.

They sometimes reply that they reject terms from the past only insofar as it is reasonably possible. However, if the use of a term from the past implies *per se* untenable views, then one can *never* use that term without re-introducing the untenable views. Thus the qualification "insofar as it is reasonably possible" does not save the situation.

to their own fancy and sometimes in a sense that cannot with any semblance of justification be considered phenomenological. As a matter of fact, the term "phenomenological" can be used only if a number of very definite and rigorous conditions are satisfied. Phenomenology means simply "philosophy," but a philosophy of a special type. Hence it is excluded that one can speak of a phenomenology of law and, at the same time, ignore the fundamental principles of phenomenological philosophy. Despite the great interest in phenomenological philosophy, it would be too optimistic to assume that everyone is familiar with those fundamental ideas. For this reason we must present here the main lines of phenomenological thought as briefly and clearly as possible. Readers who are familiar with our previous works, notably PHENOMENOLOGY AND ATHEISM, will find in the following chapter ideas with which they are mostly familiar. They can without loss immediately pass on to Chapter Six.

CHAPTER FIVE

FUNDAMENTAL IDEAS OF
EXISTENTIAL PHENOMENOLOGY

Most readers are now aware of the fact that today the terms "phenomenology," "existentialism" and "existential phenomenology" all refer to one and the same sphere of thinking, which as a unitary trend of philosophizing has become predominant in continental Europe and which is also rapidly gaining ground in America. But it is only fairly recently that it has become possible to define this unitary movement. Previously there were, of course, phenomenologists and existentialists, but no one could say exactly what constituted the phenomenological and existentialist character of their thought. This is not surprising, for philosophy is primarily a way of life; as is the case with any way of life, man knows what it is when he lives it but, at the same time, he also does not know it.

Formerly a distinction was made between two "wings" of existentialism, a left wing and a right wing, an atheistic trend and a theistic trend. Because Sartre chose to identify existentialism and atheism, or rather, to define existentialism by atheism,[1] others began to refer to the right wing of existentialism as the "philosophy of existence."[2] Gabriel Marcel even went so far as to reject entirely the term "existentialism" as a characterization of his philosophy because otherwise his philosophy would fall under the same heading as that of Sartre.[3] Marcel preferred therefore

---

[1] Although Sartre distinguishes two existentialistic trends, in practice this distinction remains unimportant. He holds the view that existentialism and atheism are the same. Cf. Jean-Paul Sartre, *L'existentialisme est un humanisme,* Paris, 1954, pp. 15-16.

[2] R. Verneaux, *Leçons sur l'existentialisme et ses formes principales,* Paris, n.d., pp. 19-20.

[3] Bernard Delfgaauw, *Wat is existentialisme?,* Amsterdam, 1952, pp. 107-118.

to call his philosophy a form of neo-Socratism.[4] All this, however, did
not eliminate the impression that all these thinkers formed part of a kind
of unitary trend of thought.

1. *Existential Phenomenology as a Unitary Movement*

We make no distinction between existentialism and phenomenology
and will speak therefore of existential phenomenology. However, it will
be useful to describe briefly how the unity of the two currents of thought
came about and only then to present the fundamental ideas of existential
phenomenology.

Brief History. Kierkegaard is the founder of existentialism, but one
could hardly call him a phenomenologist. Husserl launched phenomenology, but he was not an existentialist. Thus, there was a time when
existentialism and phenomenology had to be distinguished. What, then,
was the distinction, and how did the unitary movement of existential-
phenomenological thinking arise?

Despite the differences between Kierkegaard's thought and that of
Husserl, there is nonetheless a certain agreement in the style of thought
of these two philosophers. This agreement manifests itself perhaps most
clearly in the fact that both rose in opposition to atomism or elementa-
rism with respect to thinking about man and things human. Man is not
something like an atom. The way in which they formulated their
opposition, however, differed. Kierkegaard spoke of *man,* while Husserl
practically limited himself to *consciousness* or knowledge.

Kierkegaard conceived man as existence, as subject-in-relationship-to-
God. Man is not a self-sufficient spiritual atom, but he is, as subject,
authentically himself only in his relationship with the God of Revelation.
In Kierkegaard's view, however, this existence is absolutely original and
unrepeatable, radically personal and unique. This point is not without
consequences. Because of the emphasis Kierkegaard placed on the
unique and exclusive aspect of existence, the aspect of universality in
man's knowledge, claimed by every *science,* is jeopardized as soon as
there is question of thinking about man. The one-sided emphasis on the
unique and exclusive character of existence has as its consequence that
whatever a thinker states about existence is in principle not applicable to
any other existence than his own and has no validity for anyone else.

---

[4] Gabriel Marcel, *L'homme problématique,* Paris, 1955, p. 72.

Kierkegaard's thought is consciously and deliberately antiscientific.[5] It can in principle not tend to go beyond the monologue, the "solitary meditation."[6]

Undoubtedly, this view of what philosophy is has its own peculiar attraction. Hence it is not surprising that in the past, when existentialism was reproached for not being scientific and for being in principle unable ever to become scientific, the followers of Kierkegaard replied resolutely that existentialism *ought not* to be scientific. Usually, however, this rejection of the qualifier "scientific" appeared to be based on a certain aversion to a particular view regarding what makes man's thinking scientific. In the thought of Hegel—the black sheep in Kierkegaard's works—and in positivism man was spoken of "scientifically" in such a way that the original, unrepeatable, unique and exceptional character of human subjectivity was simply buried under verbiage.[7] Yet this type of speaking of man was considered to be "scientific" *par excellence.* Thus it is not surprising that, in reaction against those trends, some philosophers resented having their ideas called "scientific."

The difficulty, however, was not solved in this way. Even if a particular view of what makes thinking about man scientific has to be rejected, it is not at all clear that philosophizing about man cannot and may not be scientific in any sense. One who philosophizes about man can hardly escape philosophizing about man in general. He uses universal and necessary judgments to indicate universal and necessary structures of being-man and therefore speaks "scientifically." This idea led some thinkers to claim that one should perhaps have to chose between existing authentically and existentialism.[8] Those who opt for existentialism would have to speak about the general structures of being-man, while those who choose authentic existence would have to renounce existentialism as a *general* doctrine about man as such.[9]

Thinkers who seek their inspiration solely in Husserl are hardly

---

[5] De Waelhens, "Kierkegaard en de hedendaagse existentialisten," *Tijdschrift v. Philosophie,* vol. I (1939), pp. 827-851.

[6] "The point is to determine whether existence is not something that must be reserved for solitary meditation." Jean Wahl, *Petite histoire de l'existentialisme,* Paris, 1947, p. 61.

[7] J. Peters, *Hedendaagse visies op den mens,* Heerlen, n.d., pp. 228-230.

[8] "Must perhaps a choice be made between existentialism and existence?" Wahl, *op. cit.,* p. 61.

[9] "We must still ask ourselves whether the search for *existentialia* and for being is compatible with the affirmation of existence." Wahl, *op. cit.,* p. 43.

affected by the above-mentioned difficulties. Like Descartes, Husserl, who began his career as a mathematician and a physicist, was painfully struck by the divergences of views and the terminological confusion existing in the realm of philosophy. He devised his phenomenology as an attempt to make philosophy also a "rigorous science." For Husserl, philosophy is a way of thinking that ought to be characterized by the subjective and objective universality of its statements.

To realize his plans for philosophy, Husserl investigated the nature of human consciousness or knowledge. He conceived consciousness, knowledge, as intentionality, as directedness to that which consciousness or knowledge itself is not. This view of consciousness as intentionality shows an unmistakable similarity to Kierkegaard's concept of man as existence. Both are opposed to a closed, atomistic conception of man and his consciousness. In Husserl, however, the main emphasis fell on problems concerning the theory of knowledge, while in Kierkegaard the greatest stress was laid on questions of theological anthropology. Existentialism and phenomenology were distinct.

This condition was not destined to last very long. In Heidegger's *Being and Time* Kierkegaard's existentialism and Husserl's phenomenology merged, as it were, to serve as the basis of the philosophy which today is rather generally known as "existential phenomenology." Heidegger presents us with a scientific philosophy of man in general, one which does not fall into the illusions of idealism and positivism. Under the influence of the phenomenological theory of knowledge and the phenomenological ideal of science, existentialism renounced its antiscientific attitude; on the other hand, phenomenology as a theory of knowledge became enriched by borrowing numerous topics from Kierkegaard's existentialism, thereby developing into a philosophy of man in general.[10] In this way was born the unitary movement of existential-phenomenological thought, of which Heidegger, Sartre—though not in all respects—, Merleau-Ponty and the School of Louvain are the principal exponents.

The antiscientific attitude of existentialism, however, was continued by Karl Jaspers and Gabriel Marcel.[11] These two thinkers thus stand more or less outside the unitary movement of existential phenomenology, although there remain numerous points of contact.

---

[10] We do not deny, of course, that Heidegger's intervention contained more than was explained above.

[11] Marcel, *Du refus à l'invocation,* Paris, 1940, p. 193.

2. *Materialistic and Spiritualistic Monism*

One who endeavors to penetrate into the history of thought comes to the conclusion that the attempt to say what man is amounts to the search for a delicate equilibrium. The materialistic and the spiritualistic systems bear witness to the difficulties our thinking faces when it attempts to say what man is. At the same time, those systems are the result of a certain imbalance in man's thinking. Nevertheless, they are not useless, for there is no philosophy that is entirely valueless because it fails to give expression to anything real. Moments of equilibrium are relatively rare in the history of philosophy.

Existential phenomenology is such a moment of equilibrium. It manages to retain the valuable points contained in the materialistic and the spiritualistic systems without lapsing into their one-sidedness.[12] It is in the use of the term "existence," expressing one of the most fundamental and essential characteristic of man, that this balanced view of what man is finds expression.[13]

Materialism. All materialistic systems agree in considering man the result of processes and forces just as things are the results of processes and forces. A materialist, then, would say that man's being can be called a being-in-the-world, but he would mean by it that man, just as all things, is a thing in the midst of other worldly things, a part of nature, a moment in the endless evolution of the cosmos.[14]

This view is not so stupid that one can simply disregard it. It formulates a valuable vision, it gives expression to a reality that should never be forgotten, it takes seriously the indisputable fact that man is whatever he is only "on the basis of materiality."[15] Every philosopher must sooner or later face the temptation of adhering to materialism if he does not want to underestimate the significance of matter. For there is

---

[12] For a very clear explanation of the critique which the philosophers of existence address to the materialists and the spiritualists, see Dondeyne, "Beschouwingen bij het atheistisch existentialisme," *Tijdschrift v. Philosophie,* vol. XIII (1951), pp. 1-41.

[13] Merleau-Ponty, *Sens et non-sens,* pp. 142-143.

[14] "There are . . . two classical views. One treats man as the result of physical, physiological and sociological influences determining him from without and making him a thing among things." Merleau-Ponty, *op. cit.,* p. 142.

[15] Dondeyne, "Dieu et le matérialisme contemporain," *Essai sur Dieu, l'homme et l'univers,* ed. by Jacques de Bivort de la Saudée, Paris, 1957, p. 24.

only a short distance between the view that man is whatever he is only on the basis of materiality[16] and the conviction that man is a piece of matter or a passing phase in the evolution of the cosmos.[17] There exists no spiritual knowledge without sense perceptible things, without brains, without physiological processes, without schemata of sense imagination, without words. There exists no spiritual love without sensible love, no personal conscience without biological infra-structures, no artistic act without expression in matter. Thus it is possible for the biologist, for example, to speak about knowledge, love and conscience, and what he says about these matters is concerned with reality.

This example shows how a certain way of thinking can be materialistic, even if the thinker never says explicitly that man is a thing. As a matter of fact, materialism is very often camouflaged. It occurs most frequently as scientism, as the overestimation of the physical sciences which busy themselves *ex professo* with things and use categories and models exclusively applicable to things. The pursuit of the sciences, in the narrow sense of the term, degenerates into scientism when one claims that there are no other realities save those disclosed by the sciences of nature. Precisely because man is whatever he is only on the basis of materiality, the sciences *also* are able to say something about man. In principle, for example, it may be possible to indicate the physiological difference between a saint and a criminal or to claim that there is a chemical difference between a Christian and a Mohammedan conscience. Similarly, many alcoholics and prostitutes are not primarily transgressors of God's laws but rather people with bodily deficiencies who should not be punished but given medical assistance. A physiology of drunkenness or of prostitution belongs to the realm of possibilities.

One who realizes this also understands that it is very tempting to claim that the sciences can speak of any reality. Because man is whatever he is only on the basis of his materiality, there is nothing in man about which the sciences cannot say anything. Thus, it is only a short but fatal step to the position that when the man of science has spoken nothing else remains to be added. The philosopher must know this

---

[16] "Our scientific experience has revealed to us no forces that lack a material basis, no 'spiritual world' that stands outside and above nature." Ernst Haeckel, *Die Welträtsel,* Leipzig, 10th ed., 1909, p. 99.

[17] "We human beings, too, are merely passing phases in the development of the eternal substance, individual forms in which matter and energy appear. We understand the unimportance of these phases and forms in reference to endless space and eternal time." Haeckel, *op. cit.,* p. 259.

temptation if he is not to minimize the power and importance of materialism. Scientism is a materialistic theory because it holds that outside the matter spoken of by the sciences nothing exists that is worth being spoken of.

With respect to man, materialism means, as Le Senne expresses it, a "detotalization of reality."[18] The attempt of materialism to explain man, to state what it means to be man, to account for the totality of man, fails because it pays attention only to one aspect of man, albeit an essential aspect. Materialism is a kind of monism, in which there exists, in the totality of reality, room only for one type of being, namely, that of the material thing. Thus man also is a thing and man's life is a chain of processes.

If one were to restrict the claim to the statement that man is *also* "thinglike" and that his life has *also* processslike aspects, there would be no reason to quarrel with the claim. But materialistic monism disregards an essential aspect of man because the thesis that man is a thing does not take into account the irrefutable fact that man exists-for-himself and that things exist-for-man. If one rigidly interprets the thesis that man is a thing, one meets the unsurmountable difficulty of having to explain how it is possible for this thesis to be *stated* although every materialist admits that geological layers and rain storms—*things*—cannot state this thesis.

Generally speaking, one can say that a philosophy fails not so much by what it says as by what it does not say or by what it eliminates from reality. This judgment applies very clearly and decidedly to materialism. The materialist fails to pay attention to the fact that man exists for himself *as* man, i.e., that being-man has meaning and significance for man and that things also have meaning and significance for man and not for themselves or for other things. If there existed nothing but things, nothing would have any significance. Materialism, then, disregards the fact that it is only with and through man that there can be question of things and processes. No matter how "thinglike" man is, one can never take the fatal step of claiming that man is only a thing because this step would eliminate the very possibility of making this claim. To be able to claim that man is a thing, man must transcend the "thinglike" character of his essence at least to such an extent that he is able to make the claim.[19] For this reason alone the being of man cannot be like the being of a thing.

---

[18] Quoted by Dondeyne, *art. cit.*, pp. 24-25.
[19] Sartre, *op. cit.*, p. 65.

Accordingly, it is man's subjectivity that is simply negated by the materialist.[20] The being of man on the proper level of his manhood is a consciousness through which man exists for himself[21] and can give himself a name. He calls himself "I." Through the "light" of the ego, the subject, the conscious "I" that man is, exists for himself; through this "I," there is a "light" in the world of things, so that things appear to man as endowed with significance and meaning: they are-for-man.

Materialism, then, fails to recognize an essential aspect of manhood, for ultimately it does not realize that the being of man is a being-conscious. The materialist cannot defend himself against this accusation by saying that man's acts of consciousness, like all processes in the realm of material things, can be reduced to an interplay of atoms and molecules. For, he will have to admit that some of these "atoms" distinguish themselves from other atoms by the fact that they exist for themselves as atoms, by the fact that other atoms exist for them as atoms, and by the fact that they can philosophize about themselves and the other atoms. Those "atoms" we call men.

Materialism lives by the grace of a hidden contradiction,[22] for the materialist is wholly unable to be aware of his own existence as a materialistic philosopher if he holds fast to the idea that there exists only one type of being, viz., the being of a thing. The contradiction consists in this: on the one hand, the materialistic philosopher admits that geological layers and rain storms, plants and animals cannot create a philosophy, not even a materialistic philosophy; on the other, he wants to explain his own existence as a materialistic philosopher by the same categories as he uses to state what geological layers and rain storms, plants and animals are.[23] In materialism we find not only the material

---

[20] "I am not the result or the meeting point of numerous causal influences which determine my body or my 'psychological constitution.' I cannot conceive myself as a part of the world, as the simple object of biology, psychology and sociology, or enclose myself in the universe of science. Whatever I know of the world, even by way of science, I know from a viewpoint that is my own or from an experience of the world without which the symbols of science would be meaningless expressions." Merleau-Ponty, *Phénoménologie de la perception,* Paris, 1945, p. II.

[21] "In no case could my consciousness be a thing because its mode of being in itself is precisely a *being-for-itself.*" Sartre, *L'imagination,* Paris, 1948, p. 1.

[22] "Scientific viewpoints according to which I am a moment of the world are always naive and hypocritical because they tacitly take for granted the other view, namely, that of consciousness, through which from the very first a world arranges itself round me and begins to exist for me." Merleau-Ponty, *op. cit.,* p. III.

[23] Merleau-Ponty, *Sens et non-sens,* p. 143.

world, but also the materialistic philosopher[24] whose existence remains unexplained.

Spiritualism. The fact that things and processes have a meaning for man as conscious subject justifies us in assigning a certain priority to subjectivity with respect to things. One who thinks away the subject who man is *ipso facto* thinks away all meaning, so that the term "being" loses its significance. For how could this term have any meaning unless being is affirmed by a subject? Which human meanings and significations in the world of things could still be accepted as real when, in the absence of the subject, being would be nothing but being-for-no-one? Moreover, I can make the supposition that there is no subject only because and to the extent that I do not really make it. I can make that supposition only in a purely verbal fashion. The subject, then, is indeed indisputable and possesses a certain priority over the world of things.

This priority can also be explicitated in the following way. The world of things reveals itself always and of necessity as the non-I. Being-not-I belongs to the reality of the world of things. Things of this world that are not distinct from the "I" and do not reveal themselves as "non-I" are not *real*. He who wants to give expression to the *reality* of things, therefore, will always be obliged to affirm implicitly their non-identity with the subject. But this implies that it is impossible to speak about the *reality* of things and, at the same time, to deny or to eliminate the "I." For, if I deny or eliminate the "I," I cannot give expression to the world of things as the "non-I"; yet this "not being I" belongs to the *reality* of things.

Accordingly, we must accept that the "I" has a certain priority over things and for this reason it is impossible to consider the "I" as the result of cosmic processes and forces. For without the "I," those cosmic processes and forces are not what they *really* are, viz., the "non-I."

---

[24] "Materialism, which wants to reduce the whole of being to the interaction of moving particles of matter, subject only to causal explanations, cannot be refuted by *a priori* arguments. It does not contain any contradiction in terms but only a contradiction *'in actu exercito,'* i.e. in materialism we find, aside from the material system of the world with its causal laws, the affirmation of this system and the conscious pursuit of causal explanation. The latter are acts of consciousness which, in their essential structure, transcend causal determinism." Dondeyne, "Belang voor de metaphysica van een accurate bestaansbeschrijving van de mens als kennend wezen," *Verslag v.d. 12e alg. verg. der Vereniging v. Thomistische Wijsbegeerte en v.d. 3de studiedagen v.h. Wijsgerig Gezelschap te Leuven,* Nijmegen, 1947, p. 39.

How could that which without the "I" simply is not what it *really* is give being to the "I"? If that were possible, it would also be feasible for someone who is sinking away in quicksand to pull himself out by the hair.

All this indicates the direction taken by the thought of those who exploit the weakness of materialism. For the materialist, the conscious subject is not a worth-while reality; for the spiritualist, thinking about reality only begins with the affirmation of the subject. One must realize, we said, the strength of materialistic thought to understand the crass statement that man is a thing. The same must be said with respect to spiritualistic monism. As soon as one really sees the priority of the subject, one is exposed to the danger of exaggerating the importance of this subject. Without the "I" it is simply impossible to speak about the world of things and the term "being" loses all meaning. Only a slight exaggeration is needed to proceed from there to considering all things as the result of a kind of creative activity on the part of the subject or as the content of the subject's consciousness.

In spiritualistic monism this way of absolutizing the importance of the subject consists in the reduction of the being of material things to the being of the subject. The direction in which this type of monism "detotalizes reality" is exactly the opposite of that taken by materialism. While materialism simply disregards the importance of the subject, or at least considers the subject not worth mentioning, spiritualistic monism lets the density of material things evaporate into ethereal contents of consciousness.[25]

Spiritualistic monism takes seriously that which materialism disregards, viz., subjectivity's "being from itself" (*aus-sich-sein*). As a subject, man cannot result from material processes; hence the subject is "from himself" (*aus-sich*). If one exaggerates in this matter, the "from itself" is easily raised to the level of "by itself" (*durch-sich*); subjectivity is then absolutized and ultimately divinized.[26] Obviously, the spiritualists do not simply identify the divinized "I" with the "little" finite "I" that you and I are. The "little" finite "I's" lose their ownness, selfhood,

---

[25] "Transcendental idealism, too, 'reduces' the world since, insofar as it makes this world certain, it does so by considering it as thought or consciousness of the world and as the mere correlate of our knowledge; thus the world becomes immanent to consciousness and the 'aseity' of things is thereby abolished." Merleau-Ponty, *Phénoménologie de la perception,* p. X.

[26] Cf. José Ortega y Gasset, *Man and People,* New York, 1957.

distinction and consistency in spiritualistic monism because they are conceived as functions or particularizations of an all-embracing *Ego* or as moments in the evolution of an absolute Spirit.[27]   Because the subject's priority is exaggerated, the attributes assigned to him become so phantastic that this subject cannot possibly be identified any longer with the "little I" that every I is.

One who realizes the powerful attraction exercised by spiritualistic thought understands that this spiritualism can never be totally overcome in the history of philosophy.   It *should not* even be wholly overcome, in the sense that its original inspiration should disappear from man's thinking.   However, looking back to what has been attained by spiritualism, we must admit that in it little if anything remains of the original inspiration on which materialism lived.   Spiritualism irresponsibly buries under verbiage the idea that man is whatever he is only on the basis of materiality.

3. *Existential Phenomenology*

The struggle between materialism and spiritualism shows that we must try to find and intermediary road, one that takes into account the valuable acquisitions of both trends while avoiding their excesses.   As was mentioned, such an attempt is made by existential phenomenology.

A. THE EXISTENT SUBJECT AS COGITO

As should be evident from all this, existential phenomenology rightly emphasizes man's being-a-subject.   He who denies the subject can no longer speak meaningfully, for with the subject he eliminates all meaning from the world.   He is unable to affirm any being, for any affirmation presupposes a subject.   Even the denial of the subject becomes a contradiction, for any denial presupposes a denying subject.   He cannot deny any meaning, for any denied meaning presupposes an implicitly affirmed meaning.   The subject, therefore, is indisputable, and with the subject meaning also is indisputable.   The subject-as-*cogito* himself is the affirmation of meaning, the implicit, prepredicative affirmation of meaning, of which even the one who depreciates the subject speaks.   The subject-

---

[27] Dondeyne, *art. cit.* (footnote 12), pp. 27-28.

as-*cogito* is the implicit, prepredicative affirmation of meaning, and this is affirmed even in the denial of the subject; we may even say that it makes this denial possible.

All this, however, could still be understood in a wholly Cartesian sense. One who, like Descartes, divorces the subject from the world, nonetheless recognizes the subject; one who, like Descartes, places meaning within the subject-as-*cogito* nonetheless recognizes meaning. But he misjudges both subject and meaning as they really are.

Meaning does not occur as the ethereal content of the subject-as-*cogito,* but as the worldly thing itself, having its own autonomy of being with respect to the subject.[28] Meaning reveals itself as the other-than-the-subject, as the "not-I." This autonomy of being with respect to the subject, this being "not-I," constitutes the *real* being of meaning. The affirmation of meaning which the subject-as-*cogito* himself is, is equiprimordially the recognition of the autonomy of being that meaning has with respect to the subject, the recognition of meaning in its "bodily presence."[29] Thus the subject cannot arbitrarily proceed but has to observe bonds in explicitating, conceptualizing and expressing meaning. Whatever is, *is* and should be recognized as such in our speech. For our speaking takes up the implicit affirmations of the subject-as-*cogito,* and these implicit affirmations *are* the recognition of meaning in its autonomy of being with respect to the subject. Thus meaning is not a thought content of the subject-as-*cogito.*

Just as meaning is not a thought content of the subject-as-*cogito,* so also the subject is not isolated from meaning. The subject, as he really occurs, is an intentional, an existent subject.[30] The subject is not divorced from wordly meaning, he is not enclosed in himself. The

---

[28] "Truth does not 'inhabit' only the 'interior man,' rather, there is no interior man. Man is in the world, and it is in the world that he knows himself. When I return to myself after (indulging in) the dogmatism of common sense or that of science, I find, not a seat of intrinsic truth, but a subject consigned to the world." Merleau-Ponty, *op. cit.,* p. V.

[29] "The spatial thing which we see is, in spite of all its transcendence, perceived, it is our consciousness as given in its *bodiliness.* We are *not* given, in place of it, an image or a sign. One should not substitute consciousness of a sign or image for perception." Edmund Husserl, *Ideen zu einer reinen Phänomenologie und phänomenologische Philosophie,* vol. I, The Hague, 1950, pp. 98-99.

[30] "The first truth is indeed 'I think,' but but on condition that we understand by it 'I belong to myself' while belonging to the world." Merleau-Ponty, *op. cit.,* p. 466.

subject-as-*cogito* is directedness to meaning, and this directedness is called "intentionality." The same idea is expresed by the term "existence." The subject "exists," that is, places himself outside himself and in the world.[31] Heidegger uses the term *Dasein* in the same sense. The prefix *Da* points to the "ec-centric" character of the subject.[32] As intentionality, as existence, the subject *is* the immediate presence to the present reality which meaning is.[33] The subject-as-*cogito* is a mysterious self-affirmation into which merges the affirmation of the world; it is the affirmation of the world which is equiprimordially the subject's self-affirmation.[34]

"Functional Intentionality" and "Explicit Act of Intentionality." When we say that the subject-as-*cogito* must be described as self-affirmation merged with the affirmation of the world, the term "affirmation" should not be conceived as an explicit act of knowledge formulated in a judgment. On the contrary, that "affirmation" is that which makes every explicit act of knowledge possible and is presupposed by any such act. Every explicit act of knowledge, expressing a judgment about meaning, presupposes that what is expressed in the judgment is "already" meaning. But this "already"-being-meaning presupposes the existence, the presence of the subject-as-*cogito,* for without this presence there can be no question of meaning. The explicit act of knowledge, formulated in the judgment, *expresses* the meaning's autonomy of being. But this act presupposes that the subject-as-*cogito* has already recognized the meaning's autonomy of being. The subject-as-*cogito* himself is the recognition of the autonomy of meaning.

The same can also be expressed differently, as seen from the explicitly formulated judgment. Taken by itself, i.e., solely as the union of a predicate with the subject of a judgment, the judgment has no ground. This means that no one really knows what is being spoken of when he is offered nothing but the union of a predicate with the subject of the judgment. Thus no on can affirm or reject such a judgment; it simply "hangs in the air." A judgment needs a ground, a foundation, if it is

---

[31] Heidegger, *Sein und Zeit,* p. 53.

[32] Heidegger, *op. cit.,* p. 11.

[33] "If the subject *is* in a situation. . . , this is because he realizes his 'ipseity' only by actually being a body and, through this body, entering the world." Merleau-Ponty, *op. cit.,* p. 467.

[34] "In saying 'I,' *Dasein* expresses itself as being-in-the-world." Heidegger, *op. cit.,* p. 321.

really to say anything. But it really says anything only when the subject of the judgment refers to a present meaning, of which something is stated by means of the predicate. The presence of meaning, however, presupposes existence, the presence of the subject-as-*cogito,* the "affirmation" of meaning which the subject himself is; and the predicates, which in a plurality of judgments are stated of the meaning, are merely explicitations of that "affirmation." In this sense Plato is right when he says that all judgmental knowledge is really remembrance. Every judgment ultimately goes back to the subject's existence and it is there that it finds its foundation and ground.

The presence of the subject-as-*cogito* to meaning may also be called "experience" although certain dangers are, at least initially, attached to the use of this term. First of all, "experience" was usually conceived as a mirroring of reality; secondly, the term "experience" suffers from an hereditary "infection" which makes one think almost spontaneously, but unjustly, of the type of experience found in physical science as the only reliable form of experience. Besides, by thinking that experience, as the foundation of any judgment, must be conceived as the type of experience used by physical science, one loses sight of the fact that in this way no judgment whatsoever can find an indisputable foundation, for the simple reason that also the experience of physical science must be given a foundation. In this perspective it is undeniable that a scientific— in the narrow sense—judgment is based upon a scientific experience, conceived as the presence of the subject-as-*cogito* to nature in the scientific sense. But, at the same time, it is also undeniable that he who through scientific experiences appropriates what scientific judgments say, *in the last resort* still does not really know about what he speaks.[35] His judgments do not have an *ultimate* ground because in the order of knowledge scientific experience is neither first nor most primordial.

An example may serve to clarify the matter. How do I become familiar with the real meaning of landscapes, rivers and seas? Is it enough to consult books on geography and thus to absorb the scientific experiences of geographers? I can consult them, of course, but in doing so I should realize that I do not know what those experiences mean unless I accept that those books ultimately speak about the landscapes, rivers and seas I knew, before I began to study geography, through my

---

[35] "Classical science is a perception that forgets its origins and thinks that it is complete." Merleau-Ponty, *op. cit.,* p. 69.

holiday "experiences." If I do not accept that the landscapes, rivers and seas I admire when I go on vacation are the *real* landscapes, rivers and seas, then no one will ever be able to explain to me which ones are real. As anyone can see, the original experience of the world of life is much richer than the experience of the world-for-the-geographer. And the experience of the geographer is rooted in the experience of the world of life.[36]

With behaviorism, I can define speech as "certain movements of the larynx accompanied by the appropriate sound waves," yet it is evident that I only know what this description means because of the fact that I have experienced what it means simply to have spoken with someone. The latter experience is more primordial, more fundamental and richer than the scientific experience of speech. The latter is only a "secondary expression."[37]

Scientific experience is only a derived and abstract way of existing of the subject-as-*cogito* contained in a more encompassing *cogito*. Scientific experience is only an experience of a subject with a very special attitude toward a very special signification complex of the world. First in the order of "knowledge" is the subject-as-*cogito*, who through a *Gestalt* of "attitudes" is involved in the "lived world." This *cogito* is not an act in the sense in which this term is usually understood, but it is the being itself of man as existence.[38] It is the "natural light,"[39] the "light" that is the "nature" of the subject, a "light" for the subject himself and a "light"-in-the-world through which this world shows meaning, appears as meaningful.

Husserl calls this most radical form of intentionality "functional intentionality" (*fungierende Intentionalität*) or "world-experiencing life" (*Welterfahrendes Leben*); and he distinguishes this intentionality

---

[36] "To return to things themselves is to return to that world which is prior to knowledge, of which knowledge always speaks, and with respect to which every scientific explanation is abstract, significative and dependent, as is geography with respect to the landscape in which we have learned beforehand what a forest, a prairie or a river is." Merleau-Ponty, *op. cit.*, p. III.

[37] Merleau-Ponty, *ibid*.

[38] "The relationship between the subject and the object is not that *cognitive relationship* spoken of by classical idealism, in which the object always appears as constructed by the subject. On the contrary, it is an *ontological relationship*, according to which the subject, paradoxically, *is* his body, his world and his situation, and somehow exchanges himself." Merleau-Ponty, *Sens et non-sens*, pp. 143-144.

[39] Heidegger, *op. cit.*, p. 133.

from that of explicit acts of knowledge (*Aktintentionalität*).[40]   Husserl launched his phenomenology as an attempt to find the ground, the foundation of any judgment whatsoever.   Such a foundation can be found only by a return to "the things themselves," by a revaluation of the significance of the "lived world."[41]   But the lived world refers to the subject-as-*cogito,* the first and most primordial "affirmation" of meaning, of integral experience,[42] which can be nothing but man himself as existence.   In experience thus conceived philosophy attains that "radicalism of foundation" which Husserl always tried to achieve.

Existence as "Being-in."   Through the doctrine of man as existence we distance ourselves from both materialism and spiritualism.[43]   Existential phenomenology defines man as subject, but this subject does not occur without being involved in material things.   Wordly things, therefore, co-determine what man is, so that, by thinking away the world, one also thinks away man himself.   On the other hand, material things as meanings point to the subject, so that, by thinking away this subject, one thinks away also all meaning as well as man himself.

The "being-in," then, which man himself is, is a very special way of "being-in."   It cannot be compared with anything else because it is the "being-in" of a subject.   Hence one must be very prudent with the use of the expression "being in the world."   For the materialist also could use this term, but he would mean by it that man is a piece of matter in the material world or a passing phase in an endless cosmic evolution.   Besides, the "being-in" defining man is not like the being-in-the-box of a cigar or the being-in-the-drawer of a pencil.[44]   In neither case is expressed that the "being-in" in question is the "being-in" of a subject; yet

---

[40] Cf. Joseph J. Kockelmans, *Phenomenology and Physical Science,* Pittsburgh, 1966, Ch. I, Section 3, p. 40.

[41] Merleau-Ponty, *Phénoménologie de la perception,* p. III.

[42] Phenomenology "endeavors to conceive philosophy as the explicitation of integral human experience."   De Waelhens, "Signification de la phénoménologie," *Diogène,* 1954, no. 5, p. 60.

[43] "It is precisely to the credit of the new philosophy that it seeks the means to reflect on (the human condition) in the notion of existence.   Existence, in the modern sense, is the movement through which man is in the world, becomes involved in a physical and social situation which becomes his point of view with respect to the world."   Merleau-Ponty, *Sens et non-sens,* p. 143.

[44] "Being-in does not mean a spatial being 'in one another' of things that are 'at hand', any more than the term 'in' primordially means a spatial relationship of that kind.   *'In'* comes from *innanwohnen, habitare,* 'to dwell'; *'an'* means: 'I am accustomed,' 'familiar with,' 'I take care of,' in the sense of *colo* taken as *habito* and *diligo."* Heidegger, *op. cit.,* p. 54.

this is essential with respect to man's being. For this reason it is preferable to use expressions that clearly imply the subject; such as, "dwelling," "being present to" or "being familiar with."

Positivity and Negativity in Existence-as-Cogito. One who realizes that the existent subject-as-*cogito* is the ontological recognition of meaning's autonomy of being with respect to the subject, understands also that an aspect of negativity is implied in existence. Precisely because the subject recognizes that meaning has autonomy of being, he recognizes also that he is not identical with meaning. Such an assertion would not be possible in a Cartesian perspective. For Descartes, that of which the subject is conscious is not something which the *cogito* is not, for this is precisely the content of the *cogito*. For existential phenomenology the subject is an intentional, existent subject; the subject is orientation to that which he himself is not. The recognition that meaning has autonomy of being contains the recognition that meaning is not identical with the subject. The subject "nihilates" meaning, we may even say that the subject is this "nihilation" itself.[45]

Obviously, this "nihilation" should not be conceived as an explicit negation. It is an aspect of the "functional intentionality" which makes all explicit negations possible and which is presupposed by and implied in all explicit negations.[46] Just as the affirmation of meaning, so also is the negation in question here a relationship of being, an aspect of human existence itself. Sartre has grossly exaggerated and absolutized this aspect of existence, so that finally he even conceived the subject as pure "nothingness."[47] While this is going too far, we may not disregard the negative aspect in the existence of the subject-as-*cogito*.

B. THE EXISTENT SUBJECT AS "VOLO" (I WILL)

It is impossible to conceive man as a thing because man is a subject. But in the preceding pages we have spoken of this subject only as *cogito,*

---

[45] "The 'for itself' is a being for which, in its being, its being is in question insofar as this being is essentially a certain way of not being a being which it posits at the same time as other-than-itself." Sartre, *L'être et le néant,* p. 222.

[46] Nothingness "founds the negation as *act* because it is the negation as *being.* Nothing cannot be nothingness save by nihilating itself expressly as nothingness of the world; that is, in its nihilation it must direct itself expressly to the world in order to constitute itself as refusal of the world. Nothingness carries being in its heart." Sartre, *op. cit.,* p. 54.

[47] "The being by which nothingness arrives in the world is a being for which, in its being, there is question of the nothingness of its being. The being by which nothingness comes into the world must be its own nothingness." Sartre, *op. cit.,* p. 59.

i.e., with respect to the cognitive level of existence. We saw there clearly something that is disregarded by all forms of materialism, namely, that man is for himself and that the world appears as meaning. The being of man is a being-*conscious* in the world.

Some phenomenologists use strange expressions to indicate that the being of man is a being-conscious. Sartre calls man a being for which in its being there is question of its being.[48] Heidegger uses almost the same expression when he says that man is the being for which in its being its being is at issue.[49] These expressions mean that man in his being has a relationship to his being, and this relationship is an "understanding of being."[50]

If man is distinguished from a thing because in his being his being is an issue, it is obvious that this being an issue is not limited to the cognitive level. When I am bored, glad, sad or anxious, "my being is an issue for me," but this issue is quite different from the one in which I am simply conscious of myself. That my being is an issue for me, then, does not lie solely on the cognitive level but also, as the examples show, on the affective or volitive level. The fact that on this level my being is an issue for me presupposes, just as it does on the cognitive level, that I am a subject. The subject who man is exists not only as *cogito* but also as *volo* (I will).

It is important to distinguish these different levels of existence because the reproach has been addressed to phenomenology that, by omitting the necessary distinctions, it has lapsed into a kind of "monism of existence."[51] Man is defined as existence, but not everyone who admits this definition keeps in mind that this existing is realized on different levels. True, the subject is always identical with himself, but he realizes his existence on many levels.

---

[48] Sartre, *op. cit.*, p. 222.

[49] *"Dasein* is a being which does not merely occur among other beings. Rather it is ontically distinguished by this that, in its very being, that being itself is at issue. This state of *Dasein*'s being implies that *Dasein*, in its being, has a relationship to being that itself is one of being." Heidegger, *op. cit.*, p. 12.

[50] Heidegger, *op. cit.*, pp. 12-15.

[51] "If in every problem one goes directly to the 'existential project,' to the 'movement of existence,' which brings all authentically human behavior in its train, one runs the risk of failing to see the specific character of the problems, of letting the contours of the various functions merge into a kind of indistinct existential monism. This, at the end, leads to the repetition of the same exegesis of 'existence' with respect to the imagination, emotion, laughter, gesture, sexuality, speech, etc." Paul Ricoeur, "Méthodes et tâches d'une phénoménologie de la volonté," *Problèmes actuels de la phénoménologie,* 1952, pp. 115–116.

One who disregards the subject-as-*cogito* can no longer say anything meaningful, for with the subject he eliminates all meaning from the world. Something similar must be said with respect to the subject-as-*volo*. He who disregards the subject-as-*volo* can no longer recognize any meaning, in the sense of value. Yet meaning reveals itself unmistakably as value, as object of a certain "affirmation" by the subject. The "affirmation" in question, however, does not lie on the cognitive level; it is not exclusively a recognition of meaning's autonomy of being, but is a kind of "adhering to," a kind of *diligo*,[52] an affective and volitive "yes" to meaning; and this "yes" is the existent subject-as-*volo* himself. Here, too, there is no question of an explicit act of will or an express desire, but rather of that which makes possible all explicit desires, tendencies, acts of will and affections and therefore is presupposed by them. This primordial *volo* is the existent subject himself as realizing himself on the affective and volitive level; it is an aspect of the "functional intentionality" which man himself is.

With Heidegger one could call this aspect of human existence "moodness" (*Befindlichkeit*).[53] "Moodness" indicates the affective tonality of man's existence in the world. It is not a sentiment, in the sense in which the psychology of consciousness speaks of sentiments, viz., as a kind of internal commentary on an external event. So-called "internal commentaries" always presuppose the primordial tonality which existence is; they presuppose the primordial evaluation through which man already "knows" the value of his being-in-the-world. "Moodness" is the affective tone of the *Da* of *Dasein,* i.e., of the existent subject, of man himself.[54]

Positivity and Negativity in Existence-as-Volo. The existent subject reveals himself in both positivity and negativity. The subject-as-*cogito* is the affirmation and recognition of worldly meaning in its autonomy of being, and a mysterious self-affirmation is merged with this affirmation of worldly meaning. The subject is a kind of "yes" to the world and, upon

---

[52] Heidegger, *op. cit.,* p. 54.

[53] Heidegger, *op. cit.,* pp. 134-140.

[54] "Being-in-mood is not related to the psychical in the first instance, it is not itself an internal condition which then comes forth in an enigmatic way and 'colors' things and persons. It is in this that the second essential characteristic of moodness shows itself. Moodness is a fundamental existential species of the equiprimordial disclosedness of the world, of *Dasein*-with and of existence; for disclosedness itself is essentially being-in-the-world." Heidegger, *op. cit.,* p. 137.

the basis of this "yes," he is also a certain "yes" to himself. This "yes" means a certain fullness of being, a certain fulfilment and satisfaction, a certain rest and peace that can be called an existential happiness. But there is also an undeniable negativity. The "yes" to the world that the subject himself is, is irremediably affected by a "no," and with this "no" there is merged a "no" of the subject to himself.[55] Hence all fullness of being is permeated with emptiness, all fulfilment and satisfaction is saturated with unfulfilment and dissatisfaction, all peace and rest with peacelessness and unrest. Existential happiness is equiprimordially unhappiness. All this determines what man as subject-in-the-world *is*.

Being-in-the-world, then, is a being at ease in a world that must be called man's home. But, at the same time, it is also a being ill at ease in a world that is unhomely. For my existent subjectivity-as-*volo* the world is my home, a home in which I long for a better home.

C. THE EXISTENT SUBJECT AS AGO (I ACT)

The being of man as existence reveals itself not only as a being-*in*-the-world but equiprimordially as a being-*at*-the-world. Being-man is a dynamism, the dynamism that must be called history.

It is evident that being-man contains also a static aspect. Facticity, determinateness, the "already" of existence, which we express by means of grammatical predicates, indicate a certain "fixedness" of the subject. Such predicates as "dumb," "fat," "American," "boxer," and "inactive" clearly show this "fixed" character. However, there is no facticity that does not imply a certain being-able-to-be; every "already" discloses a certain "not yet."[56] Being-able-to-be is not an accidental feature of facticity but co-constitutes the reality of this facticity. On the other hand, there is no real being-able-to-be that is not based upon a certain facticity. Existence, then, is the oppositional unity of being-in-fact and being-able. This unity Heidegger calls "project" (*Entwurf*).[57] Sartre in a somewhat strange but striking way defines this characteristic of existence by saying that man is not what he is, and is what he is not.

---

[55] "Something massive and fleshy is lacking in his assent." Merleau-Ponty, *Eloge de la philosophie,* Paris, 12th ed., 1953, p. 81.

[56] "*Dasein* is always 'beyond itself' already, not as behaving toward other beings, which it is not, but as being toward the 'being-able-to-be' which it itself is. This structure of being, pertaining to the essential 'it is an issue,' we conceive as the 'being-ahead-of-itself' of *Dasein*." Heidegger, *op. cit.,* p. 192.

[57] Heidegger, *op. cit.,* pp. 144-145.

For man is not solely facticity; he is also a being-able-to-be, though not facticitously.[58]

We should keep in mind, however, that both being-in-fact and being-able-to-be belong to the subject. Man is not *de facto* fat just as a dead elephant is heavy; he is not *de facto* chaste just as a lily is white; he is not *de facto* hunchbacked just as a willow is knotty; he is not bald just as a billiard ball is smooth. Similarly, the being-able-to-be of man is not just like the being-able of a thing, "to which something can happen."[59] The project that man is, is a self-project. Man is master of his situation and holds his possibilities in his own hand.

Let us add, once more, that the project which existence is should not be conceived as a "plan" that man draws up or can abandon.[60] Man himself is a project; being-a-project has ontological significance. Man's being-a-project is the foundation that makes all concrete plans possible. Every concrete plan is drawn up as a possibility to be realized from a certain facticity. Such a plan, then, explicitly takes up what existence itself as project *is*.

Man is not only a self-project, but he is also and *per se* the execution of the self-project which he is;[61] man acts. In acting, the subject extends himself over and beyond his facticity toward the attainment of one of the unfulfilled possibilities of his existence. Once this possibility is attained, the result of man's action remains in his existence as a facticity, but one that again opens up certain possibilities. The subject-as-*ago* constantly transcends his facticity. It is even impossible for man to refuse that transcendence. Even if someone allegedly were to refuse to realize himself, he would still realize himself, albeit as a good-for-nothing, a do-nothing, a know-nothing. For in this way, too, he would give a certain meaning to existence, and of this meaning the subject-as-*ago* is the origin. If man refuses to build a human world, he still builds a world, albeit an inhuman one. To will nothing is still to will something, and to do nothing is still to do something. The constantly self-transcending movement[62] that the existent subject-as-*ago* is ceases only when man ceases to be man. Being-in-the-world is equiprimordially a being-at-the-world.[63]

---

[58] "Yet the 'for itself' is. It *is,* one will say, even if it is a being that is not what it is, and is what it is not." Sartre, *op. cit.,* p. 121.

[59] Heidegger, *op. cit.,* p. 143.

[60] Heidegger, *op. cit.,* p. 145.

[61] "The 'essence' of *Dasein* lies in its existence." Heidegger, *op. cit.,* p. 42.

[62] Merleau-Ponty, *Phénoménologie de la perception,* p. 492.

[63] Merleau-Ponty, *op. cit.,* pp. 496-520.

D. THE HUMAN BODY AS TRANSITION FROM SUBJECT TO WORLD

One who wants to speak about the human body must take all kinds of precautions to make sure that he does speak of the *human* body. He could very easily be induced to speak about the human body as one of the many bodies belonging to the great family of bodies[64] meant when someone states: "If a body is fully or partly immersed in a liquid, then its weight decreases by. . . ." One who speaks about the human body in such a way entirely forgets the human aspect of the human body. The human body is human because it is "mine," "yours," "his" or "hers," i.e. because it is the body-of-a-subject. The human body is a participation in the subject, and the subject lies immersed in the body. My grasping hands are "I who grasp"; my feet are "I who walk"; my eyes are "I who see"; my ears are "I who hear." My body does not lie as a thing among other things.[65] My hands do not lie in a graspable world; my feet do not belong to a world to be walked on; my eyes are not part of the visible world; and my ears do not belong to the world of sound. The human body lies on the side of the subject. Considered in this way, man *is* his body.[66]

Similarly, the human body is not what is said about it in biology, physiology and anatomy.[67] In books about these sciences the human body is not mentioned because they do not speak about "I," "you," "he" or "she." Obviously, we do not mean to say that biology, physiology and anatomy do not speak about anything when they profess to discuss the body, but only that they do not express the human character of the human body.[68] Moreover, those sciences do not even know what they are speaking of if they disregard the primordial "knowing about the body" which the subject as embodied *cogito* himself is.

Once this point is understood, it is easy to see that "my" body is the

---

[64] Sartre, *op. cit.*, p. 278.

[65] "My body, as it is for me, does not appear to me in the midst of the world." Sartre, *op. cit.*, p. 365.

[66] Marcel, *Journal métaphysique,* Paris, 1927, p. 301.

[67] "Regarding the body, including that of the other, we must learn to distinguish it from the objective body described by books on physiology." Merleau-Ponty, *op. cit.*, p. 403.

[68] ". . . the objective body is not truly the phenomenal body as we 'live' it, but is only an impoverished image of the latter. Hence the problem of the relations between soul and body is not concerned with the objective body, which exists only conceptually, but with the phenomenal body." Merleau-Ponty, *op. cit.*, p. 493.

transition from "me" to my world, that it is the place where I appropriate my world,[69] that it attaches me to things, that it gives me a solid or a precarious foothold in the world "clinging" to my body. It is also because I have hands with five fingers that the world can be "handled" in a certain way, different from the way I would "handle" it if I had only one finger on each hand; it is also because I have feet that the world can be walked upon in a certain way, different from the way I would do it if I had wings or webbed feet; it is also because I have ears that the world is for me a sonorous world; it is also because I have eyes that the world is for me a field of vision. It is also from the standpoint of my body that a mountain is high and the sidewalk low, that I call a star distant and my desk near,[70] that I call fire hot and ice cold. To the human body refers everything in the world that is called hard, soft, angular, sharp, sticky, red, yellow, purple, spacious, light, heavy, immovable, tasty, nutritious, fragrant, stinking, large, small, etc. A bicycle refers to an attitude and to motions of the human body; and the same can be said of a football, a bed, a door, a room or any other cultural object.

Accordingly, my body lies at the side of the subject who I am but, at the same time, it involves me in the world of things. My body opens the world to me, or rather, it opens me "toward the world" and places me in a situation there.[71] My body keeps alive the "stage" of the world; it animates and nourishes this "stage."[72] When my body disintegrates, my world also disintegrates, and my body's total dissolution means a break with my world and, at the same time, my death, the end of my being as a being-conscious-in-the-world, my being-man.[73]

Thus, when we reflect upon the human body, we meet the subject that is immersed in the body and, by way of the body, is involved in the world. We find the world which as a complex of meanings "clings" to the body that as human refers to the subject. We find man as existence.

Pact Between Body and World. All this sounds like meaningless nonsense to anyone who conceives the human body as a thing among

---

[69] Merleau-Ponty, *op. cit.,* p. 180.

[70] Merleau-Ponty, *op. cit.,* p. 502.

[71] "It is also my body that opens me up to the world and puts me there in a situation." Merleau-Ponty, *op. cit.,* p. 192.

[72] Merleau-Ponty, *op. cit.,* p. 235.

[73] "If the world falls apart into many fragments or is dislocated, this is because one's own body has ceased to be a knowing body and to gather together all objects in a single grasp." Merleau-Ponty, *op. cit.,* p. 327.

other things, as something belonging to the large family of all bodies. The same is still true for one who wants to express his view in a more subtle way and claim that the human body, as human, can be the object of the sciences, in the narrow sense of this term.   However, as long as one speaks about the human body in the way these sciences are accustomed to speak, one will always leave incomprehensible the fact that the world has a meaning which clings to the body as the subject's incarnation, a meaning which the body "already" "knows" and "affirms."   And at the same time, one leaves undisclosed the fact that all statements of the positive sciences about the body presuppose a more profound and more primordial "knowing," viz., the "knowing" in which my hands and my feet are unconcealed for me when I use tools or walk on the world.[74] In a scientistic conception of the sciences one forgets and disregards the source from which they have sprung.

It may be worth-while to dwell a little longer on this mysterious "knowing" that the human body itself is.   The body is human because it is the body of a subject.   The subject is immersed in the body, and the body participates in the subject.   We described the subject as *cogito*, as *volo* and as *ago*.   But if the body participates in the subject, then the body itself must also be called a kind of *cogito, volo* and *ago* in the world.   And this is patently so.   Before I have made any intellectual judgment about space, I have already orientated myself in space; this is the same as "having eyes" or "being able to see."   If I want to compose a scientific treatise about colors, I must presuppose that my eyes already "know" and can "distinguish" colors.   My body "knows" much better than I what is meant by hard, soft, sharp, sticky, cold, warm, fragrant, or tasty.[75]   The hands and feet of a football player "know" the field and the ball much better than this player himself when he reflects upon them. My feet "know" much better than I the stairs I climb every day, and the cyclist's body "can" ride much better than the cyclist himself.   One who has to lead a large gathering in set prayers will not forget them only if his lips "know" the prayers much better than he himself knows them. The human body, as sexually differentiated, is a bodily *cogito* and *volo* of

---

[74] "We have learned again to feel our body; underneath the objective and detached knowledge of the body we have found that other knowledge which we have of it because it is always with us and because we are (our) body.   But by thus making contact again with the body and with the world, we will also rediscover ourselves.   For, if we perceive with our body, the body is a natural 'I' and, as it were, the subject of perception."   Merleau-Ponty, *op. cit.*, p. 239.

[75] Merleau-Ponty, *op. cit.*, pp. 275-276.

the other sex, and this *cogito* and *volo* is the foundation of every personal sexual initiative.

"Under" the personal subject, then, a pre-personal subject is at work;[76] this pre-personal subject is presupposed by every personal *cogito, volo* and *ago,* and its prehistory is taken up by the personal *cogito, volo* and *ago* in the world.[77] This pre-personal—one could almost say "anonymous"—subject is the human body.[78] The body has already established a pact with the world before the personal subject begins its personal history,[79] and this pact is not rendered superfluous by any personal history.[80] This pact, however, which has been concluded in semi-darkness, becomes wholly unintelligible when the human body is replaced by the "purely bodily processes" spoken of by the sciences, in the narrow sense of the term. This is the profound truth contained in psychoanalysis, even though it may be true that Freud himself did not clearly realize this truth.[81] It would have been very surprising indeed if Freud had been aware of the importance of the human body as a pre-personal *cogito, volo* and *ago,* for in his days the human body was considered solely as an object of the sciences. Thus it was in principle impossible to recognize "officially" the mysterious *cogito, volo* and *ago* which the human body itself is. The genius of Freud consisted precisely in this that, in spite of this lack of "official" recognition, he did not disregard the mystery of the

---

[76] "There is, then, another subject beneath me, for whom a world exists before I am there and who marks my place in it. This captive or natural spirit is my body, not the momentary body which is the instrument of my personal choices and fastens itself on this or that world, but the system of anonymous 'functions' which gather every particular 'fixed point' into a general project." Merleau-Ponty, *op. cit.,* p. 294.

[77] Merleau-Ponty, *op. cit.,* p. 293.

[78] "Perception is always in the mode of the (impersonal) 'they.' It is not a personal act by which I would give a new meaning to my life." Merleau-Ponty, *op. cit.,* p. 277.

[79] "My first perception and my first hold on the world must appear to me as the execution of an earlier 'pact' between *X* and the world in general." Merleau-Ponty, *op. cit.,* p. 293.

[80] Cf. also Remy C. Kwant, "De geslotenheid van Merleau-Ponty's wijsbegerte," *Tijdschrift v. Philosophie,* vol. XIX (1957), pp. 217-272.

[81] "Whatever declarations of principles Freud may have made, psychoanalytical research *de facto* does not lead to an explanation of man through his sexual infrastructure, but to the rediscovery in sexuality of relations and attitudes which previously had been regarded as relations and attitudes of (our) *consciousness.* Hence the importance of psychoanalysis is less to make psychology biological than to discover a dialectical movement in functions held to be 'purely bodily,' and to reintegrate sexuality into the human being." Merleau-Ponty, *op. cit.,* p. 184.

human body. He realized that the "knowing," "willing" and "acting" of the human body did not lie on the same level as the knowing, willing and acting of the personally-conscious subject. Thus he saw himself obliged to introduce the category of the "unconscious psyche," in order to make it possible to express in words the truth he had discovered about the human body.

The pact between body and world is also the "place" of very many psychical disturbances.[82] These disturbances are not caused by unilateral, deterministic processes originating in stimuli coming from the "external world," nor can they be regarded as the externalization of a disorganization in the "internal world." Rather, they are breaks between the body and the world, usually on an affective level, and this break is not repaired by a personal intellectual effort or a personal decision of will, but only if the body, aided by psychotherapy, once more opens itself to the world and to man's fellow-men.[83]

E. THE ONTOLOGICAL STATUS OF WORLDLY MEANING

Far-reaching consequences are attached to the idea of existence with respect to the ontological status of worldly things. If it is true that man is existence, that he is a subject-in-the-world and that man[84] "clings" to the world, then the world also "clings" to man, so that one can never again ask what the world is without man nor claim that there is a world without man. We realize, of course, that this statement needs some clarification lest phenomenology be the butt of the most extravagant accusations.

When Husserl defined the subject as intentionality, he "bracketed" the actual existence of the worldly meaning to which the subject is orientated, that is, he suspended judgment about this actual existence. This is the first sense in which Husserl used the term "reduction," the "bracketing of being." What, we may ask, led Husserl to this suspension of judgment?

According to De Waelhens, the philosophies of the nineteenth centuries still struggled with the "critical problem," the question whether or

---

[82] Merleau-Ponty, *op. cit.*, pp. 180-199.

[83] Merleau-Ponty, *op. cit.*, p. 192.

[84] We adapt ourselves here to a way of speaking that, strictly, is not correct. It is not man who clings to the world, but the subject. Man is the unity of the reciprocal implication of subject and world. Hence, since the world belongs to that which constitutes being-man, it is, strictly speaking, not correct to say that *man* clings to the world.

not an external reality corresponded to the contents, the representations and concepts of the self-encapsuled, isolated and closed *cogito*. Idealism held that meaning was a content of the *cogito* and consequently not distinct in its being from this *cogito*; realism, on the contrary, held that meaning was wholly separate from the *cogito* and utterly foreign to this *cogito* in its being. Husserl did not want to get involved in the dispute between realists and idealists for fear that he would get stuck in this controversy and therefore be unable to ever execute the task he wanted to assign to phenomenology. Moreover, he thought that his phenomenology could make progress even if he did not choose sides in the dispute. Husserl himself did not yet realize then that the idea of intentionality he defended made it impossible to bracket the actual existence of meaning. He did not yet realize that the bracketing of this actual existence is possible only when one starts from a closed *cogito*; yet he had rejected precisely that kind of a *cogito*.

If *cogito* is intentionality, one can no longer ask whether or not the meaning to which this *cogito* is orientated actually exists,[85] but one must at once admit that the actually existing worldly meaning co-determines what the *cogito* is and that, without the actually existing worldly meaning, the *cogito* is not what it is, namely, intentionality.[86] Thus it is not surprising that the phenomenological reduction, in the sense of a "bracketing of being" does not occur in the work of Martin Heidegger.[87]

Representational Realism. The world spoken of by phenomenology is the real world. This statement may sound trivial, and it would be trivial indeed if it were not for the existence of spiritualistic monism or idealism, which lets the reality of worldly things and of the world itself evaporate into being nothing but the contents of the subject-as-*cogito*. Phenomenology precisely wants to deny this idealistic claim when it says that worldly things are real. Things are not contents of the *cogito*, but they are the solid massivity and density of the real, of that which is "bodily given." Obviously, this does not mean that I cannot make

---

[85] "One can see . . . that the problem of the existence of the external world, strictly speaking, does not make any sense at all." Marcel, *op. cit.*, p. 26.

[86] "For my part, I would say that Heidegger has shown, probably in a definitive way, that it is absurd to isolate the existent subject and, starting from this isolated subject, to ask oneself whether or not there exists a world. For, as a matter of fact, that existent subject is only an existent subject in its relationship to the world." Marcel, *L'homme problématique,* pp. 141-142.

[87] Joseph J. Kockelmans, *Martin Heidegger,* Pittsburgh, 1965, p. 20.

mistakes when I speak of the world, or that I cannot admit, through illusion, fear or wishful thinking, all kinds of meanings that are not really meanings. Evidently, all this is quite possible. However, the fact that I can distinguish an illusory world or a dream world from the real world means that, prior to all reflection, I have already "distinguished" these worlds, I already "know" that, in dreaming and illusions, I am not dealing with the *real* world facing my subjectivity-as-*cogito*.[88]

At the same time, it is clear that the "critical problem," as it was traditionally formulated, does not exist.[89] This is no reason why anyone would be entitled to reject phenomenology. For, if there exists a critical problem, the terms in which it is formulated will have to be borrowed from the *cogito* as it really is.[90] (As a matter of fact, there exists such a problem, but it differs from the traditional one.) It is not a scandal for philosophy that a valid proof for the existence of an "external world" has never been delivered; on the contrary, if there is any scandal, it must be sought in the fact that the search for such a proof still continues.[91]

Is the reality of worldly things and of the world itself perhaps the brute, inhuman reality of the realism defended by the English empiricists (Locke, Hume) and many Thomists? Is the real world a "world in itself," a collection of "things in themselves," a world that is totally divorced from man? Those who feel inclined to answer in the affirmative should realize the implications. In realism, the subject and the world occur as totally separate, isolated and divorced from each other, as entities that are self-enclosed and foreign to each other. Knowledge is then conceived, of course, as the representation or mirroring of brute reality in the mirror of a passive *cogito*. The meanings of the world, which disclose themselves only in existence as encounter with the world, are thrown out of the encounter and viewed as "in themselves";[92] hence knowledge is no longer conceived as encounter, as the immediate presence of the subject-as-*cogito* to present reality, but as a mirroring of the "in

---

[88] Merleau-Ponty, *op. cit.,* p. XI.

[89] Heidegger, *op. cit.,* p. 61.

[90] "What court is to decide whether and in what sense there is to be a problem of knowledge, what other court than that of the phenomenon of knowing and the kind of being of the knower?" Heidegger, *op. cit.,* p. 61.

[91] Heidegger, *op. cit.,* p. 205.

[92] "The return to perceptual experience, if it is a consistent and radical reform, condemns all forms of realism, i.e., all philosophies which leave consciousness and take as their datum one of its results." Merleau-Ponty, *op. cit.,* p. 58.

itself," and the *cogito* is described as dwelling with its own immanent contents of consciousness or its mirror images.[93]

David Hume saw every reason here to become a complete sceptic. For, in this interpretation of "reality," the world occurs as a world divorced from the subject-as-*cogito,* separated from the *cogito* as "affirmation" and as "knowledge," i.e., as a not-affirmed and not-known world. Obviously, a not-affirmed and not-known world can never be affirmed and known. Similarly, truth, as the agreement of knowledge with reality, becomes chimeric, for reality here means "not-known reality" so that truth would have to consist in the agreement of known reality with not-known reality. But who would be able to compare known reality with not-known reality, as is required to observe their agreement?

The "in itself" of representational realism is "reality" as "separate" from the *cogito,* as that which is foreign to the *cogito.* "Obviously, such an 'in itself' becomes nonsense as soon as it is affirmed. For it is something 'outside thought' in the strictest sense of the term and as such it is 'unthinkable.' It is reality 'as it is when I do not know it,' and with respect to such a reality one must agree with Kant that it is by definition unknowable."[94]

Phenomenological Realism. In defending the reality of the world, phenomenology rejects, on the one hand, that the world is the content of a *cogito* and, on the other, that it is a world-in-itself, in the sense in which this term is understood by representational realism.[95] But phenomenology does not reject every form of realism, for the choice to be made is not limited to either idealism or representational realism. There is also a phenomenological kind of realism, in which the reality of the world is conceived as reality appearing to the subject-as-*cogito,* as "phenomenon," not in the sense of semblance (*Schein*)[96] or mere appearance beyond which a reality in-itself would be concealed, but as "that which shows itself, the manifest," briefly, as appearing being itself.[97]   To

---

[93] Merleau-Ponty, *La structure du comportement,* p. 205.

[94] De Petter, "Een geamendeerde phaenomenologie," *Tijdschrift v. Philosophie,* vol. XXI (1960), p. 291.

[95] "The thing can never be separated from the one who perceives it; it can never be actually in itself because its articulations are those of our existence itself, and because it stands at the end of one's look, or at the terminus of a sense exploration that invests it with humanity." Merleau-Ponty, *op. cit.,* p. 370.

[96] Heidegger, *op. cit.,* p. 222.

[97] Heidegger, *op. cit.,* p. 28.

distinguish this "in itself" from the "in itself" of representational realism, phenomenology uses the term "in itself for us" or "being for us," [98] thereby expressing the autonomy of being which worldly meaning has with respect to the subject.

For phenomenology, knowledge is the encounter of the subject-as-*cogito* and worldly meaning. Meaning is the appearing being itself, which becomes appearing through the subject's dis-closing activity.[99] Meaning is the unconcealed, the dis-closed, that imposes itself on the subject in knowledge as encounter.[100] Meaning is that which is real. Representational realism, on the contrary, first accepts all meanings of the world that impose themselves in knowledge as encounter and then "realizes" them,[101] i.e., places them outside the encounter. It considers them as "given," as "existing in themselves" before and outside the encounter and then proceeds, with the aid of these "given data," to rebuild knowledge. Thus representational realism seems to think that it can transcend the encounter that knowledge is by affirming the things-in-themselves as beings. This is a contradiction, for what else is this affirmation but an encounter?

It should be evident now why phenomenology conceives the real world as radically human. For the world, in its own autonomy of being with respect to the subject, is a term of encounter; it "clings" to the subject. The being of the world is a being for man, a "being for us."[102] If phenomenology rejects the term "in itself," this should be taken to mean only and exclusively a rejection of being that is *not* a term of encounter. The emphasis on the "for us" means only an emphasis on meaning as *term of encounter*.[103] With the affirmation of the radical humanness of the world, phenomenology transcends the dilemma "either idealism or

---

[98] Merleau-Ponty, *op. cit.*, p. III.

[99] Heidegger, *op. cit.*, p. 219.

[100] "Expression is a being toward the thing itself that is. And what does perception demonstrate? Nothing but that (the thing) is the very being intended by the expression. . . . The being itself that is intended shows itself just as it is in itself. i.e., it shows that, in its selfsameness, it is just as in the expression it is shown forth, uncovered as being." Heidegger, *op. cit.*, p. 218.

[101] "For the first time the philosopher's meditation is sufficiently conscious not to endow its own results with reality in the world prior to this meditation itself." Merleau-Ponty, *op. cit.*, p. XV.

[102] Merleau-Ponty, *Sens et non-sens*, p. 187.

[103] "The phenomenological world is not the explicitation of a pre-existing being but the foundation of being. Philosophy is not a reflection on a pre-existing truth but, like art, the bringing about of a truth." Merleau-Ponty, *Phénoménologie de la perception*, p. XV.

representational realism."[104]   To be man is to dwell in the human world, to resonate with its meaning, which is inseparably connected with human subjectivity.[105]

F. WHAT PHENOMENOLOGY IS NOT

From all these considerations it should be evident that the terms "phenomenology" and "phenomenological" are to be handled with prudence. Yet in many cases they are used indiscriminately. Husserl launched his phenomenology as a "method" to find ground, to reach the indisputable, to arrive at a foundation for any statement whatsoever. Many, however, have given rather strange interpretations to Husserl's cry "Back to the things themselves." "The phenomenologically-analyzing march of the subject toward 'the thing itself' is a praiseworthy tendency which, especially in the realm of physical science, has produced results that are as surprising as they are impressive in their still incalculable importance," says Feber.[106]   He does not even seem to suspect that such an assertion exposes him irremediably to the accusation of being totally ignorant of what phenomenology is.[107]   One can make oneself ridiculous not only in the sciences but also in the realm of philosophy.

That effect is achieved also when, in the words of one critic, one considers phenomenology as a kind of "philosophical buzzing around a center that refuses to become visible" and calls such buzzing a "phenomenological description of existence."   All that has nothing to do with philosophy.

But even among philosophers there are many misconceptions of phenomenology. Phenomenology is not a form of Platonism, it is not a revival of Aristotelian realism, not a late bloom of idealism, and not a philosophy that draws the last consequences from atheism. Similarly, phenomenology is not identical with introspection, it is not merely a method supposed to lead to metaphysics; it is not a rich but nonetheless deficient preliminary inquiry preceding philosophy proper. Neither does

---

[104] Merleau-Ponty, *op. cit.,* p. 492.

[105] "The world cannot be separated from the subject. . . , and the subject is inseparable from the world, that is, a world which he projects himself." Merleau-Ponty, *op. cit.,* p. 491.

[106] L. Feber, *Existentialisme en Christendom,* Tielt, 1962, p. 124.

[107] "Without the keystone of the judgment, phenomenology can only lead to hypotheses possessing perhaps a high degree of probability. But it can never go beyond this." Feber, *op. cit.,* p. 127. One who is familiar with phenomenology cannot even venture a guess as to what such a statement wants to convey.

it suffice to say that phenomenology is a hermeneutic, intuitive and dialectic philosophy. But existential phenomenology is a philosophy whose "primitive fact" or "central point of reference" is the idea of existence, to express the essence of man conceived as "openness." We abstract here from the question whether perhaps this term "openness" must be considered to express several dimensions of openness in being-man.

CHAPTER SIX

JUSTICE AS AN ANTHROPO-
LOGICAL FORM OF CO-EXISTENCE

Justice, conceived as man's willingness to act in accordance with the demands of rights and duties is evidently a mode of co-existing, a mode of being together with others in the world. As was sufficiently emphasized in the preceding chapters, justice cannot be identified with the legal order. The legal order is established precisely in order that justice may be done, but it sometimes contains injustices; hence the two cannot possibly be identified.

We must now devote our attention more explicitly to the fact that justice lies on the level of human co-existence. There is every reason for insisting on this point, for some philosophers of law totally disregard it. Within the framework of a Thomistic theory of the natural law, Duynstee, for example, thinks that, on the basis of man's natural orientations, he can indicate man's natural rights, conceived as subjective "titles."[1] Man's nature, he says, gives man these rights. One may not be willing to argue much about Duynstee's explicitation of man's natural orientations and about their formulation as norms of the natural law. However, when these norms are "translated" as explicitations of "rights," without any mention of human co-existence, one wonders why those "rights" are called *rights*. Without any reference to man's being together with his fellow-men, a list of "rights" are enumerated. But what could the term "right" possibly mean outside the sphere of co-existence? Is such an approach not a form of thinking in categories of an individualistic ideology?

In line with this individualistic approach Duynstee *subsequently* asks

---

[1] Duynstee, *Over recht en rechtvaardigheid*, p. 29.

whether man must also respect the rights of other men.[2]   He answers in
the affirmative, of course, but his answer is not based on the evident
correlationship between my justice and the others' rights on the one
hand, and their justice and my rights on the other.   He tries to prove his
point by way of a detour, using a special argument for this purpose.[3]
All this, however, sounds unreal because justice and rights are not placed
at once in the sphere of co-existence.   Yet man as existence *is* co-
existence.

1. *Existence is Co-existence*

The statement that human existence is co-existence can have many
senses.   In general, the term "co-existence" is used to express that on no
level of his existence is man wholly "alone."   No aspect of being-man is
what it is unless other human beings are "present" in it.   The presence
of others in my existence implies that my being-man *is* a being-through-
others.   If in a "thought experiment" I would try to eliminate the being-
through-others from my own being-man, I would arrive at the conclusion that I am trying to eliminate the reality of my own being-man.
Being-through-others, then, is an essential characteristic of man.[4]

Two Objections.   Before delving somewhat deeper into this matter, it
may be useful to consider first two objections often raised against the
claim that human existence is radically social.   First of all, we said that
no aspect of being-man is what it is unless other human beings are
"present" in it.   This assertion is sometimes opposed, in various forms,

---

[2] Duynstee, *op. cit.,* p. 30.

[3] 'As a spiritual being man is ordered to the universal, the infinite good and
he tends to it by virtue of his nature.   But this universal, infinite good implies
the good of all individual men; hence one who tends to this infinite good *ipso
facto* also tends to the good of all other men.   The natural good of all men
becomes also his good. . . .   Thus he is naturally ordered to respect and will in
all other men that which they are ordered to.   This is by necessity of nature his
good, so that one can formulate a norm of the natural law: man must tend to
everything that naturally is a good for another man."   Duynstee, *op. cit.,* p.
31.

[4] "Being-with is an existential constituent of being-in-the-world.   *Dasein*-with
shows itself as a kind of being that beings encountered in the world have as
their own.   Insofar as *Dasein is* at all, being-with-one-another is its kind of
being.   This (being-with-one-another) cannot be understood as a summative
result of the occurrence of several 'subjects.' "   Heidegger, *Sein und Zeit*, p.
125.

on the following ground. The white corpuscles of man's blood obviously are "an aspect of being-man," yet who will claim that they constitute a social reality? We do not want to reply that, on the basis of man's biological origin and the laws of heredity, it would perhaps still be possible to say that man is not wholly "alone" even with respect to those corpuscles. The reason we do not wish to give this answer is that it does not lie on the level on which the question of man is posed here. The same applies here when one speaks of the human heart as a "muscle" or a "pump." When existential phenomenology speaks of man, it does not consider him as one of the many objects considered by the sciences but as the being-man that precedes the pursuit of the sciences. It considers man as existent subject, as project, as "having to be," and as the execution of that project, i.e. as history. Man is essentially history and as such he is radically social.

The second objection is as follows. If existence is *essentially* co-existence and the term "essentially" is understood as it should be, i.e. as referring to that by which man is man and not something else, then it follows that the "first man" who lived cannot be called a man. Our reply to this objection is similar to the answer to the first difficulty. To a certain extent we would be willing to accept this consequence, but not without explaining what this "extent" is. Experts in the field attach scientific value to the estimates and calculations saying that man is at least five hundred thousand years old. What kind of a man was man that many years ago? Our anthropologists still discover primitive tribes which, according to scientific estimates, are fifty thousand years behind modern civilized man.[5] One who goes to the trouble of finding out what being-man means for those primitives may even ask himself whether they can be called men. Although the answer is, of course, affirmative, there is also a standpoint from which one can give a negative reply: their being-man has not yet reached the first level of authenticity. Nevertheless, they are human beings because, and to the extent that, the way they actually are contains a possibility of rising to the level of being authentically human, and this cannot be asserted of a totem pole or any other mere thing. However, the level of human authenticity will never be reached unless their existence proceeds to realize itself as co-existence on a much broader level than before.

---

[5] This does not mean, of course, that in the present conditions an equally long period is needed to bridge the distance.

Applying this thought to the above-mentioned objection, we must answer that the "first" man was not man on the authentically human level because his existence was not co-existence. The statement that existence is *essentially* co-existence, then, applies to man on the authentic level of being-man. Besides, this level is the only one on which one can speak of man. For, if, on the one hand, the "first" man can still be called man because, and to the extent that, his actual way of being contains the possibility of rising to the level of authenticity, it is evident, on the other hand, that there can be question of this possibility only if "being man" is understood in terms of an actual level of authenticity.

The general idea of co-existence mentioned above needs to be developed in greater detail. We will do so here while following the distinctions made in the preceding chapter. Thus we will speak in turn about the existent subject as *cogito,* as *volo* and as *ago* and, at the same time, with respect to the world in which the subject is involved we will make a distinction between the cultural world and the natural world.

Co-existence and the Cultural World. The subject who as *cogito* exists in the cultural world evidently is co-existent. The perception of a simple meaning such as a chair is made possible for me by others. They do this, first of all, by the way I see them *behave* with respect to a chair.[6] Through their behavior toward the chair, the latter appears to me as a certain meaning; for the meaning of the chair "clings" to a certain way of behavior. The same can be said, in general, about the entire world of culture. Others precede me in behaving toward the cultural world. By being taken up into the history of this behavior, I am also taken up into the history of the cultural world's disclosure of meaning.

Secondly, language, even in its most elementary form of gestures or pointing, makes the meaning I perceive appear to me. Language, however, is not primarily *my* language, for the language I speak has been made by others. By participating in the speaking of others, I also begin to participate in the "seeing" embodied in that speaking.[7] If I am unable to understand a certain way of speaking, the other cannot help me to "see" what his language expresses. If I stand in front of a complex piece of machinery, I certainly do not "see" everything there is to see. Explanations of an expert in his own technical language would not

---

[6] Dondeyne, "De mens en de geschiedenis," *De mens,* Utrecht, n.d., pp. 32-33.

[7] Kwant, *Phenomenology of Social Existence,* pp. 79-86.

help me, for I would have to go first through a long history before I could begin to live in the language he speaks. Without that history, my subjectivity-as-*cogito* is not roused to "vision." For the same reason, if a native from a wholly undeveloped country is suddenly transferred to the heart of a metropolis, he does not see what others who live and work there see.

With respect to the subject-as-*volo* similar considerations can be made. The subject who on the affective level of his existence is involved in the cultural world is characterized by a certain "moodness," a fundamental affective tonality, that today differs completely from that proper to people who lived in a primitive world of culture. A long history separates these two phases of the cultural world. This history was made by others, who thereby also "made" me with respect to my "moodness." In my affective life also I am a child of the twentieth century, but I have been made in this respect by the children of the nineteenth century.

On the level of my subjectivity-as-*ago,* the co-existing character of my existence manifests itself most clearly. My action with respect to the cultural world presupposes the action of others establishing the meaning of the cultural world. The actual meaning of the cultural world is the result of a long history made by others. They have made it possible for me to project history toward a new future. This future would be impossible if I had to start from zero. In that case, if I were a genius, I might be able to invent the wheel, but the future of this invention is already past history. I would never even reach the level of that past if I had to start from zero. My activity with respect to the cultural world can be fruitful only on the basis of the history written by the activity of others. Moreover, others have to introduce me to that history and make me participate in it, by the way they act and by their language. Accordingly, the activity of history, i.e. of others, is present in my action with respect to the cultural world.

Co-existence and the Natural World. Superficially it may seem that we make it easy for ourselves in showing that the authenticity of my existence presupposes other existences, for we are constantly referring to examples of the subject's involvement in a *cultural* world. The cultural world in which I participate is by definition a system of meanings established by others. These meanings function as objective correlates of my existence as *cogito, volo* and *ago.* Thus it would be absurd to omit those other existences in the explicitation of my existence.

However, one could ask, is the same true with respect to the involvement of my existence in the natural world? That the natural world is a system of meanings already established by others is, to say the least, not as evident as the matter is in the case of the cultural world. And even if the natural world is such a system, its sense would differ greatly from that of the cultural world.

This difficulty provides us with an opportunity to put the emphasis where it belongs in this matter. It is obvious that the cultural world in which I am involved is a system of meanings established by others. The proper reason, however, why my existence must be called co-existence, why others must be said to be "present" in my existence, so that my existence is an existence-*through*-others, lies in the fact that, through their behavior and language, others *make* me participate in the cultural world. That others *make* me be, so that my being is a being-through-others, that is the proper sense of the thesis that my existence is co-existence.

One who understands this, sees also that it does not make much difference whether one speaks of the cultural world or of the natural world when one wants to show that existence is co-existence. For, even when there is question of the natural world, the behavior and language of the other *makes* me be as *cogito, volo* and *ago*. Thus the other is "present" in my existence, and my existence is co-existence.

The Social Body of Man. In this section we wanted to discuss in detail the idea of co-existence. But such a detailed discussion could easily make one lose sight of the totality. In fact man is naturally the unity of a *Gestalt* and, as such, man *makes* man *be*. The fact that in existence we distinguish *cogito, volo* and *ago,* does not mean that we want to place isolated "elements" side by side. *Man* makes *man* be. Thus we must say that this man is a New Yorker through New Yorkers, a smoker through smokers, a philosopher through philosophers, a Christian through Christians. So also a mother is a mother through her children; a sick person is really sick only when he is visited or is forgotten; a Negro is a real Negro only when he is refused permission to register in a White college; an asocial family is really asocial only when others refuse to have anything to do with it or when the social worker comes to visit it; a "cute button nose" really is a cute button nose when others notice her;[8] a hunchback is a real hunchback only when he is called

---

[8] F. Buytendijk, *Ontmoeting der sexen,* Utrecht, 1952, p. 7.

that.   These examples clearly show the complex *Gestalt* character of
making-one-another-be.   *Cogito, volo* and *ago* may and must be distinguished, but they cannot be separated from one another or from the
totality.

The fact that it is the totality of man that makes man be manifests
itself even more clearly when we direct our attention to those domains of
being-man in which man, either unconsciously or deliberately, proceeds
to the formation of groups.   This is the domain of positive sociology.
The idea that individual existence cannot reach any level of authenticity
unless it realizes itself in forms of co-existence is the same as the positive
sociologist's observation that the individual man is always found as
already belonging to certain groups whose bonds largely determine what
he is.   The positive sociologist investigates the character of the interaction and communication within a particular group.[9]   As soon as he
discovers a stability characterizing a specific group,[10] he can with a certain
measure of probability predict that certain interactions will occur between the persons belonging to that group.[11]   Thus the positive social
sciences empirically describe in detail the philosophical idea that existence
is co-existence.   They are *par excellence* "debunking" sciences,[12] for they
show how much others, the group, are "present" in my existence when I
assume that *I* think or that *I* act.   In every group there exists more or
less "dominating" views and more or less fixed patterns of behavior.   In
every group there is a more or less stereotyped way "things go."   This
expression is eloquent: it is as if the individual subjects do not matter
with respect to the group's way of acting: things run their course.

Young people, so it is said, "enter life," but especially for young people
this saying is not true.   On the contrary, they are more or less "pushed"
into it.   In "life" there is a way "things are done."   This way is
concerned with the manner of moving around, eating, drinking, taking
recreation and being bored, practicing virtue and committing sin, pursuing politics and participating in worship, applying oneself to the fine arts
and enjoying them, producing and advertising, expressing one's sexuality,

---

[9] J. van Doorn and C. Lammers, *Moderne sociologie,* 3rd ed., Utrecht, 1962,
pp. 34-37.

[10] "Neither football team nor labor union, neither family nor group of friends,
neither state nor society could be considered subject to scientific research if it
were not possible to discover in them routine ways of acting and standardized
attitudes."   van Doorn and Lammers, *op. cit.,* p. 44.

[11] van Doorn and Lammers, *op. cit.,* p. 45.

[12] Fechner, *Rechtsphilosophie,* p. 268.

working, being ill, etc. "Entering life" is at first not much more than being taken up into a way of doing things that has become the fixed pattern of a group. This being taken up into a pattern implies that the group makes the individual existences think, act and be in accordance with its patterns.[13]

It was necessary to emphasize the quasi-process by which human beings make one another be. First of all, an understanding of this point is wholly indispensable for a correct appreciation of the importance of the legal order. Secondly, we want to draw attention to the fact that making one another be is a necessary condition for the authenticity of *personal* existence. This assertion may seem to contradict the preceding paragraphs, for they seemed to say that whatever an existence thinks that it is, thinks or performs by itself, is in fact nothing but the result and the repercussion of the group's "pressure." How, then, can we now assert that making one another be is a necessary condition for the authenticity of *personal* existence? Is it still possible to speak of the "person" and the "subject" if one is willing to recognize the undeniable reality that we make one another be?

Sociologism. Sociologism answers these questions in the negative[14]: man is nothing but the product of "social processes." Any philosopher must sooner or later face the temptation of sociologism if he does not want to minimize the undeniable importance of co-existence, of making one another be. Speaking about materialism, we mentioned that the materialist is *almost* right. Materialism takes seriously the idea that man is man on the basis of his materiality. Being-man contains aspects that can be studied by the sciences, in the narrow sense of the term, and they consider these aspects as results of cosmic processes and forces. Thus the temptation is strong to represent man as *nothing but* the result of such processes. In the history of my encounters with others, my life in many groups, these encounters leave something behind in my existence. In my dealings with others on all levels of my existence, there occurs a quasi-process of sedimentation and the quasi-effect of it is my "social

---

[13] "In this inconspicuousness and unobservability the 'they' unfolds its real dictatorship. We take delight and enjoy ourselves as 'they' do; we read, see and judge about literature and art as 'they' see and judge; we even pull back from the 'great mass' as 'they' pull back; we find 'shocking' what 'they' find shocking. The 'they,' which is nothing definite, and which all are, though not as the sum, prescribes the kind of being of everydayness." Heidegger, *op. cit.*, pp. 126-127.

[14] Kwant, *op. cit.*, pp. 105-106.

facticity"[15] or my "social body."[16]   Man has not only a "natural
body"[17] but also a cultural body and a social body.   My "cultural
body"[18] is the facticity remaining in my existence as the result of my
personal actions.[19]   My "social body" is the facticity accumulating in my
existence in and through my being together with others.   In our co-
existing, the other "influences" me, but this "influencing" is not a process
in the strict sense in which the influence of one thing upon another thing
is a process.   The reason for the difference is that my social body is and
remains *my* body; it is the social body of the existent *subject* who I am.[20]
As existent, the subject is immersed in the social body and gives meaning
to this body; he "can do all kinds of things with it"—just as a hunchback
gives meaning to his bent back and "can still do all kinds of things" with
this aspect of his "natural body."   Hence, like the "natural body," the
"social body" is not an effect, it is not purely the result of unilateral and
deterministic causes.[21]   The other's "influence" is a quasi-process and the
social body is a quasi-effect.

It is precisely the significance of the subject that is disregarded and
finally eliminated by sociologism.   Man's *personal* thinking and doing
presupposes the social body accumulated in my existence in the manner
others make me be.   This making-be and its quasi-effect, i.e. my social

---

[15] Kwant, *op. cit.,* pp. 122-138.

[16] "The body in general is an ensemble of paths already traced, of powers
already constituted, it is the acquired dialectical soil on which a higher 'putting
into shape' is brought about."   Merleau-Ponty, *La structure du comportement,* p.
227.

[17] This "natural body" is, of course, not the reality of the human body studied
by the biologist, but the "lived body."

[18] Merleau-Ponty, *op. cit.,* p. 227, note.

[19] We do not want to assert that my "cultural body" is not a social reality.   It
is such a reality, for the others are "present" in my personal actions.   Indirectly,
then, the "cultural body" also is a "social body."

[20] "If my social 'I' is forced upon me, I can still *innerly* resist it.   Although I
am inexorably chained to my social being (*Dasein*) and in it maintain my self-
consciousness in the mirror of my activity, I can nonetheless put myself over
against it as 'I' myself.   Despite all social gain and loss, I can remain myself in
all changes.   I no longer coincide with my social 'I,' even though I am at the
same time in this 'I' at every moment. . . .   My social 'I,' which I do not cease
being, no less than I cease being there as a body, becomes itself for me an object
from which, at the same time, I distance myself."   Karl Jaspers, *Philosophie,*
1948, p. 320.

[21] "I am not a result of complexes of sociological factors, for I remain, by
virtue of my origin, the possibility of my self, even when I am determined by my
sociological being (*Dasein*) in everything of myself that objectively appears."
Jaspers, *ibid.*

body, make it possible for me to think and act *personally*.[22] If man does not receive his social body from others, his thinking and acting will be unable to reach any level of authenticity.   The assertion that man receives his social body from others, however, does not mean that his personal thinking and acting are nothing but the repercussion of the group's "pressure," for the very social body that is presupposed by personal thinking and acting is not unqualifiedly the effect of a social process.   The subject and the social body are not opposites,[23] but constitute a unity of reciprocal implication.[24]

The proper significance of the subject with respect to the "weight" of the social body may perhaps also be expressed with greater detail in this way.   If personal thinking and acting were *nothing but* the repercussion of the social body's pressure, then the establishment of a *new* meaning would be wholly incomprehensible.   Yet it is unmistakably true that new meanings enter history.   A meaning is new if it was not present before as it is present now.   Thus a new meaning presupposes the subject's creativity and spontaneity, and these cannot be reduced to the "pressure" exercised by what is already present.   If, for instance, Heidegger's philosophy is called "new," then this does not mean that the past is not present in his philosophy.   Heidegger, too, has a social body, without which his philosophizing would not have been able to reach any level whatsoever.   That his philosophy is new means that he cannot be reduced to the "pressure" which the philosophy already thought by others exercised on him.

Accordingly, it is not the social body "alone" that establishes meaning in the thinking and acting of personal existence.   It is the unity of reciprocal implication of subject and social body that thinks and acts.[25]

---

[22] "I want to assume my role not only in order to be materially there, but also in order to become 'I' myself. I know myself only in this role; nonetheless, I am not identical with it." Jaspers, *ibid.*

[23] "Thus we know now that concrete dialectics is the dialectics that discloses itself through the common *praxis* of a group. But we know also that the fundamental condition of historical rationality is that it is impossible for organic action to go beyond its strictly individual pattern (through the combining of the individuals' efforts). This means that constituted dialectical Reason, as the living understanding of all common *praxis,* must always be brought back to constituting rationality, which is its ever-present and ever-disguised foundation." Sartre, *Critique de la raison dialectique,* p. 643.

[24] Kwant, *Phenomenology of Social Existence,* pp. 163-177.

[25] "It is true that the individual is conditioned by his social environment and, in turn, acts on it to condition it. It is this, and nothing else, that makes his reality." Sartre, *op. cit.,* p. 52.

To the extent that the subject transcends in his creativity and spontaneity the social body's facticity, a new meaning can appear or be established in history. Moreover, it cannot be denied that the subject keeps his social body alive, lets it starve or even die in some respects. Thus the social body of man does not "live" *solely* through the group's pressure. The non-identity of the subject with his social body makes it possible for him to distance himself from it or to consent to it. This consent keeps the social body alive. If the subject is no longer able or willing to consent because the spontaneity of his subjectivity is no longer supported by his social body, then this body starves and begins to degenerate. The patterns of life in a group do not have the permanence of a rock.

Similar ideas impose themselves with respect to social facticity on the side of the world. Canals and roads, cars and airplanes, books and libraries, works of art and museums, schools and hospitals, educational systems and public health institutions, factories, production methods and organizations for the care of the poor—all these belong to social facticity on the side of the world. They constitute the "inorganic social body" of man. They are the result of a long common history. The subject has established the world's social facticity; the subject keeps this facticity alive; and the subject projects this facticity toward a new future.[26]

We have dwelt rather extensively on the phenomenology of existence as co-existence because an understanding of it is indispensable for a correct idea of justice and rights. However, the reader may have noticed that, in speaking about co-existence, we did not mention justice and rights at all. This is not a mistake. For justice is a form of co-existence that does not lie—at least not solely—on the level of co-existence spoken about above. There are many levels of co-existence. We must now consider what constitutes the specific essence of justice as a mode of co-existence.

2. The Origin of Our Knowledge About the Essence of Justice

One who inquires into the essence of justice and of its correlate, (natural) rights, abandons legal positivism. But the reasons why the

---

[26] "Hence we must see what, strictly speaking, is the rationality of action on the level of individual *praxis*. For the present, it matters little what are the collective constraints that give rise to this *praxis*, limit it or deprive it of its efficacy." Sartre, *op. cit.*, p. 166.

legal positivist is a legal positivist continue to weigh on him also as a heavy burden. He distinguishes justice explicitly from the unreserved willingness to observe the legal order; he claims that justice can sometimes demand the overthrow of the legal order; he does not sacrifice justice to legal security.[27] All this is an abomination for the legal positivist. The defenders of natural rights flagrantly contradict one another. "With an appeal to justice," the positivist says, "anyone can validate as 'sacred rights' his most extravagant claims, his lust for power, his short-sightedness and narrow-mindedness, his political aspirations, his envy and greed."[28] Who is to determine what is just?

Let us begin with this question. The question of what is just has occupied man from the moment he reached the level of authenticity on which he was able to raise this question. And from that very moment also the answer to that question became mixed with his most extravagant claims, his lust for power, his short-sightedness and narrow-mindedness, his political aspirations, his envy and greed. This is the reason why the legal positivist is a legal positivist. And this reason weighs heavily on the defender of natural rights when he rejects legal positivism. That rejection itself does not give him too much trouble, for he has history on his side: it teaches him that the so-called legal order was all too often nothing but the embodiment of the most extravagant claims, lust of power, short-sightedness and narrow-mindedness, political aspirations, greed and envy. The positivist does not want to raise the issue of what makes the legal order just. But, without raising the question, he nonetheless answers it. He does not want to run the risk contained in any reply to the question of what justice is. But he runs the risk anyhow, even though he does not see it.

Who determines what is just? This is the question to which legal positivism capitulates. The defenders of natural rights show that this capitulation contains an implicit answer. But in that case, would it not be reasonable to give up the ostrich attitude and to ask explicitly: What is just? Is it not reasonable to accept the risk implied in any answer, with our eyes wide open? One who closes his eyes to the risk no longer has any means to defend himself and others.

---

[27] "Certainly, these concepts of 'supralegal' justice (*Recht*) and legal unjustice contain grave dangers precisely for the security of right which we demand with such insistence." Radbruch, "Die Erneuerung des Rechts," *Die Wandlung,* vol. II (1947), p. 10.

[28] Bergbohm, *Jurisprudenz und Rechtsphilosophie,* vol. I, p. 133; Kelsen, "Was ist die Reine Rechtslehre?" *Demokratie und Rechtsstaat,* p. 157.

The question of what is just has two phases. It can be understood as referring to what must be done here and now to make justice reign in society. Opinions about the correct answer to this question can vary greatly. However, this difference of opinion does not at all mean that those who disagree about what has to be done here and now to make justice reign in society give, at the same time, contradictory answers to the question of what justice is. This is the first phase of the question: What is just? The questioning and searching of all those who try to determine what is to be done here and now continues to live by virtue of their implicit answer to the question of what justice is. That same question is also implicitly answered by the positivist when he refuses to abandon man to his most extravagant claims, his lust for power, his short-sightedness and narrow-mindedness, his political aspirations, his envy and greed. To prevent this from happening, hence in order that there be justice and humanity in society, the positivist defends the absolute validity of positive law. For this reason we said above that the legal positivist also gives an answer to the question about the essence of justice.

Implicit Knowledge. Man, it appears, has an implicit "knowledge of the essence of justice." Prior to any explicit statement, man has already distinguished justice from his most extravagant claims, his lust for power, his short-sightedness and narrow-mindedness, his political aspirations, his envy and greed. This "knowledge" is so certain of itself that anyone who is at least a little bit human knows for certain that the positive law by which Hitler sent millions of Jews to the gas chamber was unjust, even though Eichmann thought differently. Eichmann was simply wrong. Anyone who is at least a little bit human knows that it is unjust to pluck out the eyes of children solely because they happen to be blue;[29] and whoever disagrees with this statement is simply wrong. Anyone who is at least a little bit human knows that it is unjust to burn widows or to offer children in sacrifice; and whoever disagrees with this is simply wrong.[30]

What is this mysterious "knowledge"? It is man himself; it is the

---

[29] Pompe, "Natuurrecht," *Wezen en grondslagen van het recht,* 1957, pp. 32-33.

[30] We realize that the addition of "at least a little bit human" gives rise to many questions. Who is to determine who has become at least a little bit human? We will not avoid this question, but have to postpone the answer till later, for we want to proceed in an orderly fashion.

being of man, for man is the being for which, in its being, its being itself is an issue;[31] he is the being for which its being itself is at stake.[32]   Man has a relationship to what he is, and this relationship is an "understanding of being" (*Seinsverständnis*).[33]   The mysterious "knowing" that man himself is arises at the same moment that man as subject emerges in the evolution of the cosmos, for this "knowing" is the existent subject himself.   As "natural light," the existent subject brings light to the cosmos and constitutes it a world of meaning.   In this "knowing" the subject stands in the truth as unconcealedness.[34]   The event of the subject's emergence is at the same time the event, the emergence of truth as unconcealedness.[35]   In this sense, then, in the sense of "coming about," truth is historical.   Besides, truth is historical also insofar as the historical "event" of truth has a future, a future that is never finished so long as man is man.

The mysterious "knowing" mentioned above, which is man himself insofar as he is characterized by an "understanding of being," is an implicit kind of knowing.   It is the implicit "affirmation" by man of truth, the unconcealedness of himself, of the world and of the other.[36] In this "knowing" man does not make himself, the world and the other explicit themes of his attention, but he is simply present to himself, to the world and to the other as subject, as "light."   But that which is implicitly "known" in this immediate presence can be made explicit. Man can explicitly turn to himself, the world and the other.   These two modes of "consciousness," of "knowing" and "affirming," contemporary philosophy calls "pre-reflective consciousness" and "reflective consciousness."[37]

Consciousness is called "reflective" when I proceed from being-present-to to placing-in-my presence.   I then thematize that which was non-thematic and I make explicit that which was implicit.   All philosophizing consists in such a placing-in-my-presence, in an express return to the "world experiencing life" that I myself am.   My life is at first only the "*irréfléchi*," the "unreflected upon," but the latter is not wholly con-

---

[31] Sartre, *L'être et le néant*, p. 222.
[32] Heidegger, *Sein und Zeit*, p. 12.
[33] Heidegger, *op. cit.*, pp. 12-15.
[34] Heidegger, *Ueber den Humanismus*, Frankfurt a.M., 1947, p. 19.
[35] Merleau-Ponty, *Sens et non-sens*, pp. 186-187.
[36] "Every conscious existence exists as consciousness of existing."   Sartre, *op. cit.*, p. 20.
[37] Sartre, *op. cit.*, pp. 16-22.

cealed from me because I am present to it as a pre-reflective *cogito*. This pre-reflective *cogito* is also called "lived experience." Everything the philosopher says explicitly is already "known" in this "experience," and without this "knowing" there cannot be any explicit knowledge.[38] In this sense Plato is right when he says that all knowledge is a kind of remembering.

The "implicit" knowing that man as existent subject is can help us understand also that man already "knows" what justice is. Above we gave some examples indicating that man knows for certain that certain ways of acting toward one's fellow-men are unjust. These examples become clear in the light of what phenomenology says about "lived experience." Man indeed "knows" what justice is and what right is. If the philosopher wishes to express what justice and right are, he must remain faithful to this "knowing." Life in its non-reflective form, man's direct dealing with things and his fellow-men, is the soil from which spring the philosopher's statements and definitions. Without this soil, all philosophizing hangs in a vacuum, and the philosopher cannot convince us that he is really talking about something. In other words, philosophy may never contradict "unreflected life." To philosophize is to grasp at life in order to give expression to it. But this grasping and this expression have value only if the philosopher expresses that to which he is present, only if "lived experience" supports his reflective expression of life.[39]

3. Sociological and Ethical Forms of Co-existing

It is an unmistakable fact that no aspect of human existence, whether on the level of the *cogito, volo* or *ago,* can be understood unless we recognize that other existences are present in it. We are therefore entitled to call every aspect of existence a form of co-existence, a form of "we-being." Thus it is possible to write, e.g. a positive sociology of affective life, in which the sociologist investigates what it concretely means that other existences are present in every personal affective life. Such a study can, of course, be made more detailed; for instance, in a positive sociological work about the affective life of an officer. Even more specifically, one could write a positive sociology about the affective life of an officer in the Russian Army. Adding even more details, it

---

[38] ". . . the condition of all reflectivity is a pre-reflective *cogito*." Sartre, *op. cit.,* pp. 116-117.

[39] Merleau-Ponty, *Phénoménologie de la perception,* pp. II-V.

could become a book about the officer's affective life in the Russian Army before the Revolution. The realm of positive sociology is endless because there is such an infinite variety of sociological forms of "we-being." The same is true with respect to the more encompassing forms of "we-being" in which man is a member of a group. As a physician, a student, a teacher, a churchgoer, an American, sportsman, a football fan, a laborer, a policeman, an artist, a priest or minister, etc., man is a member of a group, and as such his existence is an unbelievably complex *Gestalt* of modes of co-existing. All these forms are studied by positive sociology.

We emphasize these sociological forms of co-existence in order to distinguish them explicitly from other forms of co-existence which we will call "ethical" forms and to which in addition to love and hatred, belongs justice. Unfortunately it is beyond the scope of this work to account for the reason why we want to call love, hatred and justice ethical forms of co-existence. Such an account would require the writing of a phenomenology of man's ethical dimension.[40] However, even without such an explicit phenomenology, it should be evident that the "we-being" contained in being a student, an American, a football fan, a policeman or an artist lies on a different level from the "we-being" of love, hatred and justice. Love, hatred and justice are not *per se* identical with any particular sociological form of co-existence, but appear capable of being realized *within* any sociological form of co-existence. Their reality seems to depend upon other conditions than does the reality of the sociological forms of "we-being." The "we" of hatred can be found within the sociological "we" of marriage, and the "we" of love can be met within the sociological "we" of an army barrack. Both the "we" of justice and that of injustice can be realized within the sociological "we" of a labor order. Sociological and ethical forms of "we-being" do not lie on the same level of co-existence.

Karl Marx failed to see this. According to Marx, work alone makes man a fellow-man. For work is productive only when it is divided, i.e. when it is executed as a common task. The product of work is always a product of common labor. Work establishes and develops society,[41] for

---

[40] Luijpen, *Phenomenology and Atheism,* pp. 235-240.

[41] "The *object* as *being for man,* as *object-being of man,* (is) at the same time *man's being for the other man,* his *human relationship to the other man,* the *social behavior of man toward man.*" Marx-Engels, *Die heilige Familie,* Berlin, 1953, p. 146.

the division of labor means that people actually work for one another. Work is really mutual assistance, as is most manifest in modern industrial labor. Man would simply disappear if he did not work. But exactly the same is expressed when we say that man would simply disappear if people do not work *for one another*. Thus work not only makes man man but also a fellow-man.[42] Co-existence in work also constitutes the connection in mankind's history. The fact that every generation finds working tools produced by past generations means that every man is intimately bound to the past and dependent upon it. Thanks to the central place of work, history is a common history. The bond between men is not guaranteed by all kinds of political and religious nonsense, says Marx, but by the continuity of the means of production.[43]

According to Marx, our co-existence in work still finds itself in the phase of negativity as long as the means of production have not yet been taken over by the proletariat. Brotherhood and peace are, it is true, presaged in the objective reality of the proletariat, for the latter possesses a "universal character through its universal suffering";[44] it is characterized by pure solidarity in suffering. After the revolution, however, this negativity will be changed into positivity. The revolution will produce the integral man, *the* man in the subjective and inter-subjective sense. The "we" of work will then of necessity be the "we" of love, the "we" of brotherhood and peace. Marx is mistaken in this matter, for the "we" of work can also be a hell. That happens when those who are together in a labor order hate one another.

4. Justice as Struggle Against Inhumanity

Even the "fiercest" legal positivist defends the absolutism of positive law only because he is interested in humanity. He sees the full applica-

---

[42] "Precisely in reworking the object world man really proves himself as a *specific being*. This production is his practical specific being." Marx, "zur Kritik der Nationalökonomie," Marx-Engels, *Kleine ökonomische Schriften,* Berlin, 1955, p. 105.

[43] "Accordingly, from the very beginning a materialistic connection manifests itself among man. This connection is conditioned by the needs and the manner of production, and is as old as mankind itself. The connection constantly assumes new forms and thus presents a 'history,' even when there exists no kind of political or religious nonsense to provide an extra bond uniting men." Marx-Engels, *Die deutsche Ideologie,* Berlin, 1953, pp. 26-27.

[44] Marx, "Zur Kritik der Hegelschen Rechtsphilosophie," *Die heilige Familie,* p. 26.

tion of positive law and the authority of the state as the only way of being "just." But, according to the proponents of man's natural rights, it is not only possible but has also frequently happened in fact that precisely this absolutism of the law makes a mockery of justice. What, then, we must ask, is that "humanity" which both the legal positivist and the defender of natural rights want?

Barbarism. The assertion that the humanity of justice must conquer man's injustice is most emphatically made by Hobbes and Spinoza. According to Hobbes, man in his natural state lets himself be wholly guided by egoism. Life is dominated by a paralyzing fear of death because in the natural state of man there exists a war of all against all. Man is a wolf for his fellow-man. There simply cannot be any question of compassion, unselfishness and love. The natural state is identical with barbarism, in which nothing human can bloom.[45]

Spinoza expresses similar thoughts. With respect to "what in man is," he wants neither to laugh nor to cry, neither to blame nor to praise, but only to observe and to understand, just as he also tries to observe and understand what happens in the atmosphere, the origin of heat, cold and thunderstorms.[46] One who assumes this attitude, Spinoza thinks, soon realizes that the various religions teach men to love one another but also that this doctrine is not very effective with respect to man's egoism, lust for power, vengeance, glory, and envy. In church people accept the doctrine of love, but in church they do not have to deal with one another. Where they have to deal with one another, in the market place or in the political arena, where their interests are in conflict, there they let themselves be guided by entirely different tendencies.[47] There they try to destroy one another.

This aspect of being-man has been unfolded in our time in unsurpassed fashion by Sartre in his philosophy of the "stare," the "look." He tries to express in it the essence of man's relationship to his fellowmen.

---

[45] Hobbes, *Leviathan,* p. 82.

[46] "I wanted to investigate the things that pertain to this science (political science) with the same freedom of mind as we have in mathematical matters. Hence I have taken great care not to ridicule, deplore or detest human actions, but to understand them. Thus I have contemplated human affections, such as love, hatred, anger, jealousy, pride, mercy and the other affections, not as vices of human nature, but as properties that belong to it just as heat, cold, storms, thunder etc. belong to the nature of the atmosphere." Spinoza, *Tractatus politicus,* c.I, 4.

[47] Spinoza, *op. cit.,* c.I, 5.

According to Sartre, the other is immediately present to me and accessible in his look. He is essentially "the one who looks at me."[48] There is, however, only one way to accurately describe the other's look: I must describe myself, as looked at, as one who looks through the key hole of a hotel room and who, suddenly hearing footsteps in the corridor followed by silence, feels that he is being stared at.[49]

In my being stared-at by the other, the latter's subjectivity reveals itself, but solely as the destruction of my own subjectivity. Under the other's stare my subjectivity is reduced to the mode of being proper to a thing: for the other as subject, I am an object in his world. As long as there is somebody, no matter who or where, by the very fact that his subjectivity emerges before me, I have an "external side," I have a "nature," I am an "object." "My original Fall is the existence of the other."[50]

As subject I am the origin of my world's meaning. But under the other's stare my subjectivity is lost, so that the world shows itself to me with quite a different face; a face that lies beyond my grip and corresponds to the subjectivity of the other as origin of meaning.[51] As subject I am a project; I am not what I am, and I am what I am not. But under the other's stare the project I am is wholly destroyed; I am what I am, just as a thing is what it is: under the other's stare I *am* indiscrete just as a table is square.[52] As subject I am the free execution of the project I am, an always self-transcending movement. But under the other's stare my transcendency freezes, my freedom grows rigid and loses its fluidity.[53] The other's stare is the death of my subjectivity. Thus the others are my hell: "Hell, that is the others" (*Huis-Clos*).

As is evident from all this, for Sartre there is only one way in which man can save or regain his subjectivity from the threat of destruction by the other's stare. I am an object for the subject who the other is, but I am never an object for an object. To liberate myself from being an

---

[48] Sartre, *op. cit.*, p. 315.

[49] "To seize a look is not to apprehend an object-look in the world (unless that look is directed to us), but is to become conscious of being looked at. The look manifested by the eyes, no matter what kind of eyes they are, is a pure reference to myself." Sartre, *op. cit.*, p. 316.

[50] Sartre, *op. cit.*, p. 321.

[51] "But with the other's look a new organization of the complexes comes to superimpose itself on the first." Sartre, *ibid.*

[52] Sartre, *ibid.*

[53] "Thus, for the other, I have stripped myself of my transcendence." Sartre, *ibid.*

object, I must make a tremendous effort, rise up and try to reduce the other to an object by my stare.[54] For, as soon as the other appears to me as an object, his subjectivity degenerates into being a "property" of the object whose appearance caused me to become his victim. His subjectivity becomes, for instance, a "property" of his eyes, just as being-blue or being-ugly are properties of his eyes. The other now "has" his subjectivity, just as a box "has" an inside. "And in this way I recoup myself."[55]

In this way all concrete human relations are determined in principle for Sartre. Either the other rejects me and reduces me to a thing in his world or I hold his subjectivity in my power by making it an object for me. There are no other possibilities. Hence intersubjectivity, in the sense of a relationship of subject to subject, is unthinkable. Nevertheless, man does not cease to tend to intersubjectivity. Love, masochism, concupiscence, hatred and sadism are attempts to realize the intersubjectivity of which man dreams.[56] All these efforts, however, are in vain.[57] Human relations are wholly encompassed by the twofold possibility of either transcending the other or being transcended by him. The essence of interhuman relationship is not "being with" (Heidegger's *Mitsein*) but conflict.[58]

It is hardly necessary to mention that what Hobbes, Spinoza and Sartre say about our being-man-together-with-others is part and parcel of reality. It is the reality of inhumanity, of barbarism. The term "barbarism" should not be understood in reference to a phase of history that is past in some parts of the world but still fully actual in others. Spinoza

---

[54] "The objectification of the other . . . is a defense of my being which frees me precisely from my being-for-the-other by giving the other a being-for-me." Sartre, *op. cit.*, p. 327.

[55] Sartre, *op. cit.*, p. 349.

[56] Sartre, *op. cit.*, pp. 428-503.

[57] "In vain one would wish for a human 'we' in which the intersubjective totality would become conscious of itself as a unified subjectivity." Sartre, *op. cit.*, p. 501.

[58] "The essence of the relationships between consciousnesses is not being-with but conflict." Sartre, *op. cit.*, p. 502. In his *Critique de la raison dialectique* Sartre does not return to his philosophy of the "look." One even gets the impression that he has dropped it. This is not surprising, for in his *Critique* Sartre defends Marxism, albeit in his own way. Now, it is impossible to believe, with Marxism, in the future universal recognition of man by man and, at the same time, to describe the necessity of rejecting the other's subjectivity on the basis of the philosophy of the "look," as Sartre did in *L'être et le néant*. If conflict is the essence of human relationships, then the universality of subjects is impossible.

says explicitly that his assertions about man can be "read" in man's *essence;*[59] and Sartre holds that conflict is the *essence* of human relations. We will not consider here whether those thinkers have the right to use such strong expressions, although we are inclined to deny it. Yet it appears undeniable to us that barbarism is more than a phase of history that is past in some countries but still fully actual in other parts of the world. What Hobbes, Spinoza and Sartre have "seen" in co-existence is part of the truth. Since a philosophy fails less by what it "says" than by what it "omits," we must now ask ourselves whether barbarism is the whole "truth about man."

The Theory of the "Social Contract." Before examining the question formulated above, we want to point out that, if man is *nothing but* willingness to destroy his fellow-man, it is utterly useless to "explain" the origin of positive law and public authority by means of a so-called "social contract." He who wants to understand the essence of positive law and the rights it "gives" must try to account for the "rightness" of these rights and the normative character of the legal order. One who points only to man's fear of his fellow-men may be able to explain psychologically that enemies visit one another and come to terms because they realize that their mutual interest demands restraint to their enmity. However, the reason why such a "contract" has normative value remains wholly unexplained. In fact, he cannot adduce any reason at all for it.

A certain "ought" can be ascribed to a "social contract" between men only if man himself *is* a certain "ought" with respect to his fellow-men. If contemporary social rights are *nothing but* a contract between master and slave, based upon a mutual dread of a war without quarter between the two parties, or if the Civil Rights Law of 1964 is *nothing but* an agreement between Whites and Negroes, based on the realization that both parties would destroy each other unless they come to an agreement, then neither party would have any reason not to repudiate that agreement as soon as it is in a situation where it no longer needs to fear the other. With respect to the essence of the legal order and its normative character a "social contract" explains nothing because fear offers no explanatory basis for the "ought" proper to the legal order. "I fear" is entirely different from "I ought."

Undoubtedly, it is true that in history fear has often been the *occasion* leading to the conclusion of a "social contract," thus preventing a massacre. But that is not the essential point. The essential point is the

---

[59] Spinoza, *op. cit.,* c.III, 18.

answer to the question why those who fear or no longer have anything to fear "ought" to observe a "social contract" or, in more general terms, a legal order. The endeavor to account for the normative value of the legal order can succeed only if the philosophy of law is able to show that man himself *is* a certain "ought" with respect to his fellow-men.

Victory over Inhumanity According to Sartre. Sartre's book *Critique de la raison dialectique*[60] is one of the most recent works in which the question of humanizing man's relationships is considered. In this book Sartre acts as if he had never written his philosophy of the "stare"[61] and adheres to the Marxist trend of thought, albeit in a way that substantially modifies Marxism.[62] But, as for Marx, so also for Sartre, the humanity of human relationships is something that has to be wrested from inhumanity.

For Sartre, inhumanity is not, at least not primarily, the fact that men act like wolves toward their fellow-men, but consists in the degeneration of personal and free existence as *praxis*. Personal and free existence is the organizing and totalizing of the world, in one word, work.[63] In *praxis* existence finds itself. The degeneration of personal and free existence as *praxis* begins when this *praxis* no longer determines itself from within but is determined from without.

This external determination of personal and free *praxis* occurs when this *praxis* is crossed by another *praxis*. When a farmer works his land, the products of his labor have meaning and signification in function of his own personal and free *praxis*.[64] The product is for him "means of nourishment." As soon, however, as the farmer's existence is crossed by the *praxis* of the merchant, who offers him money for his products, there arises in the farmer's world a meaning that is not determined by the personal and free *praxis* of the farmer himself. When the merchant presents himself, the farmer's product reveals itself as merchandise. The fact that the farmer's *praxis* is crossed by that of the merchant implies that in the world of the farmer a meaning is established which does not

---

[60] Paris, 1960. For a critical explanation and discussion of this work, see Kwant, "Het Marxisme van Sartre," *Tijdschrift v. Philosophie,* vol. XXII (1960), pp. 617-676.

[61] "It is not true that every consciousness aims at the death of the other." Sartre, *Critique de la raison dialectique,* p. 371.

[62] Kwant, *art. cit.,* pp. 673-675.

[63] "Thus, to the extent that the body is function, the function is need and the need is *praxis,* one can say that *human work* (i.e., the original *praxis* by which man produces and reproduces his life) is *wholly* dialectical." Sartre, *op. cit.,* pp. 173-174.

[64] Sartre, *op. cit.,* pp. 360-361.

work in function of the farmer's own personal and free *praxis*. This meaning is characterized by "otherness." Thus it follows that a certain "otherness" also affects the *praxis* itself of the farmer, for through the merchant's *praxis* the farmer becomes a producer of merchandise.[65] Hence the *praxis* of the second existence (that of the merchant) violates the personal and free character of the *praxis* of the first existence (that of the farmer).[66] The other robs me of my freedom. "It is freedom that limits freedom."[67]

Because existences have already crossed and recrossed one another in an infinite variety of ways, every personal and free existence lives in a world that should, strictly speaking, be called a world of meaning-for-nobody. The world as meaning-for-nobody, however, imposes itself compellingly upon our personal and free existence, for man must live in and from the world that is already constituted. His life in the world is a "passive activity" because his activity is imposed upon him by the anonymous meaning of the world. The social facticity of the world, which Sartre calls the practico-inert "field,"[68] determines the character of the personal and free *praxis,* and this means that this freedom is violated. Man produces the machine but, at the same time, the machine produces man.[69] Man produces products but, at the same time, he is the product of his products. The practico-inert field, in which every personal and free *praxis* exists and which is preserved by this personal and free *praxis,* imposes itself upon and encapsules the multitude of men; it makes the producers products.[70] In this way necessity establishes itself

---

[65] "The product really becomes merchandise. But what is important here is that this transformation imposes itself upon the free individual *praxis.*" Sartre, *op. cit.,* p. 360.

[66] "Only the free *praxis* of the other based upon the material conditions can, through reworked materials, limit the efficacy and freedom of my *praxis.*" Sartre, *ibid.*

[67] Sartre, *op. cit.,* p. 361.

[68] "Thus, just as dialectics goes beyond the material conditions while preserving them in its very negation, so materiality, as an inflexible practico-inert necessity, goes beyond each one's free *praxis,* i.e. the many current dialectical relationships, in order to preserve them in itself as the indispensable means to keep its heavy machinery rolling." Sartre, *op. cit.,* p. 376.

[69] "The machine fashions its man exactly to the extent that man fashions a machine. . . . This means that the machine, through a temporal and teleological process, constitutes the one who services it a machine to make the machine function." Sartre, *op. cit.,* p. 269.

[70] "The reign of necessity is that domain . . . in which inorganic materiality closes itself upon the multiplicity of man and transforms the producers into its product." Sartre, *op. cit.,* p. 375.

in man's freedom. The matter man works on becomes a "categorical imperative" of freedom,[71] and man's personal and free *praxis* becomes "passive activity."[72] In this consists the degeneration of personal and free *praxis,* and it is this that is the inhumanity of man.

Although every personal and free *praxis* undergoes the pressure of the practico-inert field, it is not possible to speak of a genuine *social praxis.* Of course, there is a certain sociality insofar as each personal and free *praxis* undergoes the same pressure. But the fact that the same pressure is impressed on everyone does not mean that the many constitute a genuine unity. The unity remains wholly external; the community is "serial," like the "community" of the elements pertaining to the same series.[73] The "community" of travellers waiting for a bus is imposed upon them by the practico-inert field of their existence (the system of public transportation), but in fact it does not amount to more than a plurality and interaction of "solitudes."[74]

The same ideas had already been expressed previously by Heidegger. The latter said that the subject of everyday existence is *"das Man,"* the "they," the anonymous subject.[75] True, existence is characterized by "always being mine" *(Jemeinigkeit),*[76] but in everyday existence this "being mine" degenerates into bowing under the yoke of a nameless tyrant, the anonymous subject. In everydayness it is no longer the "I" that exists, for the others have deprived the "I" of its being. Because it is so inconspicuous and cannot be pointed out, the anonymous subject is a true dictator.[77] The "self" of everyday existence is the self of the "they."[78]

---

[71] Sartre, *op. cit.,* p. 255.

[72] Sartre, *op. cit.,* p. 362.

[73] "To understand collectivity, one should understand that this material object brings about the unity of interpenetration of the individuals, beings-in-the-world-'outside'-themselves, to the extent that it structures their relationships as practical organisms according to the new rule of the 'series.' " Sartre, *op. cit.,* p. 308.

[74] Sartre, *op. cit.,* pp. 308-309.

[75] Heidegger, *Sein und Zeit,* p. 126.

[76] "The being which is an issue for this being in its very being, is in each case mine." Heidegger, *op. cit.,* p. 42.

[77] *Dasein* "itself *is* not; the others have taken away from it its being. . . . Moreover, these others are not definite others. . . . The 'who' is the neuter 'they.' . . . In this inconspicuousness and unobservability the 'they' unfolds its real dictatorship." Heidegger, *op. cit.,* p. 126.

[78] "The self of everyday *Dasein* is the 'they'-self, which we distinguish from the authentic self, i.e. from the self one takes hold of in its ownness." Heidegger, *op. cit.,* p. 129.

The problem of victory over inhumanity, conceived as the degeneration of existence in the subjective and intersubjective sense, is the main
theme of Sartre's book. We would not need to dwell extensively on it
here if Sartre had not given a very special orientation to this rather
general topic. The general question is: How can the freedom of
personal *praxis* be regained from the pressure of the practico-inert field,
and how can authentic intersubjectivity be wrested from the inauthentic
"community" of serial behavior? Strictly speaking, this problem is
concerned with the modern question of gaining or losing one's selfhood
in work;[79] it is not the problem of the victory of humanity over the
inhumanity of the wolf-in-man, which is what we want to discuss here.
However, by giving this general problem a very specific orientation,
Sartre proposes a view that is of importance for our topic. He narrows
the general question down to the problem of how it is possible to
overcome the practico-inert weight of capitalistic and colonial systems.
Obviously, the human dignity of laborers and natives is violated by
capitalistic and colonial systems in a way that is quite different from the
"affront" a public transportation system or a baseball stadium commits
against the personal and free *praxis* of people waiting for a bus or
watching a ball game. The statement that one existence crosses an other
can have any number of meanings. With respect to capitalism and
colonialism, the crossing of existences means inhumanity in the strict
sense of the term. It is victory over this *kind* of inhumanity that
occupies us here. Taken in this sense, the question is answered by
Sartre's theory about the formation of groups.

Sartre speaks of the "group" and the "formation of groups" when he
considers the authentic humanity of the innumerable sociological forms
that co-existence can assume. By "group" he means the authentic
community that transcends the "serial community" and has to be wrested
from it. What Sartre has in mind here is always and exclusively
capitalism and colonialism.[80] The representatives of these systems are
forced by their interests—their factories or plantations—which lie in the
practico-inert field, to deny the humanity of the laborers or the natives.[81]
Hence this denial of that human dignity does not arise from a subjective

---

[79] F. Tellegen, *Zelfwording en zelfverlies in de arbeid*, Delft, 1958.

[80] Kwant, *art. cit.*, pp. 658-659.

[81] Anyone can see that there is question here of a totally different kind of
inhumanity than the "inhumanity" entering the personal and free *praxis* of
human beings who have to stick to a bus schedule, stand in line or submit to
being assigned a sequence number for being served.

mentality or attitude of the capitalist or colonist,[82] but is embodied in the practico-inert field. This field itself *is* "objective violence."[83]

The victims of this objective violence remain free subjects, in spite of the fact that the practico-inert field violates their freedom. Precisely because their freedom remains freedom, they are *a priori* enemies of this field.[84] But the remnant of freedom that they retain contains the possibility of eliminating their alienation by a violent negation.[85]

This elimination comes about when the victims of the practico-inert field refuse to accept their impossible life as parts of a "series."[86] At that moment the "group," in the Sartrian sense, is constituted; "humanity reigns, that is, free relations of human beings among themselves."[87] Following Malraux, Sartre calls this moment "the Apocalypse," the moment when "seriality" dissolves into "merging groups."[88] The formation of the group is the victory of man as common freedom over "seriality." "It is the beginning of humanity."[89] It is impossible, however, that the individual through his personal *praxis* can overcome the violence of the practico-inert field. Victory and liberation can be only the result of a truly common *praxis*. The liberating *praxis* is and remains common, even though it presupposes the mediating personal *praxis* of a "third" party.[90] The storming of the Bastille was the work of the people, but it presupposed the call and the command of a leader with whom every one could identify himself. In such a leader, a *common* freedom is discovered.[91] By the pursuit of a common freedom, by violence, it is possible to overcome the objective violence of the practico-inert field.

---

[82] See footnote 25.

[83] "In other words, violence is present in the very situation for the son of the colonist. A social force produces it. Sons of colonists and sons of Moslems equally are children of the objective violence that defines the system itself as a practico-inert hell." Sartre, *op. cit.,* p. 675.

[84] Sartre, *op. cit.,* pp. 692-693.

[85] Freedom "could indeed constitute itself through the group as the violent negation of their alienation." Sartre, *op. cit.,* p. 693.

[86] "Thus the group constitutes itself as the radical impossibility of the impossible life which threatens 'serial' multiplicity." Sartre, *op. cit.,* p. 377.

[87] Sartre, *ibid.*

[88] "From that very moment, there is something which is neither the group nor the 'series,' but is what Malraux in *L'espoir* calls 'the Apocalypse,' that is, the dissolution of the 'series' into the 'merging group.'" Sartre, *op. cit.,* p. 391.

[89] Sartre, *op. cit.,* p. 453.

[90] Sartre, *op. cit.,* p. 398, *passim.*

[91] "The operation becomes defined for each one as the urgent discovery of a terrible common freedom." Sartre, *op. cit.,* p. 394.

For Sartre, then, the common freedom, exploding from the remnant-**of**-personal freedoms left in spite of the violence of the practico-inert field, is identical with the "merging group," and in the latter authentic community and authentic intersubjectivity realize themselves. The "merging group" liquidates what is practico-inert and "serial" but itself is not practico-inert and "serial"; the "merging group" is the birth of intersubjectivity.

The phenomena considered by Sartre had already been discussed by others before him, of course. No one else, however, had had the idea of identifying what Sartre calls "the merging group" in such a radical fashion with the birth of authentic community and authentic intersubjectivity. Orthodox Marxism conceives the community of the proletarians before the revolution as "pure solidarity," as "universality in negativity" because in the pure wretchedness of alienated labor the particularity of every proletarian is supposed to be wholly without significance. But, according to Sartre, this community is just as "serial" as that of the conspiring capitalists or colonialists. In other words, it is not authentic. How, then, can the "merging group" suddenly be identical with the birth of authentic community and authentic intersubjectivity?

Why would the "merging group's" experience of community be more than what Sartre himself in *Being and Nothingness* calls the experience of the "we"? According to Sartre's theory of the "stare," under the other's look I am as a thing in his world. I can liberate myself only by reducing the other's subjectivity to a thing in my world. Our relationship *is* simply nothing but "conflict." Let us now, with the author of *Being and Nothingness,* assume that a "third" party looks at us. I now experience that I am an object for him, I occur as a thing in a world that is not my own. At the same time, however, I discover that the other with whom I am in conflict undergoes the same alienation of his subjectivity. The other also is an object in the world of the third. But his being-an-object does not simply parallel mine, but I experience that we occur as equal and solidary significations in the world of the third; the third has "us" in his power.[92] In the absence of a third, I fight with the other, but under the stare of a third, I experience that "we" fight. Under the third's stare we *are fighters*. We are ashamed because a third looks at "us."

Certain situations, Sartre tells us in *Being and Nothingness,* very

---

[92] Sartre, *L'être et le néant,* p. 490.

clearly reveal the "us," the "us object." For instance, the class-consciousness and solidarity of laborers with respect to their oppressors is nothing but the experience of being-looked-at by a third, viz., the ruling class. Similarly, the Jews are solidary under the pressure of anti-Semitism, and the citizens of a country under the stare of the occupation army.[93] If the term "love" had any meaning, it could be used for this form of solidarity. To love one another means to hate the same enemy. Authentic intersubjectivity, a genuinely human "we" is impossible.[94] Recalling this Sartrian theory, one wonders how the explosion of common freedom in the common *praxis* of liberation from the practico-inert field can now suddenly and without any explanation be identified with the birth of authentic fraternity in Sartre's *Critique de la raison dialectique.*

There are reasons enough to doubt that identification. Without further explanation it is not clear where the difference lies between Sartre's formation of the group and the mass hallucination with which the nations of Western Europe plunged into World War I. Similarly, Hitler can be regarded as a "third" acting as intermediary in the clear formation of a group. But his mediation did not give birth to fraternity and peace but to the mass psychosis of hatred and unbelievable blindness. Hitler, however, was not the first and most likely will not have been the last man whose mediation ended in mass psychosis.[95] It happens that a "third" assumes the leadership of an entire nation, just as some one does with a class of weak-minded children.[96] Always, however, the group will be represented as the embodiment of fraternity and peace.

Let us now follow the essential line of Sartre's thought to the end. In spite of the fact, he says, that in and through the common action common

---

[93] Sartre, *op. cit.,* pp. 491-494.

[94] See footnote 57.

[95] "True, heroism is always possible in such cases, but it remains isolated and not understood. The rest is only contagion and blindness. Millions and more millions of men are sent to their death, without knowing exactly why and without the slightest advantage resulting from their sacrifice for those who come after them. The ease with which this happens shows with sufficient clarity how much, in spite of the contrary appearances, mankind, as identified with the masses, has regressed in the past centuries. If one scratches away a little of the verbiage covering those totalitarian disciplines, one finds only slavery. This slavery is presented as if it were a virtue because a transition is needed, but soon it will be possible to call it by its own name." E. de Greeff, *Notre destinée et nos instincts,* Paris, 1945, p. 75.

[96] De Greeff, *op. cit.,* p. 79.

freedom is born, the common plan of the definitive liberation does not impose itself through all on each and through each on all.[97] Because the liquidation of "seriality" is a temporal process, going faster in one place and slower in another, there will be conflicts. The remnants of "distinction" contain the danger that totalizing freedom may relapse into "seriality." For this reason the group must also act upon itself in order to bring about in the quickest possible way the liquidation of the remnants of "otherness."[98]

Moreover, the members of the group are only homogeneous from the standpoint of the threat that weighs upon them. As a matter of fact, every member of the group brings along a certain "liability," namely, certain biological and social determinations, and these again imply a danger of relapse into "seriality." In the common action of liberation there will be individuals who lag behind or resist; orders will be given and countermanded, conflicts will arise, and certain leaders will lag behind others.[99] These elements of "otherness" must be liquidated, and those who lag behind or offer resistance must be eliminated. Common freedom will turn against them until the orders passed around are really common orders. Then the homogeneity of fury, courage and resoluteness to battle to the finish will exclude every risk of relapse or cowardice. I will then depend upon others, but they will have given me a guarantee against this dependence.[100] My action then will be a common action, and the common action will be my action. The violence to which the group must resort before the authentic community is established does not contradict this community. First of all, this violence is nothing but the disruption of the original violence of the practico-inert field; secondly, this violence is the self-defense of the group against the attempt to re-establish the violence of the practico-inert field.[101]

---

[97] Sartre, *Critique de la raison dialectique,* p. 426.

[98] "The remnants of otherness are for the freedoms, as totalizing, a danger of 'seriality.' The group must take action against itself to hasten their liquidation." Sartre, *op. cit.,* p. 427.

[99] Sartre, *ibid.*

[100] "I depend upon all, but through freedom as practical recognition I have a *guarantee* against this dependence: they will fight *my* battle with my fierceness." Sartre, *ibid.*

[101] "Actually there is no contradiction. That common freedom draws its violence not only from the violent negation that gave rise to it but also from the reign of necessity which it has overcome but preserved in itself. This reign constantly threatens to re-establish itself as a hypocritical petrifaction, that is, as a relapse into the inertia of the group." Sartre, *op. cit.,* pp. 428-429.

As soon as the *immediate* goal of the common action is reached, the group can "read" its unity in its objectification. The merging group finds its unity in its common action. This unity is not an "ideal" of the action, but simply arises from the action's sweat and blood. The group constitutes itself as means to action, but does not exist "for itself" as a unity. It simply *is* as common *praxis*.[102] When the action is over, the group "reads" its unity in its objectification,[103] for instance, in the ruins of the Bastille. "We" visit those ruins; "we" can be proud of our victory; "we" can look forward with confidence toward the future.[104]

However, the vanquished foe can return! Tomorrow he may appear again. Therefore, the group must be united. To be able to act tomorrow against the enemy, the group must act now with respect to itself. The group must act upon itself in order to be able to last as a group in the future.[105] If the group is to be able to be a means of action *later,* it must *now* make itself its goal.[106] The external pressure disappears as soon as the immediate goal of the common action is attained. No "third" can then be an intermediary and no "orders" or slogans can be effective. As soon as the group can "read" its own unity in its objectification, that unity is in danger.[107] For this reason the group must make itself its goal.

It does so by introducing differentiation and organization into the group. Some members begin to function as sentries, others as spies, while others again man the barricades or stand armed at the windows.[108] The group is a "merging group" at the moment of the common action. At that moment common freedom is born. But, in order that this common freedom be preserved after the attainment of the immediate goal and in order that the group continue to exist, it *must* proceed to organize itself. This means that in a sense the group assumes a contradictory statute,[109] for any form of organization implies a certain inertia.

---

[102] "Although it established itself as a means of action, the group did not put itself up for itself; it put up the objective and *made* itself *praxis*." Sartre, *op. cit.,* p. 434.

[103] "When the total result is attained, the group 'reads' its unity of totalitary synthesis *in its objectification*." Sartre, *op. cit.,* p. 433.

[104] Sartre, *op. cit.,* pp. 434-436.

[105] Sartre, *op. cit.,* p. 434.

[106] Sartre, *op. cit.,* p. 435.

[107] Sartre, *op. cit.,* p. 436.

[108] Sartre, *op. cit.,* pp. 437-438.

[109] ". . . the group . . . demands a contradictory statute because it wants permanence." Sartre, *ibid.*

The group can continue to exist only if a certain inertia—organization—is established in the very heart of the common freedom.[110]   The members of the group henceforth act as functionaries; they execute the common action in a certain separation and dispersion.   This state of affairs will only then not be a relapse into "seriality" when the group imposes itself as a "lived permanence" upon all the bearers of the separate functions.[111]

At this point, the group is in real danger.   Its awareness of common interest could evaporate; individual antagonisms could once more arise; and the powerlessness of "seriality" could re-establish itself.[112]   Individual *praxis* reveals itself as the possibility of division within the group, and this possibility belongs to the structure of the group.[113]   In order to prevent division and betrayal from becoming realities through individual *praxis* within the group, in other words, to safeguard the "lived permanence" of the group in and through individual *praxis,* the members of the group take an oath, whether it be implicitly or explicitly.[114]   "The oath is mediated reciprocity."[115]   Through their implicit or explicit oath, the group makes the necessary transition from its immediate but dangerous unity to a reflective but permanent unity.[116]   As a permanent unity, the group consists of sworn membership.

This oath also justifies the terrorism of the group over itself.[117]   In the absence of external pressure, the group must present itself as pressure upon its members.[118]   To prevent the group from collapse and a return to "seriality," the group must make "absolute violence" reign in its midst.[119]   The oath establishes the statute of violence in community and reciprocity: with its sworn membership the group has compelling power. Each one's freedom demands the violence of all against the betrayal of

---

[110] ". . . this unity must be a kind of inert synthesis in the very heart of freedom."   Sartre, *op. cit.,* p. 438.

[111] "But, precisely because its otherness is real, this character of unity can be given to it only by the group imposing itself as 'lived permanence' across the (functional) dispersion."   Sartre, *ibid.*

[112] Sartre, *op. cit.,* p. 447.

[113] Sartre, *op. cit.,* p. 439.

[114] "When freedom becomes the common *praxis* to give a foundation to the group's permanence by producing its own inertia in 'mediated reciprocity,' this new statute is called 'the oath.' "   Sartre, *ibid.*

[115] Sartre, *ibid.*

[116] "It is a question of showing the necessary transition from a form that is immediate but in danger of dissolution to another form of the group that is reflective and permanent."   Sartre, *ibid.*

[117] Sartre, *op. cit.,* p. 448.

[118] "In the absence of any material pressure, the group must produce itself as pressure upon its members."   Sartre, *ibid.*

[119] Sartre, *ibid.*

anyone.[120] The oath every member takes means: "I demand that I be killed if I become unfaithful."[121] Within the group there exists an absolute reciprocal power of man over man. With its sworn membership the group's ontological statute is that of "common freedom" and the latter is "terrorism." There is no contradiction here, Sartre adds, for *this* terrorism does not divide but unites.[122] "It is the beginning of humanity."[123] To be sworn members is to be brothers. This bond of brotherhood is affirmed even when the group lynches one of its brothers because of his betrayal. The betrayer is not cut off from the group. When the group releases its violence against the culprit, it precisely affirms that he belongs to the group.[124] The bond of brotherhood between those who lynch and the one who is lynched continues to exist. "Nowhere does one find a warmer milieu than in an authoritarian party."[125] The lynching of the traitor means for the lynchers a reaffirmation of the group's birth. Every blow that is struck and every stone that is thrown is a renewal of the previous oath.[126]

All this shows very clearly that Sartre wants to identify the Communist Party and its *praxis* as the bearer and guardian of freedom, brotherhood and peace.[127] Nevertheless, it is true that Sartre deviates greatly from Marxist orthodoxy, especially in his theory of authority. According to orthodox Marxism, the objective being of the proletariat guarantees the coming of the universal man. The proletariat is represented by the Communist Party, and the Party is represented by the Party Secretary. Ultimately, then, one must say that it is the Party Secretary who guarantees the coming of the universal man in the subjective and intersubjective sense. He who opposes the Party Secretary is opposed to the coming of the new man and therefore *per se* wrong. Through its own objectivity history will give rise to the new man, and the Party Secretary guarantees this. Anyone, save orthodox Marxists, realizes that such a view no longer agrees with the reality of history but simply dreams about

---

[120] Sartre, *ibid*.

[121] "To swear is to state as a common individual: I demand that I be killed if I secede (from the group)." Sartre, *op. cit.*, pp. 448-449.

[122] Sartre, *op. cit.*, p. 451.

[123] Sartre, *op. cit.*, p. 453.

[124] "But this exterminating violence remains a bond of fraternity between the one who is lynched and the lynchers, in the sense that the traitor's liquidation is based on the positive affirmation of his belonging to the group." Sartre, *op. cit.*, p. 454.

[125] Sartre, *op. cit.*, p. 456.

[126] Sartre, *op. cit.*, pp. 454-455.

[127] Kwant, *art. cit.*, p. 667.

history. Sartre, of course, cannot be expected to hold such a simplistic view.

According to Sartre, a group has not yet gone all the way when it has made the transition from "merging group" to "surviving group" (*groupe de survivance*), for it still has to make the passage from "surviving group" to "statuary group" (*groupe statuaire*).[128] This second passage requires that the provisional organization and differentiation of the group assume the form of a permanent institutionalization. It will imply a certain inertia within the group as the "locus" of common freedom,[129] but there is no other way to safeguard the common freedom.[130]

Thus, the function of the regulating "third" must also be institutionalized. As long as the group is still in the process of merging, the one acting as "third" is constantly being replaced. Every "third" is immanent to the group because the personal *praxis* of the regulating "third" is the *praxis* of the group.[131] On the other hand, the "third" transcends the group, for the self-awareness of the group comes from his awareness and the group's *praxis* is accomplished by his co-ordination of the common *praxis*.[132] However, he is not yet a leader, a man vested with authority, in the full sense of the term. For this purpose his mediating activity has to be institutionalized. When this happens, authority is born as the specific relationship of one to all.[133] Just as the entire institutional existence of the group is a danger for the common freedom of the group, so also is institutionalized authority a danger for this freedom. Institutionalized authority belongs to the order of the practico-inert realm and to the "serial" domain,[134] but it is indispensable to prevent the disolution of the group.[135] The established leader, the

---

[128] Sartre, *op. cit.,* p. 457.

[129] "The institutionalization . . . possesses a considerable power of inertia . . . over everything and in itself because, by and in its being-inert, it presents itself as essential and describes man as an unessential means for its permanence." Sartre, *op. cit.,* p. 581.

[130] Sartre, *op. cit.,* pp. 581-586.

[131] "As a matter of fact, the group is not *my* object; it is the community structure of my act." Sartre, *op. cit.,* p. 403.

[132] Sartre, *op. cit.,* p. 409.

[133] Sartre, *op. cit.,* p. 587.

[134] "Authority manifests itself in its complete development only on the level of institutions. The latter are needed, that is, there is need for a rebirth of 'seriality' and powerlessness, in order to make Power sacred and secure its right to permanence. In other words, authority is of necessity based on inertia and 'seriality' insofar as it is constituted Power." Sartre, *ibid.*

[135] Sartre, *ibid.*

bearer of authority, is the legal leader and bearer of authority because and insofar as he is immanent to the group.[136] As such he is the "common individual." At the same time, however, he transcends the group, for he is its leader and bearer of authority. This does not mean that all initiatives and plans originate from him, but it does mean that all become the group's practical orientation because they have to pass through him.[137] With respect to legislation, for example, the group gives itself laws through the bearer of its authority.

The transcendency of the institutionalized bearer of authority over the group is both necessary and dangerous. It is necessary for the preservation of the group;[138] it is dangerous because authority implies a loss of freedom for the members of the group, even though they have freely accepted this loss. This loss of freedom is for each member a kind of "accepted mutilation."[139] However, the will of the bearer of authority is and remains an "individual will" and the *praxis* of this man is and remains the *praxis* of *this* individual man with *his* personal qualities, *his* diseases, *his* age, *his* physiognomy. Thus it can happen that his freedom no longer serves the common freedom, that his terrorism, which ought to be a brotherhood terrorism, degenerates into an "ordinary" terrorism, and that in and through his function he does not lead the group to integration but to disintegration.[140]

It sounds as if Sartre wants to say: the Secretary of the Communist Party does not guarantee the coming of the universal man in the subjective and intersubjective sense. As a matter of fact, Sartre greatly disagrees with the way Communism has developed. He considers it necessary to break through the bureaucracy and centralization and to introduce more democratic relationships. For Sartre, this means that the leader gradually gives up his "group monopoly."[141]

According to Sartre, then, there is no guarantee that humanity will be

---

[136] Sartre, *op. cit.,* p. 589.

[137] "This does not mean that all practical initiatives, all projects of reorganization, all inventions and discoveries must draw their origin from the sovereign. But it does mean that they must pass through him, be re-interiorized by him and be presented by him to the group as its new practical orientation." Sartre, *op. cit.,* p. 591.

[138] Sartre, *op. cit.,* pp. 590-598.

[139] Sartre, *op. cit.,* pp. 456, 592-593.

[140] Sartre, *op. cit.,* pp. 597-598.

[141] "The internal contradictions of the socialist world, despite the enormous progress that has been accomplished, show forth the objective need for less bureaucracy, more decentralization and democratization. By the last-named term I mean that the sovereign must gradually abandon the group's monopoly." Sartre, *op. cit.,* p. 629.

victorious over inhumanity. The "fraternal terrorism" of one man over all can degenerate into an "ordinary terrorism"; he himself can be inhuman. This is the reason why the democracies of the West have gone a different way, the way of the democratic development of the legal order. However, as we pointed out in speaking of the claims made by legal positivism, even positive law does not *guarantee* humanity—no more than the Secretary of the Communist Party.

Summary. Reflection on the theories of Hobbes, Spinoza and Sartre's *Being and Nothingness,* on the one hand, and those of Marx and Sartre's *Critique de la raison dialectique,* on the other, leads us to the conclusion that inhumanity consists in man's direct or indirect violation of the human dignity of his fellow-man. This violation is indirect when the objective structures of society in the economic, social and political realm, simply by being what they are, oppress man's subjectivity. They can oppress man because he is not an isolated subject but a subject-in-the-world. Man as subject is involved in the world, including its economic, social and political structures. These structures can be such that, by the mere fact of their existence, they simply eliminate many existent subjects. On the other hand, the objectivity of these structures should not be conceived as if they were "in themselves," separate from man. They did not come into being by the same kind of process that gives rise to geological layers or rain storms, nor can they be directly connected with the working of divine Providence. Ultimately, those structures are *made* structures; they are made by *man* and embody his intentions in the world. If, then, their mere "being there" does violence to many subjects, they constitute a violation of *man* by his *fellow-man,* albeit in an indirect way. However, this is not the last word to be said about man's being-man-together-with-his-fellow-men.

5. *The Origin of Rights and the Legal Order*

According to Sartre, humanity originates as common freedom at the moment when a group no longer tolerates its oppression by the practico-inert field and in common concert overthrows the established order. At the same time, there arise ethical obligations with respect to the common freedom, and these are implicitly or explicitly recognized in the oath. The use of violence also is made legitimate in this way.

We want to abstract here from the fact that Sartre identifies the moment of humanity's birth with that at which a group begins to resist capitalism or colonialism. We likewise abstract from his identification of humanity with the relationships existing in the Communist Party. Both these identifications make Sartre's theories irresponsibly one-sided. Nevertheless, there are in his theories two points that seem very important to us.

"A Certain Real and Practical Bond Between Freedoms." The first of these points is that, according to Sartre, the birth of humanity takes place at a *historical* moment. The second is that the use of force cannot be justified unless it is based upon "a certain real and practical bond between freedoms."[142]

Abstracting from the Sartrean context, no one can say that the inhumanity of barbarism is the final word with respect to human relations. At a given moment in the history of a society, through the intermediary of an "ethical genius," there arises a "vision" of man's essence which, *as a matter of principle,* breaks through barbarism or inhumanity, conceived as the execution of man's willingness to destroy the subjectivity of his fellow-man. No such principle is involved when man, involved in a war of all against all, "sees" that such a war is bound to terminate in the total destruction of "society" and therefore attempts to stop barbarism by means of a "social contract." The reason why such a "contract" does not break through barbarism is that no one would have any motive *not* to terminate that "contract" as soon as he thinks that he is powerful enough to do so without running any risks.

No "ethical genius" is needed to see that a social contract sometimes *de facto* establishes humanity. But a break through inhumanity is secured *as a matter of principle* when an "ethical genius" at a given moment of history "sees" man's essence as destined for the other, a destiny which man brings to execution by his "yes" to the other's subjectivity. The "ethical genius" discovers a "certain real and practical bond between freedoms" which belongs to the essence of existence as co-existence. Man's being discloses itself to the "ethical genius" as a "having to be in the world for the other," and this disclosure imposes

---

[142] "What counts is that no 'confiscation of violence' (seizure of power) makes sense unless this violence is not from the outset a certain real and practical bond between freedoms within the context of the common action. In other words, that violence must be the kind of action which the sworn group exercises upon itself insofar as this action is re-invented, exercised and accepted by all." Sartre, *op. cit.,* p. 448.

itself upon man with a binding force. For the subject-as-*cogito* is a "light" for himself and this "light" is an objective "light," i.e., it does not permit to deny that which appears in this "light."[143] Bound by the objective "light" of his subjectivity-as-*cogito,* man "sees," through the intermediary of an "ethical genius," his own essence as destined for the other. Man himself *is* a certain "ought" with respect to his fellow-man. An age-old tradition calls the execution of this "ought" "love" and it understands this love as the acceptance, the willing, supporting and fostering of the other's subjectivity, selfhood and freedom.[144]

Thus man appears to himself as a particularly paradoxical reality. On the one hand, he is a willingness to destroy the other's subjectivity, and acting according to this willingness is called "hatred" or "being a wolf for the other." On the other, he experiences himself as destined for the other, and acting according to this destiny is called "love." Experiencing himself both as a wolf toward his fellow-man and as destined for the other, man, through the intermediary of an "ethical genius," "sees" that the minimum demand contained in his being destined for the other consists in not permitting the "wolf" in his existence to devour his other destiny.

The *minimum* of the demand of love, the demand which human existence as co-existence itself *is,* can thus be formulated as the most fundamental right of the other. The other's right is the minimum of my "yes" to his subjectivity, a "yes" called for by my existence as a "having to be for the other," as an "ought" on the level of co-existence. And this "call" is not something coming from without but is I myself. Thus the other's right is a "natural right," better still, an "essential right," for it is implied in the "nature," the "essence" of co-existence. For the execution of his "having to be for the other" belongs to that through

---

[143] "In the heart and at the root of moral choice there exists a constant and immovable value-aim which we need not invent or create in its entirety but must accept and make our own. This value-aim is the recognition of the dignity of the human person and of the values constituting man's personality." Dondeyne, "Les problèmes soulevés par l'athéisme existentialiste," *Sapientia Aquinatis,* Rome, 1955, p. 468.

[144] ". . . love is the will to promote. The 'I' who loves wants above all the existence of the 'you,' and it wants also the autonomous development of this 'you.'" Nédoncelle, *Vers une philosophie de l'amour,* p. 11. "To love is to will the other as a subject." Madinier, *Conscience et amour,* p. 95. "To love is to be interested in what the other is as an 'I' and in his 'for himself'; it is to endeavor to establish him in his intimacy, to will him as freedom and a principle of initiative." Madinier, *op. cit.,* p. 127. See also Luijpen, *Existential Phenomenology,* Pittsburgh, 5th impr., 1965, pp. 240 ff.

which man is authentically man, hence to his "nature" or "essence." In a certain sense he is not a man if he does not execute it, namely, in the sense that he is not a man *on the level of his authenticity.*

Because the other is an embodied subject in the world, his "natural" right has two aspects. On the one hand, it is a "subjective" title to do something or to have something, insofar as his subjectivity occurs as the correlate of my minimal "yes"-to-his-subjectivity, called for by the essence of my existence as co-existence. On the other hand, the other's "natural" right has an "objective" side because the subject who the other is as intentional subject occurs only as immersed in the body and involved in the world. As correlates of his right as a subjective title, his body and (a part of) his world are "his," his "right."[145]

We are deeply aware of the fact that the content of the preceding paragraphs is an abomination for the legal positivist. Practically every sentence in them will have to be discussed in greater detail, but we offer no apologies for their over-all content. The ire of the legal positivist is caused by the seeming surrender of everything he calls "law" and "order" to the "subjectivism and relativism" of man's personal inspirations, and all of it with an appeal to love! This so-called subjectivism and relativism will be discussed later in an extensive way; for the present, let us simply emphasize that the above-explained view does indeed do away with the objectivism and absolutism of legal positivism. Positivism identifies justice with the willingness to act as ordered by positive law. Thus it simply *cannot* accept that justice would ever oblige man to overthrow the legal order. At the same time, positivism cannot at all justify the "ought" it ascribes to the legal order. Such an explanation is possible only if man *himself* can be called a certain "ought" with respect to his fellow-man.

In the preceding paragraphs we have indicated this "ought." The legal order is normative because it participates in, and is the embodiment of, the minimum of the "having to be for the other" which existence as co-existence is. If, however, the legal order itself does violence to the subject, then this order is unjust precisely on this ground, and man is, by virtue of the minimum demand of love, i.e. justice, obliged eventually to

---

[145] We avoid again the term "objective right" because jurists use it in a different sense than the one we intend here. Unfortunately, there is no possibility of avoiding the term "subjective right." It should be obvious, however, that we do not use this term here to indicate the "titles" which the legal order attributes to those who are subject to it. Cf. J. van Kan, *Inleiding tot de rechtswetenschap,* 8th ed., Haarlem, 1951, pp. 52, 172-182.

overthrow this legal order. Thus justice cannot be identified with willingness to observe the legal order. But justice is the willingness to respect rights, conceived as the subjective and objective correlates of the minimum contained in the "yes" of my existence to the existence of the other.

The "we" of justice, understood as an ethical form of co-existence and as the fundamental break through barbarism, i.e. as humanity, evidently cannot be identified with any sociological form of co-existence. Neither the "we" of the proletariat as conceived by Marx nor the "we" of the "merging group" in the spirit of Sartre guarantee humanity. Humanity, as the fundamental break through barbarism is born from man's "yes" to his fellow-man. But no kind of "guarantee" is connected with this birth.

Excursus: Some Objections. Before we examine the preceding ideas in greater detail, it may be useful to present, as far as possible, certain objections. First of all, we want to stress that the use of the term *natural* law or *natural* right does not at all imply as relapse into "thinglike" ideas with respect to the rights underlying the legal order. "Nature" and "natural" here mean "essence" and "essential." Natural rights are rights implied in the truth, as unconcealedness, of the *essence* of co-existence. The unconcealedness of this essence contains the demand of justice, or rather, this demand *is* the unconcealedness of the minimum of man's "having to be for the other." Precisely because this demand is unconcealed, it is possible to give expression to it. The co-existent subject, as an "understanding of being," is, as it were, the promulgating authority of the "having to be" which this subject himself is. In this sense the co-existent subject, as "understanding of being," is the "natural" *law*. As is evident, when matters are expressed in this fashion, in terms of subjectivity and intersubjectivity, of existence and co-existence, there is nothing that should bring to mind the old, naturalistic and "thinglike" view of natural rights and the natural law.

Secondly, let us add that all those are right who think that they must draw attention to the fact that our theory of justice, rights and law does not speak about the same matters which the positive sciences of law discuss. However, they go too far when they attribute this "failure" to a "lack of phenomenology," which prevents us from grasping the true character of the juridical phenomenon, and add that hardly anything else could be expected when someone who is not a jurist wants to write about the "law." Such a person may be well versed in phenomenology but his lack of familiarity with the legal profession dooms his phenomenology of the law to failure. For, obviously, in a phenomenology of the law, the jurist should be able to recognize himself, his profession and his "law."

It seems evident to us that in this objection the term "law" is taken in the sense of "positive law" and the rights flowing from it. Hence, as admitted above, our theory of right, justice and law obviously does not speak about the same matters as are discussed by the positive sciences of law. However, it is wrong to think that a phenomenology of the law is *bound* to speak about what jurists call "rights" and "law" and that the failure to do this reveals a "lack of phenomenology." The philosophy of law, which we equate with the phenomenology of law because we consider phenomenology not merely as a method but as philosophy itself, does not investigate, at least not primarily, what the nature of the juridical phenomenon in the positive sense is, but asks what the essence of man's natural right, understood as the justifying ground and critical norm of the legal order, is. Hence there is no reason for addressing to a phenomenology the reproach that it does not sufficiently or at least not primarily consider positive law, for the justifying ground and critical norm of positive law itself does not have the character of a positive law.

Finally, it may be useful to point out that when the philosophy of law speaks of subjective right as a "title," this term should not be understood in the same way as in the positive sciences of law, viz., as a title conferred upon someone by positive law. The philosophy of law is concerned with rights as correlates of justice, that is, with the justifying ground and the critical norm of the legal order. The demands of justice can, but are not of necessity, embodied in the legal order as subjective rights. When *de facto* such demands are not embodied in the legal order, one can say, for example, that in a society all members have a *right* to voting *rights,* even if positive law deprives certain persons of this right, of their subjective title in the juridical sense.[146]

Werner Maihofer's Theory of Positive Law. This may be the proper place to discuss Werner Maihofer's theory about the character of positive law.[147] Maihofer wants to follow the existential and phenomenolog-

---

[146] Van Kan, *op. cit.,* pp. 177-178.
[147] Maihofer, *Recht und Sein,* Frankfurt a.M., 1954.

ical way of thinking, but holds the view that this way of thinking cannot come to a correct understanding of positive law as long as it continues to place such a heavy emphasis on "selfhood" as is done by Heidegger, Jaspers and Sartre.[148]   If the fundamental law of human existence is nothing but "Become thyself," then belonging to a legal order with its normative, generalizing and schematizing signification can only pertain to "falling into the anonymity of the impersonal 'they'" (*Verfallenheit an das Man*).   The place of the legal order then lies in the inauthenticity of the masses.[149]   Authentic existence, according to Maihofer's conception of the philosophy of existence, implies a revolt against the "general."   Unlike Kant, the philosophy of existence cannot even ascribe to positive law the value of being a "condition for the possibility of freedom."   According to Maihofer, the philosophy of existence can conceive positive law only as an "obstacle to existential freedom."[150]   Existence has to liberate itself from this obstacle before it can attain the level of authenticity.

Maihofer, however, thinks that the philosophy of existence itself contains the principle that can lead to a more differentiating way of speaking about the authenticity of existence.   The call "Become thyself" contains, if it is thought through to its end, a call "to become common";[151] and Maihofer is of the opinion that one can find this implication in Heidegger, Jaspers and Sartre.[152]   He wants to make this implication explicit.

After a fairly long explanation of implicit knowing as the cradle of all explicit knowledge of what is right,[153] in which he closely follows

---

[148] Maihofer, *op. cit.*, pp. 17-23.

[149] "Thus we find that in Heidegger both the 'external' and the 'inner' *world of right* is relegated from the realm of authentic being in the world to that of 'deficiency,' of 'falling away to the "they".' . . . Its field is the inauthenticity of the mass's being."   Maihofer, *op. cit.*, p. 18.

[150] Maihofer, *op. cit.*, p. 22.

[151] "The more extreme this way of thinking becomes as a unique explanation of existence from self-being, the clearer also it becomes, if one draws the last consequences of this originally ontological thesis , . . . that the call 'Become thyself,' with its purely individualistic radicalism, meets with its paradoxical counter-call "Become common."   This call is a demand addressed to the self which takes away from the self the right to set its own laws according to its own norms and directs it to subject the development of its being to common criteria." Maihofer, *op. cit.*, pp. 23-24.

[152] Maihofer, *op. cit.*, pp. 24-34.

[153] Maihofer, *op. cit.*, pp. 65-73.

Heidegger[154] and greatly emphasizes the necessity of the phenomenological reduction,[155] Maihofer begins his explicitation of existence as "self-being" (*Selbstsein*).[156]

Existence as self-being understands and grasps everything which it encounters in its being-in-the-world as a means to realize itself. It does so on the twofold level of the environmental world of things (*Umwelt*) and the milieu world of persons (*Mitwelt*).[157] Involved in the world of nature and of culture, existence as self-being orders everything it encounters to itself and to ends that are strictly its own. It constitutes the world as radically its own personal living space, without which it would have no self-being at all.[158] Involved in the milieu world of persons, existence of self-being encounters other human beings, not as if those persons were things (*Personendinge*) with theoretically observable properties, but as being "what they do."[159] In this sense existence as self-being has "to do" with them. Because existence as self-being has "to do" with the others insofar as these others are what they *do,* existence always has "to do" with *this* particular somebody, and the latter is not the anonymous "they" (*das Man*) of whom Heidegger speaks.[160] All others, with whom existence has nothing "to do," although they are in the world, are not present in the world of the existence realizing itself as self-being. Hence the relations with others are what they are because they have their center in the wholly unique originality of existence as self-being. My neighbor who happens to be a judge is for me not a judge but only a neighbor. Unlike the things in my world, however, he

---

[154] "In *Being and Time* with its 'preparatory fundamental analysis of *Dasein*' Heidegger takes this way to explicitate being (*Dasein*) with regard to its being. One's own *Dasein* is, as it were, 'questioned about its being.' It is asked about the understanding of meaning which, prior to any theoretical reflection, it has of its *Da-sein*. That is, *Dasein* is asked about its 'pre-ontological' understanding of being in which, prior to any 'explicit' ontology, it already 'finds itself' in its everyday being and which it merely has to show forth, in the genuine sense of phenomenology, as something 'showing-itself-to-it' in its phenomenal givenness." Maihofer, *op. cit.*, p. 73.

[155] Maihofer, *op. cit.*, pp. 73-78.

[156] Maihofer, *op. cit.*, pp. 83-101.

[157] Maihofer, *op. cit.*, p. 83.

[158] "But without such an 'own-ec-sistence,' which can be accomplished as 'insistence' in his *own world,* the person as individual *is* not '*da*'; he has as *self,* to that extent, no *Da-sein* in the world." Maihofer, *op. cit.*, p. 89.

[159] Maihofer, *op. cit.*, p. 91.

[160] Maihofer, *ibid.*, note 40.

appears to me not as a means to my self-realization but as a goal in himself and as the center of his own autonomous world.[161]

All this does not mean that self-love is the supreme law of existence as self-being. With a reference to Romano Guardini, Maihofer argues that self-being finds its authenticity only in the self-denial of loving one's neighbor. To exist as this individual person is a giving and taking, egoism and altruism. Self-being, then, is not being selfish but being unique, unrepeatable and incomparable.[162] Man has been "thrown" into this horrible paradox: on the one hand, he is already wholly predestined for an "ownness" that is totally his own; on the other, his future is wholly undetermined and can be understood and grasped by no one but man *himself*. Such is the absolute freedom in which man as this individual person is placed. The accomplishment of his ownmost being-himself is what man wants in the finitude of his historicity. In this accomplishment lies his true happiness, whenever he succeeds in harmonizing life with the demands of the authenticity of self-being that lie at the basis of any "liberal world view."[163]

Accordingly, Maihofer demands room for the free self-development of the individual person prior to any regulations made by legal authority. This room is the domain of the "natural state" of the individual person, and this state is the basis of his inalienable right to his own property and relationships which, from the legal standpoint, are expressed in property law and personal law. That there is question here of a "natural state" does not imply that this state will be eliminated by the "citizen state" (*status civilis*) of a more civilized phase of history; on the contrary, precisely under the heteronomous regulations of the "citizen state" the "natural state" unmistakably continues to exist. In this light all legal and state regulations appear as regulations to protect the self-being of the individual person and his free self-realization against all restrictions "from without."[164]

In this way, however, any regulation becomes a big problem. For self-being's uniqueness, unrepeatability and incomparability are so radical

---

[161] Maihofer, *op. cit.*, p. 92.

[162] "Hence *self-being* is not simply *being-selfish*, but *Dasein*'s *uniqueness* and *matchlessness, understood and taken up* (this *Dasein* is in every case mine). It is a *being* in which we, 'in ourselves' as well as 'outside ourselves,' as in something unique, unrepeatable and incomparable, have 'become.'" Maihofer, *op. cit.*, p. 95.

[163] Maihofer, *op. cit.*, pp. 95-96.

[164] Maihofer, *op. cit.*, pp. 97-98.

that the question must be asked how it is at all possible to place the person under regulations. Regulations presuppose similarity, but none can be found in authentic self-being.[165] In this way Maihofer comes to the provisional conclusion that all "own" rights in the autonomous sphere of authentic self-being must be understood as the "hero's right of exception"; this right he calls "existential natural right."[166]

Maihofer explicitly acknowledges that with this theory he comes very close to the idea of "man is a wolf for man" as developed by Hobbes. He recognizes that he would have to arrive at the extreme positions of anarchism and autarkism if there were nothing other in man than the "natural state" of the uniqueness of existence as self-being. However, there is more in man. There is also the "citizen state" of existence as "being-as" (*Alssein*), in which man is not unique but "one among the others." Existence is equiprimordially self-being and "being-as."[167] Let us explain this matter.

Existence realizes itself in and through the exteriorization of self-being. In this exteriorization existence dwells not only in a strictly personal world of its own, in which it is autonomously its own law, but also a common world, in which it is placed under the heteronomous law of already established social frames.[168] For example, *as* mother, a woman has a certain relationship to her child which she herself has not invented or determined; on the contrary, she is determined by it. The same applies when an existence realizes itself *as* buyer, *as* renter, *as* judge, *as* father, *as* traveller, *as* conductor, *as* merchant, etc. Independently of this "being-as," that is, outside the roles it plays, an existence *cannot at all* realize itself as self-being. Hence "being-as" is not foreign to self-being, but existence is equiprimordially both. Now, existence as "being-as" makes me "one among the others," one who can be compared to the others. It therefore means that, in spite of my uniqueness, there is an "eternal return of the same,"[169] because I agree as conductor with

---

[165] "How could an incomparable, unique and unrepeatable being stand together with others in a *single* regulative order? For, as 'orientation,' order presupposes that there is comparability, the steady repetition of the similar, in other words, similarity." Maihofer, *op. cit.,* p. 98.

[166] "All *'own'* right, therefore, becomes in the autonomous sphere of the self the hero's right of 'exception'; it becomes a 'subjective' *right of Dasein,* an *existential natural right* originating from the uniqueness and matchlessness of the self." Maihofer, *ibid.*

[167] Maihofer, *op. cit.,* pp. 98-101.

[168] Maihofer, *op. cit.,* pp. 101-105.

[169] Maihofer, *op. cit.,* p. 105.

conductors, as physician with physicians, as merchant with merchants, etc. In and through "being-as," in and through the roles existence plays, self-being is subject to and determined by social frames and norms which existence itself has not made and which it cannot arbitrarily modify. We constantly use expressions showing that we acknowledge this point; for example, when we say: *"As* a physician, *as* a traveller, *as* a renter *one* ought to do this or that." This "one" does not pertain to the "fallen state" of existence but to the "authentic 'they' "[170] because without this "they" there could be no self-being at all.

According to Maihofer, existence's "being-as" is the foundation of "institutional natural law," contrary to the "existential natural law" which is based upon self-being.[171] "Institutional natural law" contains those rules which, on the basis of the actual social relationships, have been made legal rules.[172] But these actual relationships have several aspects. For instance, as a traveller I am "a traveller *with* travellers" and also "a traveller *to* the conductor"; as father I am "a father *with* fathers" and also "father *to* my son." Thus my "being-as" implies both "equal relations with others" and "unequal relations to others." Accordingly, the social structure reveals both a "being ordered to" and a "being ordered as equal": the former is the basis of distributive justice and the latter that of commutative justice.[173]

Critique. We have the impression that Maihofer's theories omit precisely that which makes it possible to justify the "ought" of rights. To

---

[170] "Do not law and order (*das Rechtliche*) aim precisely at the 'ownness' of this *'being-as,'* the shaping and functioning of being as buyer, renter, possessor, owner—this being that can be compared with others and has not yet been seized by 'individuality'? Do law and order perhaps aim 'fundamentally' not at man as an individual person but as the *social person* which he *also* is? This would not imply a mere *'Dasein* as a mass,' a legal regulation 'of dams locking man up in inauthenticity,' in the 'lost condition of the "they".' Is there not also an 'authentic "they",' an 'authentic' (*eigentlich*) way of being father, mother, husband, son, citizen, and do we not mean this way when we say: 'as . . . , they must do this'? Is this *'they'* really a form of everyday *Dasein's* fallenness?" Maihofer, *op. cit.,* p. 33.

[171] Maihofer, *op. cit.,* pp. 117-122.

[172] "In this way law and order (*das Recht*) become at the same time also the condition making *self-being in being-as* possible. (It makes self-being possible) not merely in the sense of that *'existential natural rights'* of the exception, but in the sense of an *'institutional natural right'* of the rule. This rule lays down and constructs in the form of a legal order and in its present historical 'ownness,' the being of the social forms required by the 'nature of the matter' and indicated by the meaningful interconnection of the social world." Maihofer, *op. cit.,* p. 121.

[173] Maihofer, *op. cit.,* pp. 119-121.

give a foundation to "existential natural law," Maihofer emphasizes the
self-being of existence so much that he has to acknowledge how close he
is to Hobbes' idea of man as a wolf toward man.[174] The reason why he
does not unreservedly adhere to Hobbes' idea does not lie in his reflection
upon self-being itself but in something else, namely, "being-as." Self-
being resists any regulation "from without" and could lead to anarchism
and autarkism. Maihofer calls anarchism and autarkism extremes that
cannot be accepted, but the reason why he rejects them lies in something
other than self-being. But if that is the case, one wonders why such a
self-being could demand as a *right* the realization and fulfilment of its
self-being. By itself, self-being is anarchist and autarkist. But why
does an existence have the "right" to the fulfilment of the demands of
this anarchism and autarkism? The individualistic character of Maihofer's thinking makes it impossible for him to recognize the true
character of natural rights.[175] This character can be recognized only in
the perspective of intersubjectivity as "having to be."

What Maihofer calls "institutional natural law" is simply positive
law. He uses the term "natural law" because positive law is based upon
the "nature" of existence as "being-as." According to Maihofer, "being-
as" modifies the anarchism and autarkism of self-being. Through "being-as," an existence is integrated into social frames which are not its
own creation. These frames govern the existence as heteronomous laws,
but it is a natural demand of existence as "being-as" to submit to these
heteronomous laws because self-being cannot at all realize itself without
"being-as." Existence is a "self-being in 'being-as.' "[176] In and through
positive law the social relationships based upon "being-as" are made to be
relationships of rights.

Again, however, we must ask whether this theory does not fail to pay
attention to the "ought" of positive law. For, what exactly does it mean
that in and through positive law actual relationships are made to be
relationships of rights? On what principle is this "making" based? If
positive law simply formulates the actual state of social relationships,
there is no reason to accept that these relationships have now suddenly
become relationships of rights. Positive law is a right only when it states
what those relationships *ought* to be. But it can do so only on the
ground of a principle. This principle is the "ought" demanded by
intersubjectivity itself. On the basis of this principle positive law can

---

[174] Maihofer, *op. cit.,* p. 100.
[175] Fechner, *Rechtsphilosophie,* p. 231, note 24.
[176] Maihofer, *op. cit.,* p. 121.

state that in some cases the actual relationships are what they ought to be and that in others they are not what they ought to be. One looks in vain for such a principle in Maihofer. He does not speak of the "ought" of positive law.

Finally, Maihofer's theory of law and right leaves us with the impression that "existential natural law" and "institutional natural law" lie side by side without being sufficiently "digested" in this theory. Maihofer himself seems to realize this, for at the end of his book a footnote proclaims the hope that through the existential dialectics of self-being and "being-as" the level may have been reached on which the ontological question of the natural law "as such" can be raised.[177]

The Mediation of the "Ethical Genius." With respect to the "definition" of the natural law, there remain several points demanding an explicit consideration. For instance, we have said nothing about the necessity of adding a legal order to what is right or about the fact that the minimum demanded by love constantly varies its limits because love itself knows no limits. Methodologically, however, it seems preferable to begin with the question what is meant by the "objectivity" of rights.

In its most current sense "objective" means "verifiable by anyone." It is in this sense that the term is used by the positive sciences. All those who devote themselves to the positive sciences, especially those of nature, endeavor to present their truth in such a way that anyone who wants to trace their path and use their technical language can control their statements. Because they are highly successful in this endeavor, the results of the research made by the positive sciences enjoy an enviable unanimity.

The philosopher of law must be resigned to the fact that the results of his labor remain "subjective" *in this sense*. Otherwise he would deprive his philosophy of everything that makes it worth-while to have a philosophy of law. Nevertheless, the authentic philosopher of law will claim that natural rights and duties are "objective." He cannot agree at all with anyone who denies this "objectivity." In his view, *everyone must* admit the "demands of the natural law" because they are "objective." What, then is the meaning of this term?

---

[177] "It leads . . . to a twofold natural-law foundation of law and order (*Recht*) : the existential natural right of the exception (of self-being) and the institutional natural right of the rule (of being-as). Because of the polarity of this 'subjective' and 'objective' natural right, it is perhaps possible to reach by way of them the level on which the ontological question of the natural law 'as such' can be raised." Maihofer, *op. cit.*, p. 125, note 128.

"Objective" means "real." Within this context all philosophers of law agree on this point, but only because the statement does not yet say anything. As soon as it is made to say anything, as soon as the sense of the term "real" is made explicit, this agreement becomes a disagreement.

As we mentioned, in the Thomistic conception of the natural law the objectivity and reality of natural rights and duties is represented as a "being in itself," as being in isolation from the subject-as-*cogito*. Even if the natural rights and duties would not impose themselves on any subject-as-*cogito,* they would still "be"—more or less as the rules of chess would "be" even if chess pieces had never been made and there were no chess players. We rejected this view of objectivity and reality as being objectivistic. For objectivism, "objective" reality is objective-for-no-body. But objective reality can only be spoken as of objective for somebody. What is objective is objective-for-a-subject. Objectivism, however, very strongly emphasizes one point, viz., that what is objective-for-a-subject cannot be left to the arbitrariness of the subject. The subject is not without *bonds.*

That there are bonds for the subject cannot be denied. The subject is tied to objective reality as "that which shows itself, the manifest."[178] That which discloses itself to the subject-as-*cogito* must be admitted. To admit what discloses itself is "release,"[179] which excludes arbitrariness in any form.[180] The subject does not produce the real;[181] he does not have power over it but is only its "shepherd."[182] Thus thinking of and giving expression to the real and objective is a listening to what *is,*[183] for thinking is bound by what *is.*[184] However, that which *is* cannot be isolated from the encounter of the subject with that which *is.*[185] What is, "is" not "in itself" but is-for-the-subject. To think of and give expression to the real and the objective is to pay attention to that which is,

---

[178] Heidegger, *Sein und Zeit,* p. 28.

[179] ". . . we surmise that the essence of thinking is 'release' (*Gelassenheit*)." Heidegger, *Gelassenheit,* Pfullingen, 1959, p. 54.

[180] "What 'being' is we are told from this, the self-disclosure, and as this. We cannot arbitrarily determine from within us what 'being' is and then lay it down in authoritative statements." Heidegger, *Der Satz vom Grund,* Pfullingen, 1957, p. 121.

[181] Heidegger, *Identität und Differenz,* Pfullingen, 1957, p. 23.

[182] Heidegger, *Ueber den Humanismus,* p. 19.

[183] Heidegger, *Was ist Metaphysik?,* Frankfurt a.M., 1955, p. 13.

[184] "Thinking is as thinking in the ad-vent of being bound to being as ad-vent." Heidegger, *Ueber den Humanismus,* p. 46.

[185] "Being becomes present and lasts only as long as through its appeal it draws near to man. For it is man alone who, in his openness to being, lets being as presence come near him." Heidegger, *Identität and Differenz,* p. 23.

which is present, discloses and reveals itself.[186]　It is "dwelling in," being "present to," "familiar with" being as that which "concerns" man.[187] The objective, the real being is the "true" as that which is unconcealed for the subject.　The being-true of what is "takes place" in the existent subject-as-*cogito:* this subject is the "place" where the "event" of truth occurs.[188]　The "occurrence" of the truth of being is equiprimordially the self-unfolding, the "self coming to be," the self-perfection of man's essence.[189]　The fact that the truth of being "speaks" to man and gives him something "to think" means that man is really man.[190]

From all this it should be evident that for us real and objective means that which imposes itself as unmistakable upon the subject within the "affirmation of being" that the existent subject-as-*cogito* is.　The real and objective is the correlate of this "affirmation of being" that the existent subject-as-*cogito* is; the real and objective is the "true" as the unconcealed and therefore unmistakable for the subject.　This "truth" is "brought about" by the "letting be" of the existent subject.[191]　It is "brought about," "happens" and "originates" at the "moment" (*Augenblick*) when the subject originates as "affirmation of being."　The "true" is "independent" of the subject, for the subject does not create it and therefore cannot speak arbitrarily of it.　However, as independent, the "true" cannot be isolated from existence as "encounter with the independent" and made an "in itself," for the existent subject-as-*cogito* "accomplishes" the independence of the independent, by "letting it be."[192]　The "true," then, as the unconcealed is historical, for it presupposes the historical moment of the emergence of the subject as "affirmation of being."[193]

From all this is should be evident that we do not conceive the objectivity of natural rights and natural duties in an objectivistic sense,

---

[186] Heidegger, *Vorträge und Aufsätze,* Pfullingen, 1954, p. 142.

[187] Heidegger, *Identität und Differenz,* p. 23.

[188] Heidegger, *Was ist Metaphysik?,* p. 47.

[189] "The appeal of being alone grants man his essence."　Heidegger, *Der Satz vom Grund,* p. 119, and *Ueber den Humanismus,* pp. 5-6.

[190] Heidegger, *Ueber den Humanismus,* p. 13.

[191] "The freedom to reveal what is open lets the being that is at the moment be the being it is.　Freedom now reveals itself as the 'letting be' of being." Heidegger, *Vom Wesen der Wahrheit,* Frankfurt a.M., 1954, p. 14.

[192] "When *Dasein* does not exist, 'independence' 'is' not either, nor is the 'in itself.' "　Heidegger, *Sein und Zeit,* p. 212.

[193] This is not the only sense in which truth must be called historical.　The other senses will be discussed later.

as is done by Thomism. There are no natural rights and duties "in themselves," just as there are no rules of chess when there are no chess players. To be objective is to be objective-for-a-subject. As soon as this statement is made, it becomes impossible to avoid the question for whom rights and the demands of justice are objective. *The* subject "brings about" the truth of rights and of justice's demands; through *the* subject the truth of co-existence "occurs" and "originates." But, who is this subject?

In our time things that formerly were done only through the love of the best members of a particular society are now affirmed as rights. This fact makes it possible to give an answer to that question. *The* subject, for whom rights and the demands of justice are objective, is, at first, to be identified with the best of a particular society and, next, with all those who, through the intermediary of the best, are able to "see" what they "see."[194] There are many difficulties in this statement but, in spite of all these difficulties, the above-formulated standpoint seems undeniable to us. A right is not objective-in-itself but is objective-for-a-subject; hence it implies a certain "seeing" or, as explained above, a certain "bringing about" or "letting happen" of the unconcealedness of the demands made by justice and their correlate called "rights." This dis-closing of the demands of justice implies, in its turn, that within co-existence the subject "brings about" and "lets happen" truth as the unconcealedness of the other-as-appeal-to-his-existence, so that in his own existence the truth of his "having to be for the other" is "brought about" and "takes place."

It would be impossible, however, that this could take place in an existence encapsuled in greed or pride or in one that is involved in a war of all against all and therefore is ready to do anything that would make it possible for him to realize himself as a pure monster. The "coming about" of justice's objectivity presupposes an "ethical genius," one in whose existence truth as the unconcealedness of "the other as appeal to his existence" and as the unconcealedness of his own existence as destined to the other is accomplished at a given moment in the history of a society. The "happening" of this truth means *in principle* the emergence of humanity, and the minimum of this humanity is formulated as the most fundamental right of the other.

The statement that the objectivity of rights is brought about in the existence of an "ethical genius" does not at all mean that by this very

---

[194] Henri Bergson, *Les deux sources de la Morale et de la Religion,* Paris, 1942, pp. 29-30.

fact humanity is effectively *established* to some extent.   The "ethical genius," that is, the "heroes and saints," the best members of a particular society personally represent the best of mankind.   But at first they stand alone: they are like voices calling in a wilderness of inhumanity and barbarism.   However, they are convinced that the demands of humanity which they discern are objective and, because they see that these demands are anchored in the *essence* of existence as co-existence, they know themselves to be "functionaries of mankind" (Husserl).   They know that, bearing witness to co-existence, they express things that must be recognized by everyone.   The "heroes and saints," the geniuses and inventors in the realm of ethics,[195] have a mediating task with respect to their fellow-men.   They make it possible for others to see what they themselves see.[196]   In spite of this, however, humanity is not yet *established*.

The demands of justice and rights only then become a reigning humanity when those who "see" put forward representatives, i.e., when they give authority and power to certain persons to realize the minimum demands of love by means of rules endowed with compelling force, thus taming the "wolf" in human co-existence.

The preceding paragraph was not written to introduce here the discussion of the need to add a legal order to the natural law.   We mentioned the legal order only to stress the risks implied in our theory of the natural law.   For this theory also says that what the best of a society "see" must be imposed in a compelling way.   But, could not their "vision" be nothing but an assumed vision, a mistake?

The "Dizziness" of Being-Man.   The affirmation of the objectivity of natural rights and natural duties presupposes that the subject "sees"; those rights and duties are not objective-in-themselves.   This "seeing" is the subject-as-*cogito* himself, who lets the truth, the objectivity, the reality of those rights and duties "happen" in his existence as co-existence.   No one has at his disposal or can appeal to truth-in-itself in order to use it as a criterion of man's searching and groping for truth-for-man.   Outside the life of truth there is no "identity card" that could be "applied" to thinking from without as a criterion of truth and thus legitimize this thinking as being in conformity with reality.[197]   That

---

[195] "There is invention in morality."   Madinier, *Conscience et amour,* p. 58.
[196] Bergson, *op. cit.,* pp. 85-86.
[197] Heidegger, *Vorträge und Aufsätze,* pp. 184-185.

which in the history of the existent subject-as-*cogito* comes to be seen by the subject through his "letting be," cannot be measured by a truth-in-itself. Thus it is possible that the thinker is wrong. His "seeing" can be merely putative, for he can dream, fancy or hallucinate, while thinking that he "sees."

To think, therefore, is a dizzy enterprise. "I have only my own judgments at my disposal."[198] Nevertheless, the precariousness and the risk involved in thinking cannot entitle anyone to deny the importance of "seeing" as the "place" where truth "comes about." Phenomenology has often stressed this point with great conviction, but its emphasis has not infrequently been badly interpreted. Sometimes matters have been presented as if the phenomenologist simply "describes what happens to his retina" and, nonetheless, thinks that such an impressionism can make an important contribution to truth. Phenomenology has protested[199]—and justly so[200]—against such an interpretation of its intentions. But this protest would miss its goal if it would leave the reader with the idea that the existent subject-as-*cogito* himself is not the letting "happen" of truth as unconcealedness and that as such he must be called a "seeing," albeit not in the above-rejected impressionistic sense.[201]

This "seeing" which, as "functional intentionality," is always "at work" is the unsurpassable origin of all explicit knowledge[202] and as such is always presupposed. This is also the case when I must admit that I made a mistake. For the recognition of my mistake and the withdrawal of my judgment is only possible on the basis of the presupposition that *now* at least I "see."[203] Hence I can never ask myself whether that

---

[198] Merleau-Ponty, *Sens et non-sens,* p. 189.

[199] Stephan Strasser, *Phenomenology and the Human Sciences. A Contribution to a New Scientific Ideal,* Pittsburgh, 1963.

[200] "The idea of 'originary' and 'intuitive' grasping and explicitating phenomena is the opposite of the naiveness of a casual, 'immediate' and unreflective 'beholding.'" Heidegger, *Sein und Zeit,* pp. 36-37.

[201] "Evidence is called a seeing, perceiving, grasping of the self-given ('true') state of affairs." Husserl, *Logische Untersuchungen,* vol. I, Halle a.d.S., 1928, p. 190.

[202] "No conceivable theory can mislead us with respect to *the principle of all principles,* viz., that *every originary dator intuition is a legitimate source of knowledge,* that *everything presenting itself to us in 'intuition' in an originary form* (as it were, in its bodily reality) *is simply to be accepted as it gives itself, though only within the limits in which it gives itself.*" Husserl, *Ideen,* vol. I, p. 52.

[203] "We only know that there are errors because we have truths in the name of which we correct the errors and know them as errors." Merleau-Ponty, *Phénoménologie de la perception,* p. 341.

which I "see" is true, real and objective, for true, real and objective is precisely that which I "see." I must always ask myself whether I "see" or dream. But the fact that I can make this distinction means that I "already know" that when "seeing" I stand in the truth as unconcealedness, but not while dreaming.[204] Thinking is a dizzying enterprise precisely because all too often purely supposed "seeing" passes for real "seeing" and because it is not possible to use an "identity card" issued by truth in itself to check my "seeing" and to distinguish it from all forms of putative "seeing." This is also the reason why we emphasize the importance of the "seeing" of the "ethical genius." The clarity of his vision makes many others also "see," when it is a question of "bringing about" the objectivity of natural rights and natural duties. However, this appeal to the "ethical genius" is not our last word.

Who Decides the Question: Who is the "Ethical Genius"? The appeal to the clear vision of the best members of society gives rise to other questions that throw light upon the "dizziness" of being-man. Granted that the clarity of vision enjoyed by the best makes many others also "see," granted even that this clarity makes so many "see" that it becomes easy to embody a certain minimum of man's "yes" to his fellow-men into a legal order, nevertheless, the question remains: Who is to determine that "the best members of society" are indeed the best? The same question can be asked when "the best members of society" want to overthrow an established legal order because they realize that this order does violence to man. Who decides who has clear vision? Who decides who is best?

Our answer is: the best members of a society themselves decide this question. To prepare the acceptance of this answer, we will first state a few questions and answers that are similar to the question and answer at stake here. Who determines who is intelligent? The answer is: Not people who are really stupid, but only those who are intelligent enough to understand what intelligence is and to determine that this quality is found in this or that person. Who determines who is virtuous? The answer is: Not those who are depraved but only those who are virtuous enough to understand what virtue is and observe that this quality is found in this or that person. Likewise, not charlatans but the best among the physicians determine what sound medical science demands; and if medical quacks were to suggest that defective lungs and kidneys

---

[204] Merleau-Ponty, *op. cit.,* p. XI.

belong to good health, competent physicians will not begin to doubt what they have always called objective demands of good health.

It can happen, however, that unintelligent or wicked people get control of public power. It also happens that such people decree that all those who hitherto were regarded as intelligent must be considered stupid and that those who were held to be virtuous must now be called wicked. But even if such public authorities by means of a "legal order" force all their subjects to act in accordance with this new "view," those who are really intelligent or really virtuous will certainly not begin to doubt the objectivity of what they have always called intelligence and virtue. They will not even wonder whether perhaps they were wrong when they followed other ideals that those now imposed upon them. They will become the victims, the martyrs of the new "order." The best decide who is best and what is best, even if it costs them their lives.

However, this, too, is not the last word, for there are pseudo-martyrs, people who give their lives for a dream, sacrifice themselves to their blindness. In such a case anyone who is not blind sees that they sacrifice their lives for nothing. Anyone who is not blind realizes that their willingness to sacrifice themselves permits them to mislead the people, but no one can open their eyes to make them see that, while intending to bring blessings, they cause catastrophic results.

Again, however, this is not the last word. It has happened in the past that men sacrificed their lives, though their contemporaries thought that this sacrifice was for nothing. They were regarded as pseudo-martyrs, but later it became evident that their contemporaries were wrong. The best have the greatest clarity of vision and the best decide who are the best. But the "seeing" on which man must always depend is *never guaranteed to anyone*. To be a man is a "dizzying" enterprise, but "philosophy is not a hospital."[205]

The Philosophy of Law as "Hospital." In his search for justice man experiences his existence as "dizziness." Efforts have been made in two directions to use philosophy as a kind of "hospital" to cure man of this "dizziness." Legal positivism is one of these efforts. "Anyone," says the legal positivist, "can appeal to his 'vision' of the demands of justice to defend as 'sacred rights' his most extravagant ideas, his lust of power, his narrow-mindedness and short-sightedness, his political aspirations, his

---

[205] Merleau-Ponty, "Deuxième entretien privé," *La connaissance de l'homme au XXe siècle, Rencontres internationales de Genève,* 1951, p. 247.

envy and greed. He can consider himself called to overthrow the legal order." But there is no one who can determine what is just and therefore humanity is only guaranteed if everyone submits without reflection to the legal order." Such a position simply palliates the dizziness involved in the search for humanity. It does not cure this dizziness, for the legal order itself can also be inhuman. Humanity is never guaranteed by law alone.

An objectivistic view of the natural law also fails to recognize the precarious character and the risk involved in the search for the demands of justice. It fails to realize that the subject is involved in a true "search" and does not pay attention to the fact that objectivity "comes about" and is "accomplished" in the existent subject-as-*cogito,* without possibility of measuring the truth-for-the-subject with truth-in-itself. One who claims that he can, does not cure man's "dizziness" but fails to realize that man is "dizzy." Who could cure man of his being-man?[206]

---

[206] "The human (element) in man remains alive only in taking risks." Fechner, *Rechtsphilosophie,* p. 263.

CHAPTER SEVEN

THE NATURAL LAW AND THE
LEGAL ORDER

A society is not worth what the inscriptions on its monuments say or what the slogans of its orators proclaim. Its worth depends on the value of the actual interhuman relationships existing in that society.[1] In the same spirit one could say that a society is not worth what the "seeing" of its "ethical geniuses" is worth, but what its legal order is worth. This assertion is based upon the conviction that only a legal order permanently *establishes* humanity, conceived as the minimum of man's "yes" to his fellow-man.

1. Properties of the Natural Law

As the reader must have noticed, after describing right and justice as the correlate of the minimum of man's "yes" to his fellow-man, we did not yield to the temptation to list a "catalogue of natural laws." Not only positivists but also many non-positivists, especially among jurists, object to such a catalogue. It appears to us that their objections are not without a solid foundation.

"Catalogue of Natural Rights." With respect to the rationalistic view of the natural law, a catalogue of natural rights is open to the same objections as that rationalistic view itself. They have been sufficiently discussed in the preceding chapters, so that there is no need to enter into details here.

---

[1] Merleau-Ponty, *Humanisme et terreur*, p. X.

With respect to non-rationalistic views of the natural law, it must be noted that their proponents, generally speaking, are very modest in their enumeration of natural rights.[2] Even so, they usually fail to carry approval. The reason for this failure lies in the qualifications traditionally ascribed to the natural law: it is supposed to be immutable, eternal and valid for all men at all times and in all places. Much can be said, of course, about the interpretation of these qualifications but, no matter how they are interpreted, those who admit them will, at least implicitly, hold them to be valid also for their catalogue of natural rights. Hence it is with respect to that catalogue also that there are difficulties and objections.

Hans Welzel has examined such a catalogue in the works of Coing, and he comes to the conclusion that Coing's catalogue is suspiciously similar to the Constitution of Weimar.[3] In the past representatives of the rationalistic view of the natural law, belonging to different nations, have tried to draw up complete catalogues of immutable and eternal natural rights that are valid for all men at all times and in all places. The same era saw the codification of human rights in the Austrian, the Prussian and the French codes; yet these codes were clearly different.[4]

The various objections and difficulties against any catalogue of natural rights can perhaps be best summarized in the following way: "Every catalogue of natural rights and natural duties is actually nothing but an enumeration of those concrete rights and duties which, at a particular phase of *history,* became undeniable because at that time the subjective inspiration of love 'encountered' *de facto* existing concrete and historically determined relationships and conditions. Of such an enumeration,

---

[2] In general it is explicitly observed that the natural law does not produce more than "a few general outlines; everything else is left to positive law." V. Cathrein, *Recht, Naturrecht und positives Recht,* Freiburg i.Br., 1909, p. 279. M. E. Schmitt (*Recht und Vernunft,* Heidelberg, 1955) suggests that there exists a system of natural rights comparable to that of positive law, but he does not elaborate the point.

[3] "On closer inspection of the catalog listing the supreme fundamental principles, one is surprised to note its similarity to the catalogs of fundamental rights listed in new constitutions, especially that of Weimar. This constitution lists not only the traditional fundamental rights to life, freedom and property, but also the rights to protection of the realm of private secrets, of free expression of opinion, of free scientific, artistic and religious activity as 'a necessary part of *any* legal order.'" Welzel, "Naturrecht und Rechtspositivismus," *Festschrift für Hans Niedermeyer,* p. 281.

[4] Welzel, *Naturrecht und materiale Gerechtigkeit,* p. 160.

therefore, one can never say that it formulates rights and duties which are supposed to be immutable, eternal and valid for all men at all times and in all places."[5]

It seems to us that this quotation truthfully expresses what a "catalogue of natural rights" really is. With respect to the traditional qualifications of the natural law, however, the following remark should be added. The assertion that the natural law is immutable, eternal and universally valid is usually understood in an objectivistic sense. Thus it is not surprising that, precisely because of this objectivistic interpretation, these qualifications are rejected. It is meaningless to claim that the natural law is immutable, eternal and universally valid in the sense in which the rules of chess would be immutable, eternal and universally valid even if there were no chess players. Nevertheless, it does not follow that the natural law *in no sense* can be said to be immutable, eternal and universally valid. These qualifications do not of necessity imply an impossible objectivism.

For it is undeniably true that *every* truth is immutable precisely insofar as it is truth. This assertion may seem to contradict the historicity of truth so greatly emphasized in this book. The statement that truth is historical means, first, that as unconcealedness it presupposes the "moment" (*Augen-blick*) of dis-covery by the subject-as-*cogito* and is therefore in principle "datable"; secondly, it means that the history of dis-covery is never finished but always still has a future.[6] But the historicity of truth should not be understood in the sense that today's truth is true *because* today is today and that today's truth will be tomorrow's untruth because tomorrow will be tomorrow. On the contrary, we should rather say that in the historical dialogue of the existent subject-as-*cogito* with reality the "already" of unconcealedness is taken

---

[5] We do not agree with Welzel's view, who says: "Generally speaking, Coing's book has not done any good service to the cause of the natural law. For he has confirmed the old suspicion that the defenders of the theory of the natural law make eternal prescriptions of the natural law out of the political desires for rights prevailing in their time or even out of their personal wishes." Welzel, *art. cit.,* p. 281.

[6] "The effective possession of the true idea, therefore, does not give us any right to affirm an intelligible abode of adequate thought and absolute productivity. It establishes merely a 'teleology' of consciousness which, with this first instrument, will forge more perfect ones, and from these in turn still others more perfect, and so on endlessly." Merleau-Ponty, *Phénoménologie de la perception,* p. 453.

up into the "now." The truth of "now" does not destroy the truth of the past but makes it more profound and integrates it.[7] In this sense every truth is immutable.

For the same reason truth must be called eternal. This assertion does not mean a return to truth "in itself"; for truth "comes about" in the historical dialogue of the subject-as-*cogito* with reality. Similarly, the affirmation of truth's eternity does not mean as Heidegger thinks,[8] that from all eternity there have been human beings and that for all eternity there will be human beings who "bring about" truth in their existence. Every truth is eternal in the sense that whatever in any phase of man's common history has ever forced the subject to *affirm* it on the basis of its unconcealedness will demand the same affirmation in every subsequent phase of history; hence no subject can ever be justified in *denying* the same unconcealedness. The existent subject-as-*cogito* is, as "functional intentionality," the historical "bringing about," making "happen" and letting "arise" of that which we call the "transhistoricity" of truth. (This term contains both immutability and eternity of truth.)

Finally, it should be clear that the transhistoricity of truth implies also the validity of truth for all men at all times and in all places. Truth is intersubjective. But this qualification also can be misunderstood. The intersubjectivity of truth is a matter of *principle*. In principle, no subject has the right to deny any unconcealedness whatsoever, but *in practice* subjects very frequently contradict one another. However, no subject can be satisfied with this state of affairs, for in any real affirmation every subject, as it were, epitomizes all real and possible subjects who would want to speak of the same unconcealedness and "on behalf of all" he makes his affirmation; hence he cannot agree with those who deny the unconcealedness which he affirms. It is absolutely excluded that

---

[7] "I think, and this or that thought appears to me as true. I am aware that it is not unconditionally true, . . . but that does not prevent the fact that at the moment I think, I think something, and that any other truth, in the name of which I would like to discount this one, must, if it is to be called a truth for me, agree with the 'true' thought of which I have experience." Merleau-Ponty, *op. cit.,* pp. 455-456.

[8] "That there are 'eternal' truths will be adequately proved only when one succeeds in demonstrating that *Dasein* has been and will be for all eternity. As long as this proof is not delivered, the assertion remains a fantastic claim. Its legitimacy is not improved by the fact that philosophers generally 'believe' it." Heidegger, *Sein und Zeit,* p. 227. Let us note that philosophers who "believe" in eternal truths do not "believe" in them in the way Heidegger assumes that they "believe."

anyone could agree with me when I deny precisely that which he affirms. My denial attacks his very affirmation because every affirmation is always made "on behalf of all." Obviously, we are referring here to the affirmation and denial of the same matter in the same respect. Affirmation of something from one standpoint does not exclude, of course, its negation from a different standpoint because in such a case the two do not refer to "the same."

Transhistoricity and Intersubjectivity of the Natural Law. If we apply the preceding theory to the natural law, it should be obvious that there is no natural law which as an "in itself," of either a real of an ideal nature, is immutable, eternal and valid for all. The objectivity of the natural law must be "brought about" by an historical act in the co-existence of the "ethical genius." This genius, however, "brings about" the truth of co-existence on behalf of all those who call themselves human beings; he "brings about" a truth that is in principle intersubjective.

As such, this "bringing about" of an intersubjective truth on behalf of all is not very significant yet. An "ethical genius" would also "bring about" a truth that is in principle intersubjective when, afflicted with a toothache, he would let "happen" the reality, truth and objectivity of his toothache. He can never agree with anyone denying his toothache, without destroying his own affirmation. But the negation of his affirmation would not trouble him in this case because it would not affect his *essence*. The matter is entirely different, however, when there is question of "bringing about" the reality, truth and objectivity of the natural law. In that case the "ethical genius" "brings about" the truth of the *essence* of existence as co-existence; he "brings about" the truth of that by which man is man, even if it be provisionally on a very modest level of authenticity; he "brings about" truth about man as such, that is, an objectively universal truth, a truth applicable to "all men at all times and in all places."[9] This objectively universal truth is in principle intersubjective.[10]

---

[9] "In saying that man is responsible for himself, we do not mean to say that he is responsible for his individual being alone but that he is responsible for all men." Sartre, *L'existentialisme est un humanisme,* p. 24.

[10] "As a matter of fact, there is not one among our acts which, while making us the man we want to be, does not at the same time create an image of man as we think that man should be. . . . And nothing can be good for us without being good for all. . . . Thus, our responsibility is much greater than we could imagine, for it involves all mankind." Sartre, *op. cit.,* pp. 25-26.

Often and in many places, however, many men *de facto* do not "bring about" the objectively universal and fundamentally intersubjective truth, reality and objectivity of the natural law. This means that in those places and at those times there is no natural law. It is even possible that the truth of the natural law is absolutely denied there, if not in theory then at least in practice. Nevertheless, none of this makes the "ethical genius" doubt what he "sees" as a demand of humanity; he "brings about" the truth about the essence of co-existence "on behalf of all."

The natural law, we pointed out before, conceived as the correlate of the minimum of love, constantly changes its boundaries because love itself knows no boundaries. Hence the natural law is never "finished," but takes part in an endless history. Keeping this in mind, we realize that many societies at many times and in many places live in many different historical phases of the natural law. They live on different levels of humanity. It stands to reason that this condition causes great difficulties in the mutual relationship of different peoples.

Nevertheless, there is a standpoint from which it can be said that the natural law is immutable and eternal. The natural law derives a certain immutability and eternity from the immutability and eternity of the initial demand of justice.[11] Even though the truth of the natural law is an endless history,[12] the "already" of the initial demand of justice can never be destroyed by the "now" of this same demand. The "already" of the natural law's unconcealedness is taken up and integrated in its "now." In this sense the natural law is immutable.

The eternity of the natural law is connected with all this. Anything

---

[11] "However, if a moral system never represents anything but a historical acquisition, how can its content be justified since it will be subject to constant revision and development? The only answer to that question is to show that this content remains faithful to the initial moral demand, that it brings about for the present and for the future a recognition of man's dignity." A. Wylleman, "L'élaboration des valeurs morales," *Revue philosophique de Louvain,* vol. 48 (1950), p. 245.

[12] "An entirely new situation arose in the philosophy of law through the 'concept of historical essence.' The 'either—or' of timeless 'natural law' and sheer 'positivism' of ontic history would be overcome in favor of an 'historical natural law.' Viewed from the standpoint of the customary opposition between nature and history, this expression seems almost as paradoxical as that other possible expression 'existential essential law' appears to be from the standpoint of the traditional opposition between essence and existence. But what would come to the fore in both expressions is the unarbitrary necessity characterizing being's historicity." Max Müller, *Existenzphilosophie im geistigen Leben der Gegenwart,* p. 105.

which in any phase of history has ever become unconcealed as a demand of the *essence* of co-existence and which, on the basis of this unconcealedness, has ever compelled man to a fundamentally intersubjective affirmation, will compel him to the same affirmation in every subsequent phase of history; thus in no phase of history will the denial of the same unconcealedness ever be justified for any subject.

2. *Natural Law and Positive Law*

In the preceding chapters justice was described as the subjective and objective correlate of the sliding minimum demanded by man's "yes" to his fellow-man, a minimum that *in principle* breaks through the inhumanity of the "wolf" in man, his "no" to his fellow-man. At the same time, however, we emphasized that this *principle* does not yet *establish* humanity. When the "ethical genius" invents the natural law, no one *actually* has as yet a *really existing* "title" and the things that are "his" are not yet *actually* "his"; he is not yet *effectively* protected against any "wolf." All this comes about only through the establishment of the legal order with its positive rules of law and legal institutions; they effectively break through man's barbarism.

The Necessity of the Legal Order. To show the necessity of the legal order one could appeal to all the arguments that induce the legal positivist to be a legal positivist. The positivist wants *matter of fact* humanity, *matter of fact* order and *matter of fact* peace. He is so fascinated by the undeniable importance of the legal order for the *attainment* of humanity that he simply loses sight of the justifying ground and the critical norm of that order.

Above, the minumum of man's "yes" to his fellow-man was called the justifying ground and critical norm of the legal order. Thus we stand on the side of what Erich Fechner calls the "ideal views" regarding the origin of man's consciousness of right and the legal order. These "ideal views" place most emphasis upon the spontaneity and inspiration of the subject. However, we did not conceive this spontaneity as the power of a "clear and distinct idea" of an autonomous reason (Thomasius, Pufendorf, Wolf), nor as a formal *a priori* in the Kantian sense (Stammler), nor as a "feeling" or "intuition" of values making the ideal being-in-themselves of values accessible to man (Scheler, Hartmann, Coing). But the subject's spontaneity is the "having to be" whose reality, truth and objectivity as the *essence* of co-existence are "brought about" by the "ethical genius" in an act of "letting be" that is in principle intersubjective.

In and through its embodiment in a legal order this subjective inspiration must be *made* an actuality, a humanity that actually rules society. In attempting to do this, the subject's spontaneity encounters the actually existing relationships of a biological, economic and political nature—in general terms, the sociological forms of co-existence—as well as the facticity of the world, with all its possibilities and impossibilities, in which every sociological form of co-existence is involved. With respect to the establishment of a legal order, in spite of all the spontaneity of the subject, the latter's "sensitivity" to the way conditions and relations *de facto* are is so important that the representatives of what Fechner calls the "realistic views" regarding the origin of man's consciousness of right and the legal order are *almost* right. This consciousness of right and the legal order are not, as the realistic views claim, a passive mirror image of the actual relationships; nevertheless, the "passivity," the "sensitivity" of the subject for these relationships is so important that without it the legal order would simply be meaningless, for it would not humanize any actual relationships.[13]

The demands of justice become a *ruling* humanity when a positive rule of law, imposed with coercive force and thus embodied in the existing relationships, is formulated as that which imposes itself as a demand of humanity encountered in man's "yes" to his fellow-man with its actually existing conditions and relations. This "process" of embodiment in the existing relationships is indispensable,[14] for if the demands of humanity

---

[13] Our view of right, justice and the legal order was criticized in a friendly fashion by J. Loeff ("Gedachtenwisseling over 'Phaenomenologie van het recht,'" *Annalen v.h. Thijmgenootschap,* vol. 48 (1960), pp. 96-97). However, he is not as far distant from our view as one would be inclined to think, for he himself says: "Moral values become juridical values as soon as they qualify for embodiment in the relationships lying on the lower level of the good pertaining to human life. In the same way the community-of-persons, which manifests itself on the spiritual level in friendship and a community of love, becomes a community of rights in man's consciousness on the level of the lower types of sociality, i.e. that of political societies and organizations pursuing a specific purpose." Loeff, "De sociale grondrechten van de mens," *Handelingen der nederlandse juristenvereniging,* vol. 83 (1953), p. 118.

[14] "To give concrete form to the minimum demands of love, we need a legal order whose rules of law clearly determine the required objective performances and which, through its legal institutions, makes it possible to force recalcitrants to comply with the demands of the law. Thus the existing laws mirror what, at a given moment, is established as the minimum demands of love or humanity in a particular society." L. Janssens, "De inhoud van de rechtvaardigheid wordt steeds rijker," *De gids op maatschappelijk gebied,* 1960, p. 127.

are not embodied in the existing relationships by a coercive legal order, man would be "left to the mercy" of his fellow-man's spontaneous love, at least if the latter belongs to the best of a society. And if his fellow-man does not belong to that category, man would simply be left to the "mercy" of "wolves." This would be true even in the case where the spontaneous love of the best of a society shows "lapses," moments of weakness.[15]

Accordingly, the legal order is wholly indispensable for making the minimum of love "rule" and guaranteeing it as much as possible. The establishment of a legal order is the first step on the road to the *effective* humanization of many sociological forms of co-existence, the first success in taming the "wolf," the first victory over barbarism. The legal order takes the necessary steps to effectively establish and preserve humanity; it guarantees a measure of stability to whatever degree of humanity has already been attained.[16] In the legal order ruling a particular society one can "read" how far that society has gone in taming the "wolf." The stability of the legal rules is the expression of the firm will a society has to resist sinking below a certain level of humanity.[17] The legal order is the barrier which permanently robs the "wolf" in man of his chances.[18] The fact that there does not yet exist any significant body of international laws is very eloquent in this matter. It shows that the nations have not yet reached that minimum of love for one another in virtue of which one nation accepts the collective subjectivity and selfhood of the

---

[15] "The law compels. But precisely at this limit, its bearing becomes clear, the law becomes a support in the hour of weakness." Fechner, *Rechtsphilosophie*, p. 241.

[16] "Positive law reveals a static aspect because it is an expression of what, at a given moment, has been reached by civilization: it preserves what has already been accomplished in the development of human society lest society lose conquered ground and lapse again into man's exploitation by his fellow-man. Love keeps guard lest we abandon what its energy and inspiration have already achieved in human relationships and laid down in positive laws. To clarify this static aspect of the law, justice has been described as love which maintains its conquests but does not go beyond them." L. Janssens, "Naastenliefde en rechtvaardigheid," *Kultuurleven*, vol. XIX (1952), p. 15.

[17] "The moralist observes this pressure of justice on law. When he considers justice in man's conscience, where it is a virtue, he can define it as a will not to go backward on the road travelled by our forefathers' work of love." Nédoncelle, *Vers une philosophie de l'amour*, p. 87.

[18] "Justice is the ensemble of the rules which 'charity' has invented to establish itself safely and permanently among men. These rules are a safety catch and a railing; they represent a certain state of unity and harmony below which a society does not want to sink." Madinier, *Conscience et amour*, p. 128.

other.   On the level of international relations, the situation is still wholly inhuman.

Authority and Power.   Legal rules cannot establish humanity in a *compelling* way unless they are imposed by an authority endowed with power.   When the truth of a natural right is "brought about" in co-existence through an "ethical genius," it depends to a large extent on the response of the society whether or not humanity will actually be established.[19]   Many will not see what the "ethical genius" discerns as a demand of justice.   Thus the best members of the society have the primary task of educating their fellow-men and to make them see so that they also may understand the demands of justice.[20]   As soon as this has been done in a sufficient way, society will put forward, or rather "elevate," one or more persons who, as bearers of authority, will see that justice is realized.   These persons derive their authority from the "having to be" that co-existence itself is and, on the basis of this "having to be," the rules they establish are normative.[21]   As bearers of authority, they represent the "having to be" of co-existence, and only to the extent that they represent this "having to be" are they bearers of authority.[22]

This idea has important consequences.   Speaking about justice, the natural law and the legal order, we do not intend to write a kind of "history."   Hence when we say that a society "elevates" one or more persons to be bearers of authority and sees to it that justice is realized, "history" is not uppermost in our mind.   What we aim at is an understanding of the essence of co-existence as "having to be" and an understanding of what is of necessity implied in its realization.   Historically speaking, however, it does happen that, as soon as a society wants to "elevate" one or more persons as bearers of authority, this society realizes that the position of authority is already occupied by others who look upon the land and the people as their personal property to be exploited

---

[19] "Here the question is asked at once: How will society react to their message?   This reaction is just as important as the intuition of the individuals. In the experience of justice this reaction functions as the counter pole of the individuals' intuition."   Gits, *Recht, persoon en gemeenschap,* pp. 335-336.

[20] "He merely counts on a long effort of mankind and on a slow educational process to 'form' men and to make them constantly more reasonable.   Meanwhile it is important to be on guard against the offensive returns of a vigorous egoism."   Lacroix, *Personne et amour,* p. 13.

[21] We abstract here from the ways and techniques through which legal rules are established.

[22] Gits, *op. cit.,* p. 332.

for their own benefit. Historically speaking, such a situation often leads to a revolution and, philosophically speaking, our theory is a justification of such a revolution. However, here also it is true that being-man is a kind of "dizziness." But we will revert to this question later.

In other cases it happens that the person or persons "at the top" are forced to "change their character." By conforming to the demands of justice, a tyrant can become a legitimate bearer of authority. Thus it is striking that the constitutions of most modern states, basing themselves on the United States Constitution and the Declaration of the Rights of Man and of the Citizen made by the French National Assembly of 1789, primarily formulate the individual's rights of personal freedom with respect to the authority of the state.[23] Likewise, the first part of the General Declaration of Human Rights of the United Nations is mainly negative: it formulates the limits of governmental authority.[24] Only to the extent that bearers of authority represent the "having to be" of co-existence are they really bearers of authority.[25]

To exercise their authority, however, they need power. Positivism has greatly emphasized this point, and justly so. As late as 1932 Radbruch wrote in the third edition of his *Rechtsphilosophie:* "He who is able to enforce the law thereby proves that he is called to make the law."[26] To make justice and right actually *rule,* power is essential.[27] This is true to such an extent that those who identify power with right are *almost* correct. To defend this identification does not always mean a cynical disregard of justice. "Power ideologies are often connected with pessimistic anthropologies. Such pessimism can be a matter of principle but also the effect of certain political experiences, in which case it must be regarded as the expression of a disenchanted and disappointed idealism. Power is then exalted not for its own sake but as the only and last means to prevent chaos."[28] Humanity must become an accomplished fact, and this requires power. Those who are interested in making

---

[23] Loeff. *art. cit.* (footnote 13), p. 103.

[24] F. van der Ven, *Sociale grondrechten,* Utrecht, 1957, pp. 89-97.

[25] Gits, *op. cit.,* p. 332.

[26] Quoted by Welzel, *loc. cit.* (footnote 3), p. 279.

[27] "Every right expresses a certain relationship of powers. A right that is not sustained by any power can perhaps manage to appear as a right for a brief time, but it will not fail to collapse and reality will soon replace mere appearance. Thus, it is not enough to say that right without power is inoperative, but we must say that such a right does not exist." Lacroix, *op. cit.,* p. 15.

[28] R. F. Beerling, *Kratos,* Antwerpen, 1956, p. 177.

humanity rule but have never experienced the temptation to identify right with power[29] do not yet understand the human importance of power. Humanity cannot be established as the actual rule by mere "expressions of love."[30]

Our own time makes us painfully aware of this truth. There is no significant body of international law because there exists no supra-national authority. One who would like to consider the United Nations as such an authority cannot ignore the fact that the action of this international organization will remain weak as long as it cannot dipose of its own supra-national armed forces.

Radical pacifists and anti-militarists likewise make a mistake when they minimize or deny the importance of power.[31] They want a just peace but no armed forces; they want justice without power. This is a utopian view and an anthropological error. As a matter of fact, at present anti-militarists are able to defend their error only because there are others who fulfill their military duty and stand guard over the anti-militarists' countries.

In spite of the necessity to use force in order to make justice rule, it is wrong to identify right and power. Since this point was sufficiently discussed in previous chapters, we need not insist upon it here.

Positive Rules of Law. The rules of law established by authority and enforced through proper means derive their normative character from the "having to be" that co-existence itself is.[32] Humanity cannot exist without those rules.[33] If there were no rules of law, there would be no orientation in the innumerable actions, direct or indirect, done toward one another by men involved in an infinite variety of sociological forms of co-existence. The orientation to be observed by those actions, if they are not to violate the minimum of love whose demand has been discerned within a particular society, must be indicated by "guide lines." Because

---

[29] "Those who are more or less inclined to attribute greater weight to the factual character of the law than to its normative character will tend to occupy this standpoint." Beerling, *op. cit.,* pp. 173-174.

[30] "The great danger of the present, especially for Christians, is that of a kind of *disembodied supernaturalism,* which is ready to give us power, ignores the role of law and imagines that all problems can be solved by professions of love." Lacroix, *op. cit.,* pp. 29-30.

[31] Lacroix, *op. cit.,* p. 14.

[32] "But justice is born from love and, if it establishes a system of rules, those rules have, as it were, been laid down by love." Madinier, *op. cit.,* p. 128.

[33] Gits, *op. cit.,* pp. 337-344.

man is also a "wolf" for his fellow-man, many human actions go against these "lines." For this reason many legal rules are formulated in a negative way: they simply prohibit all kinds of actions.[34]

Above, we expressly distinguished men's actions toward one another as "direct" or "indirect." For the simple fact is that the economic, social and political structures of a society imply a certain way of acting indirectly with respect to others. Those structures are not "just there"; they did not arise through a natural process just as a rain squall arises through natural processes and forces; they cannot be directly connected with a divine Providence; they are *made* by man. They show the "real" intentions of man, that is, the intentions he has embodied in the world. The fact that they "are" and "continue to be" point to actions of man. But, because they are structures of society, they are significant for many human beings: they can imply freedom or slavery for others. Thus the fact that they "are" or "continue to be" means that some men give freedom to others or reduce them to slavery. The existence of economic, social and political structures in a society, whether primitive or highly developed, implies an indirect way of man's acting with respect to his fellow-man. Accordingly, when we refer to the "wolf" in man, we refer not solely to man's *direct* willingness to destroy the subjectivity of his fellow-man, for man can also destroy indirectly his fellow-man.

We have now reached the point that can perhaps best serve to explicitate the contingency prevailing in the arduous labor of formulating the rules of law. The point is that from the essence of justice and of the natural law one cannot deduce any positive rule of law. Laws are made to safeguard the minimum of our "yes" to man as a subject. But the subject that man is, is incarnated in a body and, together with many other subjects, involved in a common world. One who realizes what this *concretely* means for the subject knows also that the making of laws is an endless task. One would have to mention here all *concrete* bodily conditions, all *concrete* relationships within all sociological forms of co-existing, and all *concrete* meanings of the world. One would have to speak of weather conditions, geographical situations, soil fertility, population density, etc.; one would have to discuss the different phases in the history of concrete relations and conditions in various areas of the world. For the subject is an involved subject; he does not occur without a body and without a world. The encounter of the subjective inspiration's

---

[34] Gits, *op. cit.*, p. 340.

"yes"-to-the-subject with the concrete conditions and relationships calls for rules of law, in order to effectively humanize these conditions and relationships. But it is precisely the concreteness of the conditions and relationships that burdens the establishment of legal rules with an insuperable contingency. There simply have to be many different systems of positive law.

There is more, however. To the penetrating mind it is clear that the "dizziness" mentioned in connection with the "bringing about" of the reality, truth and objectivity of the natural law, is even greater on the level of bringing about a legal order. The "coming about" of the truth of the natural law is never *guaranteed*. But an even greater risk is involved in bringing about a legal order, for the positive laws intend to *establish* humanity. No one, however, can guarantee that in fact they will not effect precisely the opposite of what they intend. So much is needed to see truthfully the reality of the concrete conditions and relationships! Who can foresee how history will judge a law which one expects will establish humanity? Who can prevent a law which gives freedom to some from implying slavery for others? Who has so many positive data at his disposal that he can carefully measure the proportional equality of rights demanded by justice?

This is the reason why several philosophers of law who think along the lines of the philosophy of existence strongly—and justly so—emphasize that there is an aspect of "decision" and risk in establishing a legal order.[35] The struggle for right laws implies that man makes decisions and accepts risks which in reality establish precisely the opposite of that which his "minimum of love" wants to establish. There is no escape from this "dizzying" condition. One who, in order to escape the precariousness and risks of all decisions, prefers not to make any decision also makes a decision.[36] His decision is to leave everything as it is. It is only in the execution of a decision that it becomes evident whether or not

---

[35] "Moreover, the decision that is not guided by any norm is a risky undertaking which can succeed or fail." Fechner, *Rechtsphilosophie,* p. 260.

[36] "If I am fearful of the consequences of my action, I may perhaps imagine that it is possible to avoid guilt by abstaining from becoming involved in the world and by doing nothing. . . . But *doing nothing* itself is doing something, namely, failing to do something. It has consequences. . . . In my situation I bear the responsibility for what happens because I do not intervene. If I can do something and I do not do it, I am guilty of the consequences of my failure to act. Accordingly, whether I act or do not act, both have consequences, so that in either case I inevitably become guilty." Jaspers, *op. cit.,* p. 507.

a certain pattern of co-existence is successful.[37]   What is good shows itself in its realization.[38]   No one possesses a magic "philosophers' stone."[39]

The Ever-Recurrent Misunderstanding.   The philosophers of law who emphasize the aspect of "decision" in the establishment of a legal order call making a decision a "risk" *because* one cannot find any "given norms."   Erich Fechner, for example, expresses himself very strongly in this matter.   He says: "We must hold fast to the fact that there are no readily available objective norms";[40] "The philosophy of existence—to this we must hold fast—denies that norms are pre-given";[41] "Thus the decision that is not orientated by any norm is a 'risk' ";[42] "The fundamental rights are very fragile and in great danger because they do not solidly rest on pre-given norms."[43]

Because there are no "given norms," Fechner says, the decision on which the legal order depends lies wholly in man's *freedom:* "The philosophy of existence . . . puts the decision fully in the freedom of man; his being (*Dasein*) must be formed from within man himself because there are no obligatory models above or outside him."[44]   And: "At some time the idea of freedom dawned upon man for the first time. At some time he decided not to destroy the life of other members of his species in an arbitrary fashion."[45]   "The fundamental rights and the rights of freedom are not at all, as is claimed wrongfully by the Bonn Constitution, 'foundations of any human society.'   Societies can be conceived and can exist without them.   The rights of freedom are one of the great and original creations of Western man."[46]

The criticism levelled against this form of thinking is always the same.

---

[37] "The voice that says 'yes' when a form of being-together-with-one-another succeeds is inaudible. . . .   But, aside from this voice, there is the voice of doubt which does not cease to admonish when a legal regulation, a form of human togetherness is not entirely 'in order.' . . .   But all this does not happen before the decision, but the certainty arises only later.   Only *in* its implementation does the decision prove right or wrong."   Fechner, *op. cit.*, p. 258.

[38] Jaspers, *Philosophie,* Berlin, 2nd ed., 1948, p. 460.

[39] Fechner, *op. cit.*, p. 220.

[40] Fechner, *op. cit.*, p. 258.

[41] Fechner, *op. cit.*, p. 253.

[42] Fechner, *op. cit.*, p. 260.

[43] Fechner, *ibid.*

[44] Fechner, *op. cit.*, p. 253.

[45] Fechner, *op. cit.*, p. 250.

[46] Fechner, *op. cit.*, p. 260.

If there are no "given norms," so the critique goes, and if the decisions in which the legal order is rooted lie in man's freedom, then those decisions and the legal order based on them are left to man's arbitrariness. Hence it is utterly meaningless to speak of a natural law and natural rights because such a view denies "given norms," which are precisely what the use of the term "natural law" legitimates. This criticism is voiced, for example, by A. Hartmann and H. J. Hommes against Erich Fechner. "He who declares that before such a decision there are no objective, ontological guide lines for it has fundamentally abandoned the idea of the natural law."[47] "One who speaks here of several possibilities from which man must choose by a decision of will without a norm abandons the idea of the natural law."[48] "Where [the philosophy of existence] turns into the denial of any ontologically pre-given, objective norm, where it essentially places the origin of rights in the realm of the subjective, it fundamentally divorces itself from a metaphysics of the natural law."[49] And: "Creative freedom in the existentialistic sense cannot bear any objective bond, and vice versa."[50]

These critics note, of course, that Fechner nonetheless assigns a place to bonds within his theory of the natural law and that he does not accept arbitrariness. Fechner himself is very clear in this matter. He says, for example: "It goes without saying that in this respect justice is something other than 'positing' laws arbitrarily and because one has the power."[51] "In the sense of the philosophy of existence also a genuine 'decision to law' is not arbitrary."[52] And: "The objectivity of this orientation means, if we look at it in reference to the position of man in this orientation, that man finds this objectivity already 'pre-given' in a sense that will be explained in greater detail later. Man does not proceed to arrange life as he wills, he is not the criterion of this orientation, in the sense that he 'posit' whatever laws he wants. . . . The orientation is given *together with* man because man is man only through this 'guide line.' "[53] "From all this it follows that 'just laws' always obey being, that 'just laws' are always 'just with respect to being.' "[54]

---

[47] A. Hartmann, "Besprechungen," *Scholastik,* vol. 33 (1958), p. 111.
[48] Hartmann, *ibid.*
[49] Hartmann, *art. cit.,* p. 112.
[50] Hommes, *Een nieuwe herleving van het natuurrecht,* p. 141.
[51] Fechner, *op. cit.,* p. 256.
[52] Fechner, *op. cit.,* p. 261.
[53] Fechner, *op. cit.,* p. 209.
[54] Fechner, *op. cit.,* p. 210.

Fechner's critics give full weight to these texts and thus are led to the conclusion that he is inconsistent and full of contradictions. Fechner, they say, "in the context of such a metaphysics seeks to find the ultimate foundation of the individual's rights of freedom in the ontological relationship of individual and society and, beyond this, in a polarity that dominates the entire realm of being open to us. Thus he seems to base the rights of freedom on an ontological foundation, a pre-given criterion. However, the idea of an existential decision as the ultimate foundation of the origin of natural rights cannot be reconciled with" that assertion.[55] And: "It is a contradiction to attribute (juridically) binding force to a natural right originating in such a free creation. If the natural law arises in a wholly subjective way from creative freedom, how can it contain norms of so-called 'objective validity' since the ethical values also are made to respond to human freedom and at least have no longer any objective validity?"[56]

These and other similar disputes are based on unfortunate misunderstandings, giving rise to unnecessary disharmony among philosophers. We earnestly hope that the following pages can help remove at least one of such superfluous disputes.

When Fechner, following existentialist and phenomenological thinkers, claims that no norms or values are "given," he wants to say that there are no norms or values having being-in-themselves in the representationalistic, objectivistic and essentialistic sense which we discussed in Chapter Four. Fechner does not claim more than that, but his critics find it difficult to admit that this is all there is to it. For Fechner says also that, since there are no "given" norms and value, the *decisions* on which the entire legal order is based are wholly rooted in human freedom. And by saying this, the critics argue, he removes *precisely* that which makes it possible for a philosopher of law to speak of a natural law, for decisions without given norms are arbitrary. This arbitrariness is exactly that which is rejected by the affirmation that there is a natural law. In this "rebuttal" the misunderstandings show themselves.

Generally speaking, one can say that most philosophers now are aware of the fact that the objectivist's position is impossible and that representationalistic realism contains an internal contradiction. But, as soon as one understands that the truth of norms and values is not a representationalistic-realistic "in itself," one must also admit that truth-as-

---

[55] Hartmann, *art. cit.,* p. 111.
[56] Hommes, *op. cit.,* pp. 141-142.

unconcealedness needs to be "brought about," needs to "happen," and that it is made to "happen" by the existent subject-as-*cogito*. Now, contemporary philosophy refers to the subject as "freedom" because the subject is not the deterministic result of "blind" cosmic processes and forces. To be a subject means a certain transcendence beyond deterministic results and is therefore called to be free.[57] This being-free makes it also possible to speak of truth as unconcealedness; we may even say that the existent subject-as-*cogito* himself is the "standing" in, and the "letting come about" of truth as unconcealedness.[58] Thus one can say that freedom *is* the "letting come about," the "bringing about" of truth; hence it is not possible to interpret being-free, in the sense spoken of here, as arbitrariness. The subject-as-freedom *is* a bond with the unconcealed.[59] This point was sufficiently stressed in the preceding chapter.

Today *we* modern men find it "normal" that our legal order contains norms which prohibit murder, declare the bond of matrimony unbreakable or at least breakable only under certain conditions, and assign rights of freedom to the human person so that he is not wholly subservient to the state. Of these norms Fechner says: "All this was *decided* by human freedom without 'pre-given norms.' "[60] His critics object: "Then those norms are *arbitrary* decisions denying the natural law."

Certain prudent distinctions need to be made here lest a needless misunderstanding arise. First of all, it should be evident that the norms of positive law *as* positive norms of law are *made*, that is, they arise from free human *decisions*. Secondly, it cannot be denied that the norms of the natural law which are supposed to underlie the positive legal norms do not exist "in themselves" in the representationalistic-realistic sense. It is in this sense that Fechner denies "given norms." Thirdly, Fechner explicitly and repeatedly denies that the above-mentioned decisions are arbitrary decisions, even though they lie in the realm of human freedom.

What does it mean, according to Fechner, that these decisions arise from human freedom? There cannot be the slightest doubt about it: for him freedom means the denial of causal determinism. "The legal status," he says, "of matrimony and the family has a limited biological

---

[57] Luijpen, *Phenomenology and Atheism,* pp. 230-234.

[58] See footnote 191 of Chapter Six.

[59] "The entering into the unconcealedness of a being does not stop there, but develops into a 'stepping back' before this being, so that it may reveal what it is and how it is and (thus) serve as a norm for its approximating expression." Heidegger, *Vom Wesen der Wahrheit,* p. 15.

[60] Fechner, *op. cit.,* pp. 250-251.

explanation. But the fact that in certain conditions matrimony becomes a juridically unbreakable bond or a bond that can be broken only on certain conditions which do not coincide with those biological necessities *cannot* be explained by *any causal determination*."[61] This norm, therefore, arises from a decision of the subject, as being superior to the results of causal processes. "Whether we decide to let the individual person fundamentally merge with the state or to bring about as much collectivity as is needed and try to attain as much freedom as possible, is *no longer determined* but is based on a human decision."[62] Hence, the fact that a human decision makes rights of freedom exist in the legal order means for Fechner that nothing determined man to put those rights into that order. Who would be willing or able to deny that point? Thus, for Fechner, freedom means "subjectivity" and not "arbitrariness."

However, one could ask, does not the absence of norms in this not-being-determined ultimately amount to arbitrariness? And if so, Fechner's emphatic rejection of arbitrariness would still make his theory self-contradictory. In reply, we may point out that for Fechner freedom is not the absence of norms while not-being-determined. He rejects, and justly so, norms existing "in themselves," but he recognizes that freedom has bonds as "standing in truth as unconcealedness." True, his work does not contain any developed phenomenology of this "standing in the truth as unconcealedness," but the idea of it is unmistakably present. He says, for example, "Order is given *together* with man because it is only by this gauge that man is man. His freedom and dignity consist in knowing and recognizing this, just as he must recognize the rest of the world order, the physical laws and the laws of thinking, if he wants to be what he is able to be. Like concepts and laws of thinking, so also the statements of justice are in this sense not formed but modeled, not invented but discovered."[63] And: "The natural law, correctly understood, does not consist in a rigid claim to absoluteness of what is contained in statements of law but in the consciousness of an objectivity, that is, a validity that is independent of human fancy. This objectivity, however, is not visible and given beyond any doubt but is hidden; it must be discovered and 'risked' because it is given to man as a task."[64]

Accordingly, Fechner explicitly recognizes the bond which ties free-

---

[61] Fechner, *op. cit.,* p. 250.
[62] Fechner, *op. cit.,* p. 251.
[63] Fechner, *op. cit.,* pp. 209-210.
[64] Fechner, *op. cit.,* p. 220.

dom to truth as unconcealedness. True, he calls it decisions of our freedom that in our legal order there are norms prohibiting murder, declaring matrimony unbreakable or breakable only on certain conditions, and conferring upon man rights of freedom. But he recognizes the bond connecting freedom with truth as unconcealedness so expressly that he never asserts that, if people living in other societies make decisions containing the contrary of those norms, they would just as much stand in the truth as those who decided the above-mentioned norms.

This leads us to the conclusion that only those who conceive "given norms" as norms-in-themselves cannot agree with Fechner. As was repeatedly pointed out, however, their standpoint contains a clear contradiction. Nevertheless, it must be added that Fechner himself has contributed to the misunderstanding of his view. Let us see why.

It is confusing to reject "given norms" *unqualifiedly* if one simply intends to reject a particular interpretation of this "givenness" that is bad and untenable. Unfortunately many contemporary philosophers are guilty of this kind of carelessness. In a previous work we have given a list of examples illustrating this point.[65] The worst and most untenable sense is fastened on a term and then, by rejecting this term absolutely, one implies that the term cannot be used in *any* sense. This is a horrible procedure, for it can only lead to confusion and misunderstanding. One who denies the objectivistic interpretation of "givenness" with respect to the natural law and therefore rejects the term "given" *absolutely* cannot help but reject also whatever truth is contained in objectivism. No other theory rejects subjectivism and arbitrariness with respect to the natural law as uncompromisingly as does objectivism, though it does this without the necessary distinctions. Thus it is to be expected that he who rejects the term "given" *absolutely* will be accused of subjectivism and arbitrariness. To defend himself against this accusation, he cannot avoid pointing out that the subject's freedom is not without bonds, that is, that something is "given," albeit in a different sense from the untenable one. He can then expect to hear that he contradicts himself, for he has re-affirmed that norms are "given." Fechner himself returns to the use of the term "given" when he says that "order is given together with man."[66] All such difficulties and misunderstandings could be prevented by a more careful way of expressing oneself.

---

[65] Luijpen, *Phenomenology and Metaphysics,* Pittsburgh, 1965, pp. 146-149.
[66] "Fechner, *op. cit.,* p. 209.

3. Life in and According to a Legal Order

In the preceding chapters we described justice as the willingness to do what is right, conceiving the latter as the correlate of the minimum required by love, and we demanded that this minimum be embodied in a legal order. The objection against all this is sometimes made that such a position loses sight of an undeniable fact, viz., that living according to the law is altogether different from living a life of love. Justice is not love.

Living According to the Law and Living a Life of Love. The way this objection is formulated provides us with an opportunity to penetrate more profoundly into the specific character of humanity expressed by the term "living according to the law." Undoubtedly it is true that living according to the law is not the same as living a life of love. Justice and law derive their *origin* from love, understood as the orientation of subject to subject. "The" subject who, in orienting himself to the other, affirms the latter's subjectivity is, at first, the "ethical genius" who in his own existence "brings about" and lets "happen" the truth of co-existence as "having to be." The struggle of this genius for justice and law is a struggle for the general recognition of the minimum of love within a particular society. This struggle finds a terminus in the establishment of a legal order. In and through the legal order humanity begins to "rule" because it is forcefully imposed.

What exactly is this "humanity" that begins to "rule" through the legal order? In the existence of the "ethical genius" this humanity is a subjective ethical sentiment toward others which induces him to perform or to omit certain *external* actions. For the subjective orientation to the other's subjectivity always and necessarily embodies itself in external actions because the other's subjectivity is always incarnated in a body and involved in the world. Man's "yes" to the other as subject always and necessarily embodies itself in the doing or the omitting of actions with respect to his body and world—in other words, in *external* actions. Unless there is such external action with respect to the other's body and world, our "yes" to the other as subject will always be illusory, for the other is not a "pure" subject.[67]

When, however, humanity is imposed in and through a legal order and

---

[67] Janssens, *art. cit.* (footnote 14), pp. 123-124.

begins to rule a society, it cannot be conceived as a subjective ethical sentiment. Such a sentiment can never be imposed from without, for by its very nature it is constituted in and through acts of the subject-as-freedom. The humanity that begins to rule in and through a legal order consists in nothing other than this: certain *external* actions are done or omitted,[68] *even without the sentiment that animated the "ethical genius."*

Here lies the power of the legal order. Within a juridically well-ordered society, *in a certain sense* it does not matter what individuals think about the relationship of man to man; *in a certain sense* their subjective sentiment toward their fellow-men is unimportant; *in a certain sense* the level reached by their personal ethical action is irrelevant. Precisely because and to the extent that a society is juridically well-ordered, the "rule" of the legal order with its sanctions means that all members can be assured that certain external actions will be done and that others will not, even if some members *personally* would not be inclined to take such a course. Thanks to the power of the legal order, even the "wolves" among men act humanly, even if it be only in an *external* way. The legal order, as it were, "produces" humanity and at least makes it possible for man in a society to be secure against the "wolf" in man.

Considered in this fashion, living according to the law obviously is not the same as living a life of love. Justice, in the juridical sense, i.e., the willingness to comply with the demands of the legal order, is not love. On the legal level, the appeal to love becomes a juridical *demand,* being at the other's disposal becomes a juridical obligation, the reciprocity of love becomes a proportional juridical equality of rights, and the spontaneity of love becomes a juridical enforcement. The "we" of life according to the law is not the "we" of the life of love.

It has become almost commonplace today to claim that life according to the law makes us human beings live side by side as strangers and in mutual aloofness, and that only love establishes authentically human relations because only the community of love offers man the "communion" to which he is called as co-existence.[69] We do not want to deny this claim at all, provided it is not meant to discredit the *human* significance

---

[68] "Justice belongs to the domain of our objective relationships. . . . It has as its object the minimum of objective elements and relations needed to make love possible and safeguard it." Janssens, *art. cit.* (footnote 16), p. 12.

[69] "The law still leaves us 'outsiders' and, as it were, strangers to one another. It is by love alone that we establish genuinely human relationships, become mutually united by making ourselves 'transparent' to one another. Love is the only human society because it is communion." Lacroix, *Personne et amour,* p. 14.

of the legal order. For, "testimonies of love" do not suffice to tame "wolves," and there is no form of "communion" that does not have its moments of weakness. At such moments only positive law can save a minimum of humanity. Even the intimate "we" of the wedded "communion" and the "we" of a religious community cannot continue to exist without juridical rules.

From all this it should be evident also that living in and according to the legal order provided by the legislative, executive and juridical organs of a society, precisely insofar as it is living according to the law, has nothing to do with man's ethical life.[70] One who drives a car while under the influence of alcohol, who violates public morality, who commits an economic crime or murder is punishable before the law. He is not punished because he has committed "sin" but because he has transgressed positive laws with external actions. Of course, we do not want to claim that drunken driving, violating public morality, stealing and murder are not immoral acts. But that these acts are immoral does not mean that the legal order and any of the people who take care of this order have anything to do with their immorality. The legal order is concerned with humanity but only insofar as this humanity is constituted by external, juridically prescribed actions. Even if a judge endeavors to assess the delinquent's degree of responsibility, his aim is not to pass judgment on the culprit's "sinfulness" but to determine, insofar as possible, the latter's ability to behave as a bearer of legal rights and duties among his fellow bearers of such rights and duties. Thus, in and through the legal order humanity is, as it were, materialized. It is this that gives this order its strength.

The "Pressure" of the Legal Order as a Quasi-Process. When in Chapter Six we spoke of existence as co-existence, we emphasized that man is whatever he is, *partly* through others. In every society there are more or less commonly accepted views and more or less fixed patterns of actions. Every society has a more or less stereotyped way of "doing things." At first, man as a *person* has little to do with life, for things "run their course" in his life. When "life begins" for him, it means at first not much more than being introduced to the way "things are done," a way that has become more or less an established pattern. The group

---

[70] "The premise must be that law and morality have different objects. The law aims at man's behavior as manifesting itself externally, while morality is concerned with the internal orientation of his will. For the law results come first, but for morality the internal disposition." *Wezen en grondslagen van het recht,* 1957, p. 16.

makes the individual existences think, act and be. This quasi-process of making one another *be* is the indispensable condition for the authenticity of *personal* existence. For the "pressure" of the group establishes in the individual existence a "social body," so that the "soul" of authentic, personal existing can emerge. Without a "social body," no individual existence can attain any level of authenticity.[71]

This idea applies *par excellence* to the legal order as materialized humanity. Authentic, personal existence presupposes a social body, which is established by social facticity. The legal order is an aspect of this social facticity. The "ruling" law "runs its course" and "functions." Those who live in a society experience its "pressure." They try to abstain from "deviations" because they know that any violation of the legal order "automatically" puts this order into motion against them. The legal order "reacts" at once. When a legal order has been established, it begins, in a sense, to lead a life of its own and "acts" normatively on those who are subject to this order. If anyone tries to escape from its "pressure," he faces a trial, in which legal justice is blindfolded.

It is of the greatest importance that the members of a community undergo the "pressure," the "action" and the "reaction" of the legal order. For in this way a "social body" is established in their individual existence, and this body *is* a materialized humanity. Through it, they share in the results achieved by past struggles against the inhumanity of the "wolf" in man, even though they themselves had not part in those struggles. They can lead a life that is to some extent human; but they owe this, at least in the first instance, to the fact that they *themselves* do not live. They are as human as they are just as simple technicians are what they are because they *themselves* did not need to invent first the wheel. Because living in and according to a legal order establishes a "just social body" in man's individual existence, many human existences live on a relatively human level, a level which they would not reach if

---

[71] "Awakening at any time in a historically created situation, man has new possibilities in every generation, but only because he has a support in a 'life capital' handed down to him by tradition. If the situation were to throw him into the 'worldlessness' of an 'atom-like' solitary existence—a supposition that can be conceived only as the extreme limit—, then he would have to live on the nothingness of his inauthenticity (*vitalen Verstandesdasein*). He would then live in a painful but blind despair, not knowing what he really wants; he would seize scattered things lacking all transparency and he would suffer cramping agonies in the empty endurance of nothingness." Jaspers, *Philosophie*, p. 263.

they *themselves* had to be just. And even when they *themselves* are just, their being-just always presupposes the "social body," for the latter makes possible man's "soul," his selfhood.[72]

Is This View Anti-personalistic? Does not this emphasis upon social facticity and the social body established by it mean a denial of personalism with its accent on the subject? It must be admitted that there are philosophers of existence and phenomenologists who pay little or no attention to the importance of being "ruled" by a legal order and who therefore fail to show any appreciation of it. Some greatly emphasize the wholly original and unrepeatable aspects, the radically personal and unique facets of existence, and these thinkers will hardly find those aspects which they emphasize so much in a description of the legal order as anonymous and materialized humanity. For, does not the anonymity of the "they" deny the authenticity of the subject?

There are, indeed, philosophers of existence and phenomenologists who seem to imply such a view in their writings. For Kierkegaard, to exist means to be "unique," and the unique being that man is, is characterized by "passion," "decision" and "risk."[73] For Heidegger, man's being is a "being with," which realizes itself only in the mode of the impersonal "they." He describes this "they" as "inauthenticity" and "fallenness."[74] Man's conscience calls him from the "lost state" of the "they"[75] to authenticity, to his most "own" being-able-to-be,[76] to "resolve" with respect to his "being toward death." The authentic existing of the subject who has escaped from the "they" is "resolve" (*Entschlossenheit*).[77] Then man is authentically himself but at the same time lonely.[78] Now, if man finds his authenticity only in the loneliness of a

---

[72] "Authentic self-being is not based upon an exceptional condition of the subject, a condition detached from the 'they,' but is an existentiel modification of the 'they' as an essential existentiale." Heidegger, *Sein und Zeit,* p. 130.

[73] Welzel, *Naturrecht und materiale Gerechtigkeit,* p. 187.

[74] Heidegger, *op. cit.,* pp. 166-180.

[75] Heidegger, *op. cit.,* p. 274.

[76] "The call . . . , as an appeal to *Dasein's* ownmost being-able-to-be-its-self, is a calling forth (forward) of *Dasein* in its ownmost possibilities." Heidegger, *op. cit.,* p. 273.

[77] "Resolve" is "the silent projecting of oneself upon one's ownmost being-guilty, ready for dread." Heidegger, *op. cit.,* p. 297.

[78] "When *Dasein* thus stands before itself, all its relationships to the other *Dasein* are dissolved. . . . Thus death reveals itself as the ownmost, non-relational, unsurpassable possibility." Heidegger, *op. cit.,* p. 250.

desperate "resolve" toward death, must we not say that the calculative, calibrated, enforced and processed security of life in and according to a legal order is a form of inauthenticity?[79]

Similar ideas are expressed by Jaspers, although he differs in some respects from Heidegger. For Jaspers, the social dimension is that aspect of man in which his existence occurs as one of a species, having the same rights and the same duties as others of the same species. As such, the social dimension belongs to the inauthenticity of man as subject: "As this social 'I,' I become 'all of us.' "[80] With respect to the rules of law that regulate the rights and duties of men as "copies" of the human species, Jaspers therefore says that they are "as it were, mechanical and lifeless," that they always say the same thing and make actions predictable.[81] The social dimension acquires an authentically human meaning for Jaspers only in the "being together" which he calls "existential communication."[82] But this communication occurs only between two subjects in their "uniqueness,"[83] and any attempt to live in "communication" with more than one other subject means of necessity superficiality and inauthenticity.[84] The superficiality and inauthenticity of man's being-together is the being of the "mass man," the one in the crowd, the "they."

On the basis of these and other similar statements Hans Welzel thinks that the philosophy of law can expect nothing from existential and phenomenological thought. He sees this way of thinking as nothing but the expression of extreme subjectivism.[85] If the subject is an authentic subject only in uniqueness, exception passion, decision, risk, resolve and existential communication, then the subject-in-the-legal-order must be called an inauthentic subject. Welzel even goes so far as to claim that the philosophers of existence and the phenomenologists cannot escape

---

[79] Maihofer, *Recht und Sein,* pp. 17-19.

[80] Jaspers, *op. cit.,* p. 320.

[81] Jaspers, *op. cit.,* p. 603.

[82] Jaspers, *op. cit.,* p. 345.

[83] "In the communication, in which I know that I myself am involved, the other is only *this* other: the *uniqueness* is a manifestation of the autonomy of this being. Existential communication cannot be made by way of example or imitated; it simply is in its actual uniqueness. It exists between two selves; and these two are only these two, they are not representatives and therefore they cannot be replaced." Jaspers, *op. cit.,* p. 345.

[84] Jaspers, *op. cit.,* p. 347.

[85] "The philosophy of existence is the expression of a subjectivism in an extremely intensified and profound form." Welzel, *op. cit.,* p. 187.

from the conclusion that a legal order is "existentially" more meaningful according as it functions less well.[86] "Subject" and "legal order" are incompatible. If nonetheless there exists a legal order, Welzel adds, then, on the basis of what the existential philosophers and phenomenologists say, this order can be understood only as the result of pure power politics, as Hobbes had already suggested.[87] Hommes also comes to similar negative conclusions in his inquiry of the value the philosophy of existence and phenomenology could possibly have for the philosophy of law.[88]

After this brief survey of opinions, let us now turn to the question itself. Does the emphasis we have placed on the significance of the pressure exercised by the legal order, conceived as materialized humanity, imply the denial of the subject's authenticity? Is our view anti-personalistic?

Those who answer in the affirmative disregard the fact that the philosophers of existence and phenomenologists cited to show the incompatibility of "subject" and "legal order" speak with greater caution and more distinctions about the "subject" than is conveyed by certain summaries, e.g. those of Welzel and Hommes. Emphasis upon the subject's authenticity and upon the demands made by this authenticity means neither *per se* nor always in fact the denial of the importance of the social body, of the world's social facticity and of the "pressure" exercised by the objective structures of society. Just the opposite is the case. For Heidegger, the subject's authenticity, his own *self*-being, is not an exceptional state divorced from the "they," but an existential modification of this "they" that must be conceived as an *essential* dimension of existence.[89] Thus, according to Heidegger, social facticity is not denied by the subject's authenticity, but is first presupposed and then transcended. Jaspers manifests a similar conviction when he says that the existence of an order is necessary for the individual,[90] that society is indispensable for the existence of that order,[91] that tradition and authority must be

---

[86] "In this way the philosophy of existence must come to this paradoxical conclusion: the less perfectly the law functions as a general rule, and the more it is determined in terms of an exceptional situation, the more perfectly it is 'existentiel' and the more opportunity it gives for an 'existentiel' commitment." Welzel, *op. cit.*, p. 189.

[87] Welzel, *op. cit.*, p. 193.

[88] Hommes, *op. cit.*, p. 135.

[89] Heidegger, *op. cit.*, p. 130.

[90] Jaspers, *op. cit.*, p. 607.

[91] Jaspers, *op. cit.*, p. 349.

listened to,[92] that dutiful acting is a condition of authentic acting,[93] that established relations are needed in the contacts which even existentially united human beings cannot do without,[94] so that their being-together will always be a mixture of "fellowship and communication."[95] For Jaspers, social facticity is the basis of any form of the subject's authenticity. Authenticity always presupposes a "heritage," and this "heritage" is the history which others have made.[96] If the subject does not make this history his own, he is uprooted and perishes.[97] Hence, says Jaspers, there can be no question of doing away entirely with tradition from time to time, in order to give man an opportunity to start afresh. Man must continue to live in the tension between the conservative preservation of an already established order and the unlimited risk of total destruction.[98]

From all this we can conclude that even for those philosophers who occasionally put great—perhaps even too great—emphasis on the subject, there is no contradiction between "subject" and "social body" and therefore neither between "subject" and the "ruling legal order."[99] On the contrary, there is a unity of reciprocal implication between authentic subjectivity and social facticity. Social facticity is the "body" which makes it possible for the "soul" to be "soul."

But, one may ask, how many human beings are there who really "have" a "soul" of some importance? How many are authentic sub-

---

[92] "Hence, in order not to slide into a bottomless pit, the man who philosophically wakes up *entrusts* himself *to tradition* as a possible existence, as long as there does not occur a contradiction that destroys him. He *obeys* authority. . . . His very self-being feels a *desire for* authority because the self does not yet reach clarity on its own." Jaspers, *op. cit.,* p. 266.

[93] Jaspers, *op. cit.,* p. 157.

[94] Jaspers, *op. cit.,* p. 377.

[95] "Actually everywhere the compenetration of fellowship and communication, of the social 'I' and the possibility of self-being defies disentanglement so much that a *tension* between these two and a struggle of the individual *for* genuine communication belongs to the essence of being with our fellows." Jaspers, *op. cit.,* p. 379.

[96] Jaspers, *op. cit.,* p. 858. For other pertinent quotations of Jaspers see Fechner, *op. cit.,* pp. 231-237.

[97] Jaspers, *op. cit.,* p. 210.

[98] "It is false to argue: from time to time everything should be destroyed and a fresh start made. In historical existence (*Dasein*) it is in harmony with the truth to maintain the tension between conservative preservation and the unlimited risk of destruction." Jaspers, *op. cit.,* p. 759.

[99] Jaspers, *op. cit.,* pp. 608, 631.

jects? How many are there whose *selfhood* is ready for such humanity that *of themselves* they do what is prescribed by the legal order? No one, of course, can answer this question. But everyone knows that in any society there are always many who do not reach the same level of being-human as the "ethical geniuses" whose vision and deeds gave rise to the legal order. This is the reason why it is a great good that *all* members of a society undergo the "pressure," the "action" and "reaction" of the legal order. The "ruling" of the legal order gives to all existences a "social body," whose "weight" "drives" them to act in a certain way. This "weight" is the weight of materialized humanity. In its turn, this weight "produces" humanity. This view is not antipersonalistic, but simply recognizes the undeniable fact that, although all men are called to the authenticity of being a subject, many do not attain any level of authentic subjectivity.

Accordingly, the term "justice" can have a whole scale of meanings. Of the "ethical genius" one can say that he is just, but also of the young criminal whose father has taught him to be wary of the police and who therefore carefully abstains from murder. That, too, is important. If only mankind had an "international police," the fear of which would prevent states and nations from taking each other by the throat!

4. Mutability of the Legal Order

If the encounter of love's subjective inspiration with the actually existing relationships among men and the actual conditions of the world gives rise to a legal order, then it should be obvious that every legal order must constantly undergo change. For neither love's inspiration nor the actual conditions and relationships are fixed realities.

Love Knows No Bonds; the Legal Order Is Never "Finished." In the preceding section we spoke of the legal order as materialized humanity and the importance of the "pressure" and "operation" of this order. We referred there not to the highest but to the lowest form of life in a legal order. Those who are simply forced to realize this lowest form of life in a legal order in their existence do not even see where this life has its origin and where it leads. Their life is a quasi-process.

The situation is quite different for the "ethical genius," for the best of a society. If the legal order is the embodiment of the minimum demanded by love, then again the best of a society cannot be satisfied with any result that has already been achieved. Because love knows no bounds, the legal order is never "finished." The love of the best members of a society makes them see with clarity what humanity demands but, at the same time, every step forward on the road toward the humanization of society also means that the "ethical genius" begins to occupy a standpoint from which it is possible to discern demands of humanity with even greater perspicacity.[100] Thus the seeing itself of the "ethical genius" is an endless history. What being-destined to the other implies becomes accessible and clear only in the history of man's effective love of his fellow-man.[101]

In this way it should be obvious that we do not wish to represent matters as if the "ethical genius" has *a priori* a perfect and transparently clear "idea" of humanity and from it is able to deduce particular applications. In reality, at first a very vague "seeing" without much content leads to an equally vague and poor idea that is enriched and rendered more profound in a never ending history of "seeing" but can never be made fully transparent.[102] Every phase of "seeing" opens a new future of "seeing," and a "seeing" that does not open up toward a new future is not a *real* "seeing."[103]

In many places and at many times men live in different phases of humanity. An "ethical genius" is needed to induce a society to abolish the burning of widows as inhuman. The idea of humanity needed for this, however, is not so transparently clear that one can also see in it the widow's right to a pension. The view that such a pension is required requires a long history of humanity. It is within that history, and not outside or above it, that the idea of justice really lives. Because this

---

[100] "The concrete content of that ideal cannot be determined *a priori*. It has to be *discovered* progressively. . . . (The best among us) are equipped to occupy the standpoint that is needed to see and find something." Janssens, *art. cit.* (footnote 14), pp. 127-128.

[101] Wylleman, *art. cit.* (footnote 11), pp. 243-246.

[102] "For an absolute, presuppositionless evidence to be possible, for my thought to be able to penetrate into itself, 'catch' itself and arrive at a pure 'consent of itself to itself,' it would, in the language of the Kantians, have to cease to be an event and become wholly act; in the terminology of the Schoolmen, its formal reality would have to be included in its objective reality; to speak with Malebranche, it would have to cease to be a 'perception,' 'sentiment' or 'contact' with the truth to become pure 'idea' and 'vision' of the truth." Merleau-Ponty, *Phénoménologie de la perception,* p. 453.

[103] See footnote 6.

history is never "finished,"[104] there is room for "inventions" also in the realm of justice.[105]

As soon as an "invention" is made in the realm of the demands imposed by intersubjectivity, the legal order becomes antiquated, at least in a certain sense.   That order then embodies only a phase of humanity's history which has already been passed in the life of the best of a society. If the legal order would not be changed then, this very order would become an obstacle for the authentic *life* of co-existing men.   True, the legal order has inevitably and of necessity *also* a static aspect, precisely because this order must establish security with respect to human rights. However, it can happen that exclusive attention to this static aspect makes the jurist and others lose sight of the origin and purpose of the legal order.[106]   It can happen that the rules and institutions of law begin to lead a kind of separate and isolated existence and that jurists handle these rules and institutions as if they were autonomous entities.   Such people deserve to be called "dehydrated jurists,"[107] and their "justice" is, in Nédoncelle's words, only capable of "settling old bills" without having any creativity.[108]   A petrified legal order is not much more than a sediment of humanity and, at the same time, an obstacle to the attainment of a greater humanity.[109]

The assertion that the minimum of love constantly shifts its boundaries makes it possible to understand that things which formerly were

---

[104] "Juridical concepts are human constructions which are always subject to being perfected, thereby bringing us constantly closer to the eternal Idea of love." Lacroix, *Personne et amour,* p. 29.

[105] "There is no human dignity that can be objectively conceived.   The progress of justice consists precisely in inventing a human dignity of ever higher rank and greater wealth.   Progress does not consist in constantly coming closer to an ideal of human dignity *conceived* before this progress is made." Madinier, *op. cit.,* pp. 57-58.

[106] "Far too often the static aspect of justice causes forgetfulness of justice's origin and nature." Nédoncelle, *op. cit.,* p. 87.

[107] "I recognize that this is a danger for the jurist, but jurists who study only the law are, in my opinion and that of many other jurists, nothing but dehydrated jurists." W. Pompe, "Gedachtenwisseling over de 'Phaenomenologie van het recht,'" *Annalen v.h. Thijmgenootschap,* vol. 58 (1960), p. 101.

[108] "Justice is love with its eyes blindfolded and endowed with a stubbornly active memory; it creates nothing but settles old bills with a severe precision." Nédoncelle, *op. cit.,* p. 87.

[109] "If the law is described in terms of the moral ideal, it amounts of necessity only to a rather poor 'sediment' of a moral life that is much broader and richer. If, on the other hand, the law is described in terms of the bottom layer of the group's life, it reveals itself to us as the first manifestation of a new life that makes itself felt in the group." Gits, *op. cit.,* p. 357.

considered acts of love are now viewed as duties of justice.[110]   What the
love of the best formerly did for one's fellow-man is now demanded of
everyone and enforced by the legal order.[111]   Because justice prescribes
only the minimum requirements of love, it stands to reason that traditional ethics considers obligations in justice more serious than obligations
in charity, for man has a graver obligation to a minimum than to that
which goes beyond the minimum.[112]

The Changeable Character of Actual Conditions and Relationships.
The importance of the actually existing conditions and relationships for
the establishment of a legal order was frequently mentioned.   If man
does not show himself "sensitive" to their reality when he wants to
establish a legal order and relies exclusively on the "inspiration" of his
love, then the legal order established by him will be an ethereal system
built in a vacuum.   A legal order intends to put order in actual
conditions and therefore demands a realistic view of those conditions.

When those conditions and relationships, i.e. the sociological forms of
co-existing, change, then this is a direct sign that the legal order also
must be modified.   If this is not done, real life outgrows the man-made
frames and structures, with all the consequences this implies, as history
has repeatedly shown.   The supporters of the *Ancien Régime* and of
liberalistic capitalism tried in vain to contain changed actual conditions
within the structure of a static legal order.   Some colonizing nations also
attempted to do so and some still continue the attempt even today.   All
such efforts are ultimately doomed to failure.

---

[110] Janssens, *art. cit.* (footnote 16), p. 15.

[111] "It suffices to have a brief look at our modern fundamental rights: man's
right to his life and the integrity of his body, to his honor and reputation; the
various public freedoms: freedom of movement, of thought and of religion,
freedom of education, freedom of organization and assembly, freedom of the
press and of correspondence; the rights of ownership: acquisition of property
through occupancy or work; contracts: the obligations arising from freely made
agreements, the possibility of disposing of one's property among the living and
the dead; the rights of work: the right to work, the right to the product of one's
work, the right to a minimum needed for existence; political rights: the equality
of all citizens for the law, the right to a legally determined way of obtaining
one's rights and of being judged, the abolition of privileges, the right to
participate in the country's government and to be admitted to public office. . . ."
Gits, *op. cit.,* pp. 367-368.

[112] "At the same time it is evident that the duties of justice are most urgent
and must first be fulfilled.   This does not mean that justice ranks higher than
love or can be separated from it.   But justice deals with the strictly necessary
minimum of love's obligations." Janssens, *art. cit.* (footnote 16), p. 12.

The same idea applies also in a more modest realm which jurists deal with almost every day. The relative equilibrium reached by a society in a particular phase of its history can never last long. As soon as the rights and duties with respect to certain matters have been balanced and laid down in legal rules, something has already happened in the actual conditions and relations that makes new measures necessary. For example, rules may have been laboriously established to protect laborers involved in a production process. These rules assume that, say, electricity is used as the source of energy. By the time the protective rules are finally formulated, some factories have already abandoned the use of electricity and replaced it by atomic energy. At once then an important part of the laboriously constructed legal order becomes antiquated, so that new regulations are required.[113] Every historical situation differs from all others and therefore requires appropriate provisions. For example, man's right to traffic safety demands different regulations depending on whether a society uses donkeys, bicycles, automobiles or jets for its transportation.

"The Nature of the Matter." As was sufficiently emphasized, the concrete rules of law needed for the changing actual conditions and relationships cannot be deduced from the inspiration of the subject's "yes" to man. This is just as impossible as it is for a painter to deduce from general aesthetic principles what should be painted here on this wall and how it should be done. Love's inspiration does not imply knowledge of the facts pertaining to jet plane traffic or of the technocratic labor order, just as the affirmation of an aesthetic principle implies no knowledge about the size of a wall, its relation to the ceiling and other walls, and the angle of light. To become familiar with such matters, man must look at them and study them.

Does this mean that the changeability of the actual conditions and relationships *alone* is the source of new laws? In the philosophy of law this question is raised *inter alia* as that of "the nature of the matter." But the "nature of the matter" is a rather vague concept.[114] To prevent endless disputes, let us give a few examples to show what the concept is intended to convey.

The "nature" of the new-born child, so it is said, is such that it needs the care of its parents much longer than do the young of animals. Thus

---

[113] Gits, *op. cit.*, pp. 326-327.
[114] Wolf, *Das Problem der Naturrechtslehre*, pp. 44-49.

it follows from the "nature of the matter" that certain concrete rules of law are required to protect the child's life.[115]   In a sales contract the "nature of the matter" requires that the buyer receive good wares and the seller his money; hence certain concrete rules of law are needed to safeguard both buyer and seller.[116]   With respect to working in the modern technocratic order, it is the "nature of the matter" that no large scale private initiative is possible unless it is preceded by smaller initiatives.   In any private initiative there is present the result of initiatives previously taken by others.   For example, the "private initiative" of Anton Philips, founder of the giant Dutch electrical corporation in Brabant, presupposed the work of the religious congregations that labored in that underdeveloped region to raise it from the state of analphabetism; the results achieved by their work made Philips' private initiative possible.   Thus it lies in the "nature of the matter" that every initiative is social, and this social character demands certain laws, such as those that prescribe profit-sharing or the payment of taxes.

It seems to us that this so-called "nature of the matter" does not essentially differ from what we have called "actual conditions' and relationships."[117]   If this is true, then the mutability of the legal order does not find its origin *solely* in the changeability of the "nature of the matter," just as the legal order does not exclusively originate in the actual conditions of a society.   It may be true, of course, that, for example, the "nature" of modern technical work differs from the "nature" of work in the time of the guilds; furthermore, it may be that precisely in the realm of work man's being is a being-through-others. Nevertheless, solely on these grounds one cannot conclude to the necessity of social laws.   This necessity imposes itself only when man recognizes that he is destined for the other, i.e. it imposes itself only within the inspiration of love.   One can explicitly recognize that *his* "private initiative" is made possible through the initiatives of others and that in

---

[115] Fechner, *op. cit.,* p. 250.

[116] Fechner, *op. cit.,* p. 146.

[117] Dernburg defined the "nature of the matter" as follows: "The relationships of life, when they are more or less developed, contain their norm and order within themselves.   This order dwelling within things is called the 'nature of the matter.'   It is to this 'nature of the matter' that the thoughtful jurist must return when a positive norm is lacking, when it is incomplete or not clear." Quoted by Fechner, *op. cit.,* p. 147.   Wolf describes the "nature of the matter" in this way: "The 'nature of the matter' means the 'order' or structure needed by any being in accordance with its destiny or task (function).   With respect to the social realm of life it means the harmony of the historical order precisely with this necessity of the matter."   Wolf, *op. cit.,* p. 44.

his work that of others is "present" but, at the same time, be blinded by egoism and unable to discern the minimum demands of love. Such a person will not be inspired to establish a system of social laws but will simply find it "natural" that his fellow-men cringe like slaves before him. From man's essence as being-through-others it does not follow that his being must also be a being-for-others. If, contrary to work in the time of guilds, modern work reveals itself as social by its very "nature," it does not follow from this change *alone* that it is necessary to modify the legal order. The mutability of this order finds its explanation in the encounter of the ever-changing minimum of love with changing actual conditions and relationships.[118]

The Necessity of Love. All this also shows that the theories of Marx and Sartre about the history of humanity are one-sided. As early as his critique on Feuerbach, Marx expressed his conviction that love is unimportant. He berated Feuerbach for abolishing religion on the one hand, and introducing a new religion on the other, namely the religion of men's love for one another. If Feuerbach had been sensitive to the importance of *praxis,* he would have noticed that not love but work, with its socio-economic structures, brings men together and unites them. But for this unity Feuerbach substituted the unity of the human species, the internal and dumb universality that connects the many individuals in a natural way.[119] This unity is an "abstraction." *Real* unity among men comes about through social life;[120] the continuity of history is secured by the continuity of the means of production and not by all kinds of political and religious "nonsense."[121]

According to Marx, the objective reality of the capitalistic system contains the fall of this system, independently of the capitalists's intentions. Private ownership propels itself toward its own destruction but solely through a development that is independent of the capitalist, of

---

[118] "To be sure, the new legal order (*Recht*) is based not only on a new vision but also on a new 'having to' and a new wanting. The 'nature of the matter' found a collaborator in the idea of justice (*Recht*), the demand for social legislation (*Recht*) to protect those who are economically weak, which finally opened the law-giver's eyes to situations that had existed for a long time already. The labor laws are an example of how the idea of justice and the 'nature of the matter' must work together in the birth of new legal concepts." Radbruch, "Die natur der Sache als juristische Denkform," *Festschrift zu Ehren von Rudolf Laun,* Hamburg, 1948, p. 174.

[119] Marx, "Thesen über Feuerbach," *Die Deutsche Ideologie,* Berlin, 1953, p. 595.

[120] "All social life is essentially practical." Marx, *ibid.*

[121] Marx-Engels, *Die Deutsche Ideologie,* pp. 26-27.

which he is not aware and which he does not want, but which is conditioned by the "nature of the matter," viz., the production of a proletariat with its own objective laws.[122]   The Communist future is contained in the objective reality of the proletariat, independently of the intentions this proletariat may have.[123]

Obviously, in such a theory the subject is unimportant, as is the subject's turning to another subject in love.   Marx called the liberalistic-capitalistic legal order the mirror image of the actual capitalistic conditions and relationships.[124]   After the revolution, Marx thought, these conditions and relationships will be different, and this difference will find expression in a new legal order, the Communist order.   On what grounds, however, can Marx call the capitalistic legal order unjust and the Communist order just?   If a legal order is nothing but the mirror image of actual conditions and relationships, one can never say of any order whatsoever that it is just or unjust.   *In reality* Marx could call the liberalistic-capitalistic legal order unjust only because he saw this order as a violation of his fellow-man's subjectivity and because Marx's entire personal life was encompassed by his attempt to embody in a new legal order *his* "yes" to his fellow-man, his love.   But that which inspired Marx's entire personal life does not occur in his philosophy.[125]

Nor does Sartre ascribes any significance to love for building up man's being-man-together-with-his-fellow-men.[126]   Unlike Marx, he does not even accuse the capitalists of egoism, at least not in the sense of a subjective inspiration or attitude.   For Sartre, there is only a "class hatred."[127]

---

[122] "Private property's national-economic movement, of course, propels itself toward its own destruction, but it does so only because of a development that is independent of it, unconscious, against its will and conditioned by the nature of the matter; it does so only because it gives rise to a proletariat as proletariat." Marx-Engels, *Die heilige Familie,* p. 137.

[123] Marx-Engels, *ibid.*

[124] Engels, "Ludwig Feuerbach und der Ausgang der klassischen Deutschen Philosophie," MEAS, vol. 2, pp. 369-370.

[125] Nevertheless, Marx accuses the capitalists of greed: "The only wheels that put the national economist into motion are greed and war among the greedy, viz., competition." "Zur Kritik der Nationalökonomie," Marx-Engels, *Kleine ökonomische Schriften,* Berlin, 1955, p. 97.

[126] Sartre, *Critique de la raison dialectique,* p. 189.

[127] "We are far removed from the egoism or that 'hardness' of which the capitalists of the 'paleo-technical' era used to be accused as if their barbarism was something proper to them.   There is no question here of a character feature but of a class hatred."   Satre, *op. cit.,* p. 693.

Thus we arrive at the conclusion that the mutability of the legal order finds its explanation neither in love *alone* nor in changed conditions and relationships *alone*. But it is precisely in the encounter of these two aspects of human co-existence that the necessity of new legal rules makes itself known.[128]

5. *Peace: the "Nations' State of Grace"*[129]

There can be or there can remain no justice without a legal order, but a legal order can degenerate and become a menace to justice. There can be or there can remain no legal order without authority and power, but both of these can also degenerate and make a mockery of the legal order. In order to wrest the humanity of being-men-together from being-"wolves"-together, man has created the legal order, authority and power. They are *essential* conditions of humanity but, at the same time, they contain the possibility of destroying man. One could be tempted to eliminate this possibility by eliminating the legal order, authority and power themselves, and be inclined to leave humanity to the inspiration of love. But that temptation cannot last more than a brief moment, for the elimination of that embodied humanity would also give freedom to the "wolf" in man. Hobbes and Spinoza were not entirely wrong.[130]

Violence as Resistance to Violence. In the past man has used his power for the sake of humanity. He has made use of violence and resorted to war in order to make justice and rights prevail. When he did this, he described his violence as resistance to violence. Even when this description was evidently false, he always attempted to present the war he waged as just wars. If a war was not to appear as a form of barbarism, it simply had to be called just, even when it was patently not possible to do so. Man always "knew" that *sheer* power is not a real, permanent power; he "knew" that consciousness of waging an unjust war would make powerless the hands that wielded the sword, even

---

[128] J. J. van der Ven seems to provide a concrete illustration of this theory in his article "De vijftigjarige wet op de arbeidsovereenkomst," *Ars Aqui,* vol. VIII (1958-59), pp. 106-113.

[129] Lacroix, *Personne et amour,* pp. 14, 30.

[130] "Those who are shocked by the theories of Hobbes and Spinoza—which are quite different—would do better to start understanding these theories and recognizing the element of truth which they contain." Lacroix, *op. cit.,* p. 18.

though it is true that a power not sanctioned by justice can manage to maintain itself for a very long time.[131]

The inhumanity of war in the past does not *per se* contradict human greatness. Because war was in the service of humanity, or at least was supposed to foster humanity and peace, they were noble who preferred death to slavery. They refused to surrender the freedom that makes man human to the "wolf" in their fellow-man and sacrificed their lives in order that others could continue to live as free human beings. They considered "peace at any price" below man's dignity and a violation of the human dimension of man.[132] There were but very few who looked upon the killing of "wolfish" fellow-men simply and solely as the killing of fellow-men and who therefore refused to take part in war or give war any support. Theirs also was a noble attitude, for they realized that it would cost them dearly. They stripped war of all romanticism and made the conscience of those who ordered war pause to think. On the other hand, however, it is evident that they could not fail to realize that they were able to continue to lead a life worthy of man only because humanity was defended by others with the arms of violence. It was not expressions of love that defended their children against the threatening pack of "wolves," but the weapons taken up by others. Not the anti-militarists but the soldiers liberated the world from Hitler.

The doctrine of violence to resist violence, that is, of the just war, is really very old. It was developed by St. Augustine, Thomas Aquinas, Cajetan and Francesco de Vittoria and gave rise to an elaborate system of "cases." We will not delve into them but mention only that one of the conditions for making a war just is that the importance of the rights and freedoms involved must balance the sufferings and destruction caused by the war.[133] This required condition is the reason why some authors think that in our era there can no longer be a just war.

The Impossibility of a Just War. Today there are many who deny that a just war is still possible. They think that a future war will of necessity be a nuclear war and that, even if it begins as a war with conventional weapons, it will develop into a nuclear war.[134] A nuclear war, so they argue, means the end of the human race and its history, for

---

[131] Bernhard Welte, *Ueber das Wesen und den rechten Gebrauch der Macht,* Freiburg i.Br., 1960, p. 23.

[132] Lacroix, *op. cit.,* p. 17.

[133] Messner, *Das Naturrecht,* p. 567.

[134] We are referring here solely to war between nuclear powers.

nuclear weapons are so destructive that their use will make all human beings become their victims. There would be neither victors nor vanquished but only corpses. Because a war can be called just only if the importance of the rights and freedoms balances the suffering and destruction caused by the war, it is evident that a war which puts an end to man's history is unqualifiedly immoral. For the same reason, so they add, it is also evidently immoral to manufacture, stockpile and threaten to use nuclear weapons. One cannot *really* threaten unless one is *really* ready to use these weapons if necessary. But such a use is immoral, for in a nuclear war there is nothing to defend because everything will be annihilated.

We fully agree with these ideas. It would make little sense if, on the basis of the classical doctrine about the just war, we would examine "moral cases," i.e. ask ourselves whether it is really true that a nuclear war utterly destroys everyone and everything, whether or not there is an essential difference between nuclear weapons and conventional weapons, whether a war fought with conventional weapons must *per se* degenerate into a nuclear war, and whether or not a distinction ought to be made between "threatening" and "using" as well as "attack" and "defense." All such questions seem to make little sense to us, for, even if today's war between nuclear powers would not *per se* mean the end of history, tomorrow that would no longer be the case because of the enormously accelerated rate at which weaponry develops.

The classical doctrine of the just war is made obsolete by the changed character of man's weapons. For the same reason war is no longer a suitable instrument for politics. Rights and freedoms can no longer be defended by means of war because a nuclear war would utterly destroy everything. Man's reflection on war and peace in our era has entered an entirely new phase, viz. the phase of war's *impossibility*. Any attempt to justify the possibility of war is wrecked by harsh reality and is itself immoral. Reflection on war and peace can merely affirm the *necessity* of peace and, on the basis of this affirmation, seek the means to make peace become a reality.

It is not our intention to enter into details regarding the concrete possibilities of peace. All we are concerned with here is a general theory of peace understood as the fruit of justice. The concrete possibilities and difficulties belong to the realm of those who devote themselves to the positive sciences and not to that of philosophers. The existence of nuclear weapons changes all conditions and relationships between nations, and it is the task of the positive sciences to familiarize us with the new conditions. But this they must do with the conviction that war is impossible and that peace is a necessity. The alternative now is either peace or the end of history. If the existence of nuclear weapons changes everything, then man's thinking also must change.[135] Until recent times it was possible to consider war a usable means to implement a just policy, but it is so no longer.

The Impossibility of a Just Pacifism. From the affirmation that it is immoral to use, manufacture and stockpile nuclear weapons and to threaten to use them some conclude that it is also immoral for the individual to collaborate in any of these things. They hold that only one attitude is morally justifiable, viz. the one that endeavors to attain total nuclear disarmament.

Again, we fully agree with this idea. Anyone with a minimum of intelligence sees at once that all actions contributing to the production or preservation of nuclear weapons are immoral. Unfortunately, however, this is not the last word. For just as it is evidently immoral to possess nuclear weapons, so also is it evidently immoral not to have them. Anyone with a minimum of intelligence sees at once that a power without nuclear arms will never be able to tame the "wolf" with nuclear weapons but invites him to proceed in establishing his inhuman domain; this is why nuclear weapons will never be abolished. Hence, all those who promote one-sided disarmament, in Sartre's words, "have dirty hands." To keep their hands clean, they do not even want to touch the dirty weapons. In vain! Their hands are dirty nonetheless. The moral problem facing our era is not raised but simply buried under verbiage when one limits oneself to the statement that it is immoral to have nuclear weapons and then decides not to touch them.

Above we said that it is meaningless to appeal to moral "case" studies in order to try to justify the possession of nuclear weapons. We just as firmly refuse to have recourse to it to find a justification for not having nuclear weapons. By not having these weapons, one abandons the whole of mankind and its history to the "wolf" with nuclear arms. That, too,

---

[135] "This much is certain: Something has to happen that has never happened before if the world as we know it and man as we know him is to be saved: man must think in terms of peace from the ground up and remain faithful to this idea in all the phases of his thinking." Reinhold Schneider, *Der Friede der Welt*, Insel-Verlag, p. 108.

is immoral. If the pacifists had their way, packs of "wolves" with nuclear arms would terrorize mankind. And if these pacifists would then be asked by their children why they did not defend them, they could reply only that they did not "will" the catastrophe but merely "permitted" it. The pacifists speak of peace, but their peace is not a peace-in-the-world; they speak of defense, but their defense does not *really* defend against the "wolf," they speak of policy, but their policy is at a given moment no longer made by man but only by God.[136] Meanwhile they claim to be the representatives and bearers of this divine policy. In the name of God they demand one-sided disarmament,[137] and whoever disagrees with this one-sided disarmament is in their eyes a blind disbeliever.

This attitude contains a dangerous illusion. Only those who realize that both having and not having nuclear arms is immoral, only those who *after* affirming the truth of both horns of the dilemma, try to say something meaningful about the matter come face to face with the moral problem of our era.[138]

Nevertheless, there is an aspect of greatness in the immoral attitude of the radical pacifist. He is willing to bring the offers implied in being ruled by the "wolf" with nuclear arms. There is no reason to doubt the sincerity of his willingness.[139] However, the radical pacifist must resign himself to the fact that he cannot "prove" his willingness as long as he continues to live in that part of the world that others defend by means of nuclear arms. He lives thanks to the others' immorality.

We realize, of course, that there is a "contradiction" in our theory. But there is no escape from that. For as long as life itself is a

---

[136] "We do not need to throw the bomb. For God Himself . . . is the Great International Politician, the Guardian and Protector of the world and of the Church. . . . God's promises and commandments are our foundation in political matters. . . . A limit has been reached; we must now leave matters to the Great Politician." H. Berkhof, "Het synoderapport en hoe verder?" *Militia Christi,* July 6, 1963, p. 99.

[137] "One thing can be stated with full conviction: we may not participate in modern warfare with nuclear arms or with conventional weapons. We are not permitted to do this, in the name of Christ." *Militia Christi,* November 17, 1962, p. 165.

[138] "In political terms this one step means that one seizes the opportunities directly connected with the present situation and that one does not run away from history and from the structure of the world. For I refuse to do that, and I refuse to do that as a Christian." C. L. Patijn, *Oorlog en vrede, Congresboek,* Utrecht, 1960, p. 75.

[139] Cf., for example, *Het vraagstuk van de kernwapenen,* a pastoral letter of the General Synod of the Dutch Reformed Church, The Hague, 4th ed., 1963.

"contradiction," a theory can remain free from "contradiction" only by burying life's reality under verbiage. In real life meaning and meaninglessness are interwoven; they compenetrate each other. The scientist bears witness to this compenetration when through his knowledge and skill he stands in the front ranks of mankind and then joins the rear guard carrying a sign reading: "I protest." The same applies to the protesting civilian whose daily work contributes to the level of economic life that makes it possible to manufacture nuclear arms.[140] But—must life remain a "contradiction"?

Does History Have a Meaning? This question is wrongly interpreted if it is taken to mean whether *outside* history there is somewhere a fixed point to which history must move, so that history can be moving either in the "right" or in the "wrong" direction. When there is question of history's meaning, this term can be correctly understood only in the sense of referring to the direction which the demands living *in* history itself invite man to take. Because man is history on many levels of his existence, the question about history's meaning can be raised on many levels; for example, the question about the meaning of science, technology, art and religiousness. In the context of this book, then, asking about the meaning of history means to seek the direction that is prescribed by the demands immanent in existence as co-existence and implemented or not implemented by politics. Thus the answer to the question imposes itself at once: the meaning of the history made by politics is peace. This meaning disclosed itself at a given moment of history because man, through the intermediary of the "ethical genius," let "happen" and "brought about" the truth of his existence as co-existence. This truth invites man to go in a certain "direction" and therefore imposes demands upon him. It is *man* who understands or fails to understand these demands, who executes them or fails to execute them. It is man who makes history meaningful or meaningless.

Because man is a contingent subject and makes his history as a contingent subject, nothing is *a priori* guaranteed to him. If history were a process, it would literally run its course like an alarm clock. Those who know the forces at work in this process could predict its outcome. Now, however, there is no "destiny of fate" on which he can hope.[141] He can merely try to understand the immanent demands of history and seize the opportunities offered to him.

---

[140] Schneider, *op. cit.,* pp. 93-94.
[141] Merleau-Ponty, *Eloge de la philosophie,* p. 61.

On the level of history as co-existence which is made by politics, the impossibility of war is a possibility of peace greater than any ever offered to mankind.[142] Until recent times it was still possible to use violence, i.e. war, to establish humanity. Until recently peace was not much more than a breathing space between two wars. Now, however, peace means the impossibility of war. But this impossibility is a precarious, suspect and immoral peace, for it is based on the power to annihilate history. It is wholly uncertain whether man will survive his own inventions.[143] It is not impossible that mankind may fail on the way and be like a sentence that remains unfinished (Merleau-Ponty).

The impossibility of war lies contained in the "nature of the matter," in the actual conditions and relationships of our era. Whether or not this impossibility will lead to real peace depends upon the practical answer to the question of whether mankind is willing to *think* in terms of this impossibility with respect to its actions. But this is not enough. The powers that have nuclear weapons at their disposal already think in terms of their certitude that war is impossible. But they do not go beyond an implicit "social contract" based on a balance of terror. True, this is already something not to be despised or rejected, as would be done by a unilateral abolition of nuclear arms. The chance for peace offered mankind for the first time in history through the balance of terror may not be thrown away by unilateral disarmament.

Nevertheless, this "social contract" is no more than a *chance*. This chance will become a reality only when the nuclear powers, facing each other as collective subjects, through the intermediary of an "ethical genius," let the truth about their being-together as collective subjects "happen" and "come about" and then implement this truth through their "yes" to each other—a "yes" that affirms *at least* the acceptance of each other's collective-being-a-subject and wills it.[144] This "yes" takes away something from the absoluteness of the two collective subjects' self-affirmation, i.e. both abandon the absolutism of their national sovereignty. But this will become a reality only when within the community of a mutual "yes" certain persons are pushed forward or rather raised, in order to be vested with the authority that the "having to be," the being destined for one another of the collective subjects *itself is*. This supranational authority will then make rules or norms, it will establish a positive system of supranational laws, to "guide" the many activities that

---

[142] W. Schuyt, "Strategie van de vrede," *Pax Christi,* Nov. 7, 1961, pp. 6-7.
[143] Schneider, *op. cit.,* p. 97.
[144] J. A. Weterman, "Samenvatting," *Oorlog en vrede,* p. 181.

collective subjects perform with respect to one another.[145]   This "guid-ance" must be such that it safeguards at least the minimum of love, i.e. it must rob the "wolf" of his chances. As such, it requires, first of all, the gradual and controlled destruction of the weapons by which the nations can annihilate each other. We say "gradual" and "controlled": the destruction must be gradual to preserve the balance of terror, and controlled to prevent either party from acting as a "wolf" while the other disarms.[146]   Such a disarmament cannot effectively be made unless a supranational authority can impose supranational law with suprana-tional power. For even the "wolves" which of themselves are unable or unwilling to grant a minimum of humanity must be "tamed."

Conclusion. Is not this theory utopian? As long as the collective subjects are not ready to speak the minimum of the "yes" to each other, there will never be peace, security and humanity. There is nothing in history giving man any guarantee whatsoever that this "yes" to each other will ever be implemented. Man is a contingent subject, and he *himself* either makes history or annihilates history. In economic life this "yes" can impose itself as a necessity, as it can in the precarious, objectionable and immoral existence of nuclear arms. But there is nothing that can "produce" that "yes." It has to be "spoken" and this can be done only by subjects. Is all this not utopian?

Many so-called utopian ideas have been realized in the course of history. At the time when Florence and Siena warred with each other the unity of Italy was utopian. France and Germany fought three bloody wars within a single century. For a long time the idea of peace between certain nations or states seemed utopian, but now war between those same states is no longer thinkable.

In a similar way universal peace is not utopian. It presupposes the minimum of "yes" to one another, a minimum whose boundaries con-stantly shift. That is, it presupposes the "natural law," which in the "encounter" with the actual conditions and relationships about which the positive sciences enlighten us, makes rules of law imposed by a suprana-tional authority with supranational power. Only in this way will the protest against inhumanity be more than an emotional form of powerless-ness. Only in this way will there be a future for mankind.

---

[145] B. V. Röling, "Koude oorlog en vreedzame coëxistentie" (Aspecten van de koude oorlog), *Polemologische Studien,* vol. IV, Assen, 1964, pp. 123-124.

[146] Patijn, *op. cit.,* p. 74.

INDEX OF NAMES

243

INDEX OF SUBJECT MATTER